The Althouse Press

*Hare* / **What Makes a Good Teacher**

# What Makes a Good Teacher

REFLECTIONS ON SOME CHARACTERISTICS

CENTRAL TO THE EDUCATIONAL ENTERPRISE

William Hare
*Dalhousie University*

THE ALTHOUSE PRESS

First published in 1993 by
THE ALTHOUSE PRESS
Acting Dean: B.B. *Kymlicka*
Director of The Press: D. *Gutteridge*
Faculty of Education, The University of Western Ontario,
1137 Western Road, London, Ontario, Canada N6G 1G7

**Editorial Assistant:** Katherine Mayhew
**Cover:** *Design* - Antony Hare; *Artwork* - Louise Gadbois, U.W.O. Graphic
Services

**Canadian Cataloguing in Publication Data**

Hare, William
 What makes a good teacher

Includes bibliographical references and index.
ISBN 0-920354-36-X

1. Teachers. 2. Teaching. 3. Teachers - Training of.
I. University of Western Ontario. Faculty of
Education. II. Title.

LB1025.3.H37 1993   371.1'1   C93-093765-1

Printed and bound in Canada by Kromar Printing Ltd., 725 Portage Avenue,
Winnipeg, Manitoba R3G 0M8.

For my son Andrew —
  with affection and admiration

# CONTENTS

# Acknowledgements

The idea for a book dealing with the virtues and qualities which teachers should possess took shape in my mind during a sabbatical term spent at the University of Sydney, Australia, in 1989, and preliminary work was undertaken at that time and continued after my return. An invitation to contribute to the Ethics Lecture Series at the University of Prince Edward Island in May 1991 provided the impetus to organize these developing ideas in a tentative way in a lecture entitled "Virtues for our teachers", where I sketched out the basic ideas on humility, courage, impartiality and empathy. I am very grateful to U.P.E.I. for that timely opportunity. Versions of certain chapters have been presented at the Learned Societies and at the Conference of Atlantic Educators. Chapter 3 has appeared in the *Journal of Philosophy of Education* 26, 2, 1992, and is reprinted here with permission. I wish to thank all those who, in these various contexts, have made useful suggestions, and also my students in philosophy of education at Dalhousie University who have given me the benefit of their criticisms. I am especially indebted to my colleague Robert Bérard for numerous discussions on these issues, and for drawing many examples and cases to my attention. Once again I am indebted to my wife, Niki, for helpful comments at every stage as these ideas developed.

**William Hare**

# Preface

xxxxxxxxxxxxxxxxxxxxxxxxxx

> The essence of an educator does not lie in technical expertise,
> but in a complex of pedagogical qualities.
>                     Max van Manen, *The Tact of Teaching*

Who should teach our children? The question is posed by Socrates in the *Apology* and it constitutes an early formulation of one of the basic problems in philosophy of education.[1] Who has the necessary wisdom and judgment? Who can be trusted with this immensely important task? Who, in Socrates' words, is the expert in perfecting the human and social qualities? The question matters at every stage of the educational process. The reference to our children above is not intended to identify a certain age-group but to underline the serious implications of the decision we make when we choose a teacher; and the teacher is anyone, at any level, who seeks to help others to learn. Very often, of course, and regrettably, parents and students have little direct choice in the matter except to walk away when things become impossible, but we can influence matters indirectly by trying to formulate a conception of the qualities and attributes we would wish to see exemplified in the teaching profession.

Socrates did not in fact merely raise the question, though this itself would have been a sufficient achievement. He pointed us in the right direction as far as an appropriate answer is concerned. This direction, however, is still resisted by teacher-education institutions, school boards, the teaching profession and sundry educational "experts", a term which has deserved scare quotes since Socrates' warnings. The dominant tendency has always been to reduce teaching to a set of trainable skills and measurable competencies, but this approach is objectionable in principle. Socrates put the point bluntly in emphasizing the difference between human beings and horses as far as suitable upbringing is concerned. There are deep and open questions about the kind of life a human being should live which simply do not arise in the case of horses and cattle.[2] People disagree about the good life, and the existence of controversy means that we must be sceptical about claims to expertise in this area.

The basic distinction between mechanical learning and genuine education has reverberated throughout the history of philosophy of education. Kant echoed Socrates' point when he remarked that horses and dogs are broken in and a human being may also be broken in, but it is of far greater importance that a child learn to *think*.[3] There is much written today about critical thinking, but even here one sees a tendency to reduce this notion to general skills in which children can be drilled. There is much less emphasis on the attitudes which need to accompany the skills one learns, on the need for judgment in the application of such skills, and on the necessary prerequisite of sound and relevant knowledge without which critical thinking cannot begin. Kant observed that "all education which is merely mechanical must carry with it many mistakes and deficiencies because it has no sure principle to work upon. If education is to develop human nature so that it may attain the object of its being, it must involve the exercise of judgment."[4]

However, what it must involve and what actually goes on in the name of education are quite different, and in the closing years of the last century John Dewey deplored the "blind observance of rule and routine": "The machine teacher, like the empiric in every profession, thus becomes a stupefying and corrupting influence in his surroundings; he himself becomes a mere tradesman, and makes his school a mere machine shop."[5] Dewey, of course, is the great champion of experience, but Dewey was at pains to point out that experience does not mean mindless repetition: "It is a certain quality of practice, not mere practice, which produces the expert and the artist."[6]

Too much attention in teacher education continues to be placed on rule and routine, on particular techniques which research is supposed to have deemed effective in promoting learning. This is partly because we are afraid to use our judgment in selecting and approving those who have desirable intellectual, moral and personal qualities and so we fall back on observable and measurable behaviours; and partly because we work with an impoverished concept of education itself which continues to be seen as nothing more than the acquisition of information and skills. At a time, moreover, when it is evident that many of our children fail to make minimally satisfactory progress in school, and when international comparisons of students can cause acute embarrassment in some quarters, there is naturally even more pressure to concentrate on effective and efficient techniques.

The reflections in this book represent a deliberate turning away from the present and typical emphasis to a consideration of certain virtues and qualities which ought to characterize the teacher as a person. Dewey took the view that "to depend wholly, or even chiefly, upon the knowledge and use of 'methods', is an error fatal to the best interests of education."[7] Naturally, there are things to avoid and advice one can profit from, and much to be gained from practical experience. Any skills or techniques which teachers acquire, however, need to be employed by a person who possesses certain attributes and excellences. We should remember that the sophists were not lacking in skill or technique.

This book examines humility, courage, impartiality, open-mindedness, empathy, enthusiasm, judgment and imagination, eight qualities which are rarely or inadequately discussed in the context of teacher education and only lately finding their way into philosophy of education. Any teacher, I contend, would be better for possessing these qualities. They go some way to giving an answer to Socrates' query about the kind of person we want to teach our children. Such a person, needless to say, is not an *expert* in perfecting the human and social qualities, but someone who is sensitive to the problem to which Socrates calls attention and who possesses and displays certain human and social virtues. I also think that teachers would be better for having thought about these virtues in a rationally reflective manner, since misconceptions and sheer neglect frequently get in the way of such qualities being displayed or recognized.

One kind of response to such a list is an objection to the effect that no one seriously disputes the value of these qualities, so who is to profit from this discussion? First, however, many do in fact fail to agree that these are of any great significance for teachers. They are thought of as vaguely desirable, but of little consequence compared with strategies and methods. Their mention is apt to produce an awkward embarrassment, and a sense that woolly idealism is creeping in. Second, what these general virtues mean in the context of teaching is not always well understood, so a critical examination is in order. Third, it is helpful to appreciate their value in the context of a wider and more adequate conception of teaching and education.

Currently, a fashionable watchword in education is excellence, and this is vague enough that all can claim to be in favour of it. Who, after all, would not support excellence? If something is worth doing at all, presumably it is worth doing well. This book looks at excellence in education indirectly by way of considering various excellences, in the sense of highly desirable attributes, which ought to characterize our teachers. If I have little to say directly about subject-matter competency as an excellence, this is not because it is unimportant, but because it is presupposed in the flourishing of the other excellences examined here. Humility, courage, enthusiasm and judgment lose their significance in the absence of the knowledge and understanding which sustain them.

Suffice it to say that minimum content preparation in effect now means, in the North American context,[8] a four-year university degree which concentrates on central aspects of the one or two subjects one intends to teach. In the case of those who teach across the curriculum in the elementary grades, the only difference is that all the subjects to be taught should be represented in the degree programme. No one should be teaching mathematics in grade one who has not studied some mathematics at the university level. School boards need to make provision for teachers to take a university course in one of the subjects they teach at least every five years, and having made such provision, taking the course should be a condition of on-going employment. Furthermore, a system of sabbatical leave needs to be introduced into the school system to permit teachers to return for longer periods to the study of their subject(s) and the study of educational theory.[9]

Many of my examples come from the Canadian context but I hope that sufficient detail has been provided so that those previously unfamiliar with these cases will have no difficulty appreciating their significance. I would be very surprised if readers outside Canada were unable to find very similar examples from their own context. My impression is that the problems raised here, and the kinds of cases cited, are just as common in Britain, Australia, the United States and many other countries. I hope that those who disagree with my interpretation of particular cases and with the opinions I express will share Russell's view that what matters in education primarily is the *way* in which one's opinions are held.[10]

Following an introductory chapter in which I indicate that there is a need to regain perspective in education, I present an overview of the eight excellences singled out for attention, followed by a more detailed study of each of these in the subsequent chapters. There is, of course, no suggestion that the list of excellences is complete or perfect. The claim is simply that the qualities examined are very important and somewhat neglected. My hope is that the discussion will be of general interest to all who are concerned with the quality of education offered to our children at every level.

# CHAPTER ONE

# Distance: Regaining Focus

〰〰〰〰〰〰〰〰〰〰〰〰〰〰〰〰〰〰〰〰〰〰〰〰〰〰〰〰〰〰〰〰〰

> Glued to the phenomena, the mind can no more attain
> perspective than can the viewer with eyeballs glued to the
> painting.
>
> Israel Schetfler, *Reason and Teaching*

## Ideals Under Suspicion

Talk of ethics—or of general ideals, virtues, qualities, or excellences—in the context of teaching is met with some resistance and scepticism. Overworked teachers no doubt fear that high-minded idealism will ignore the sober reality of actual working conditions. Many will have read about Horace's compromise in Theodore Sizer's book of that title,[1] and know full well that it is one thing to say that a teacher has a responsibility to evaluate the students' work carefully and conscientiously, and another matter to have to evaluate the work of one hundred and twenty students at a time. Horace ends up cutting corners, all but the most essential ones Sizer reports, and who can blame him? The word "compromise" was well chosen in this title, because it is itself morally ambiguous. We are unaware how to feel about compromises. Sometimes the suggestion is that a compromise would involve giving up a fundmental principle. Socrates had reason to refuse the compromise offered at his trial. On other occasions, however, a compromise enables everyone involved in a dispute to achieve some part of their aims, and the result is seen as fair and sensible.[2] Only a fanatic would hold out for everything.

Again, it is easy to say that teachers should have a sense of judgment, imagination, open-mindedness, empathy, enthusiasm and other general qualities, but these may remain little more than popular catchwords tempting us to believe that the reality of teaching matches the rhetoric. If cynicism is to be avoided, we need to have a critical awareness of the nature and value of such qualities in the context of teaching. We also need to recognize how these can be undermined if they are misinterpreted and misunderstood.

We must not, of course, allow ourselves to be persuaded that present practices and conditions are fixed and final, or even defensible, but there is something in the philosophical slogan that 'ought implies can'. It is irresponsible and unfair to ignore the constraints Horace faces in his teaching situation. Nevertheless ideals are useful, since they serve to remind us of what should be if only it could be.[3] They function as distant goals giving direction and justification, when particular decisions are made. If they themselves cannot be fully realized, they can help assure that other goals are met. Sometimes, in attempting to satisfy our ideals, we manage to achieve what would otherwise have been impossible. Such attempts can give us a new sense of what is possible. Think of the perilous work of Canadian doctor, Chris Giannou, in desperate circumstances in various parts of the world. Moreover, ideals can help to focus attention on how awful present conditions are, and thus they can be seen not as *ignoring* reality but as *exposing* it.

Another source of resistance, surely, is the feeling that ethical judgments about other people are too uncertain, partly because of the controversy which often surrounds ethical issues and partly because of the difficulty in ascribing ethical traits to others. Similar doubts arise about the subjective elements involved in ascribing qualities like enthusiasm, imagination, and judgment. The excellences to be introduced and reviewed in the next chapter and subsequently examined in more detail cannot be simply added to a checklist a supervisor or principal might carry into a classroom where a teacher is being observed. We need to resist the familiar tendency to reduce complex qualities to particular observable acts witnessed in a brief encounter.

It is, however, valuable for teachers to reflect on their own practice with these virtues and traits in mind, and important for those who supervise teachers to look for more than behavioural conformity. It is, of course, notoriously difficult to judge well in our own case, but the Delphic "know thyself" (*gnothi seauton*) is also an ideal worthy of our attention. In some cases, of course, we will have to make these difficult assessments about other people, as we shall see. As far as controversy is concerned, there is no denying that some ethical issues resist universal agreement, indeed provoke violent and profound animosity. It is not wise or accurate, however, to judge the whole field of morality by the most controversial elements in it. We have a very different picture of ethics if we turn from abortion, for example, to the matter of child abuse. Similarly, qualitative assessment of teachers with respect to rather general talents such as judgment and imagination is notoriously difficult but nevertheless vital. It will be useful also to ask ourselves how far the nature of teaching and education can suggest appropriate excellences to serve as our ideals.

## Close Proximity and Critical Perspective

Having recommended the ideal of self-knowledge, and having hinted at the possibility of shared values, we may be faced with the suggestion that teachers and other professionals be left to their own good sense to apply sound ethical judgments in their practice, and to strive to meet high standards of excellence. What need is there of philosophers, or other would-be experts, to intervene, especially when they are not as familiar with the actual context as those whose work brings them into daily contact with the issues and problems? Something like this attitude could be detected some years ago when people first began raising issues about genetic engineering. Close proximity, unfortunately, is no guarantee of awareness and can militate against it. It was recently reported that a parent in Oklahoma had sued the local school district for locking her thirteen-year-old son in the cafeteria closet for three days, from 8:25 a.m. to 2:45 p.m. each day, for fighting. The boy had to urinate in a bottle.[4] The school officials involved in this episode have lost perspective. Maxine Greene's powerful metaphor of "teacher as stranger" brings home the point that there is the danger of what she called unthinking submergence in the social reality that prevails.[5] It is not easy to gain the necessary distance from our practice which would enable us to see things in perspective and to notice what we are doing and what is missing. Consider, for example, how influential philosophers, notably Peter Singer, managed to open our eyes in the recent past to what was happening *all around us* with respect to the treatment of animals.[6]

The point may be sharpened by noting that *acceptance* of a value, respect for students say, does not entail *recognizing* that a question about our own performance with respect to that value arises. This may be because we have not adequately considered the various forms which respect can take, or because we simply have not seriously considered the possibility that we may have personal shortcomings in this connection. An example in the context of schooling would be the matter of privacy rights of students. Surveys conducted in Canada in the 1980s showed that few jurisdictions had *any* clear policy on this matter.[7] Philosophers have argued, however, that the right of privacy is an important aspect of what it means to show respect to others, and these ideas are only now beginning to engage our attention.[8] The traditional task of stinging people into awareness continues to be valuable, for the virtues can turn into empty clichés, inert ideas in Whitehead's phrase,[9] dead dogma to echo John Stuart Mill.[10] If these consequences are to be avoided, we need to go on thinking about ethical ideals and their justification, and we need to try to *apply* them in particular contexts to see what they come to. Sometimes, we discover that an appreciation which exists at a general level dissipates at the level of application to context.

We have been thinking here of the kind of close involvement in a role which prevents us from seeing what we could see if we managed to turn around and take notice. This is difficult enough. But a problem of a different order arises when a person so closely *identifies* with a certain role, or with aspects of that role, or when a role is narrowly defined, that moral issues and controversial matters are quite deliberately set aside as *irrelevant*. One's role is so construed that such considerations are altogether excluded, and the only criterion is to succeed at whatever cost. There was a report quite recently about a lawyer in the United States whose considered view was that he would conceal a client's admission of guilt even if an innocent person would be executed for the crime of which his client stood accused.[11] I have reread that passage many times to convince myself that I was not misremembering. There is no such mistake. Indeed, Stephen Gillers, a New York University law professor, is quoted in the same article as saying that "lawyers, especially criminal defence lawyers, are amoral agents". The defence lawyer's task is to defend, and this tautology comes to mean seeing that one succeeds in getting one's client off regardless of considerations of justice.

We are a long way here from Socrates' attitude during his own trial when he refused to engage in histrionics in a desperate effort to gain acquittal: "The jury does not sit to dispense justice as a favour, but to decide where justice lies."[12] At least Socrates was clear that justice *is* the relevant ideal. Isn't justice, however, a complex and problematic notion requiring the wisdom of Solomon? Of course, but can anyone believe that justice is served when an innocent person is convicted, let alone executed? What has happened, it seems clear, is that *success* has become the goal. We find, to put it bluntly, the philosophy attributed to Vince Lombardi. The attitude in question is notorious in sports where the idea that winning is the *only* thing originated. There we commonly find the kind of bifurcation which enables people to shut out ethical considerations when they are playing, and empirical studies have apparently confirmed that athletes and non-athletes alike use lower-level egocentric moral reasoning when thinking about dilemmas in sport.[13] Similar stories could be told in other walks of life. The tragic fate of the late Lee Atwater led him to admit to having had just this sort of amoral attitude in his approach to politics.[14]

With these points in mind, we might reflect on a case reported in the Canadian media in 1990. It was written up in one newspaper under the headline "Whiz kids beat stock market".[15] The story originated in British Columbia where more than one hundred high-school teams were engaged in a competition which involved mock trading on the Vancouver Stock Exchange. Each team started out with a hypothetical $50,000.00 and were to buy and sell stocks in order to produce the maximum gain by the end of the allotted period. Unfortunately, the rules of the game, sponsored by the exchange and a local newspaper, contained a fatal flaw. The exchange had agreed, apparently for reasons having to do with administrative convenience, to accept orders to buy and sell based on the closing price of the previous day. Assuming that the previous day's price had risen, it was possible to buy and to sell immediately, thereby securing an *assured* profit, an opportunity regrettably not offered in real life. Mock trading which became a mockery, we might say. The object of the competition had been to see how well the teams could read the trends in the market, and the flaw made the exercise completely pointless.

We can profit, however, from reflection on the reactions of those involved in the game. It is reassuring to note that some schools kept to the spirit of the competition and did not attempt to exploit the loophole. Many teachers noticed the opportunity but, to their credit, did not alert their students, leaving them to play the game as was intended. Some schools, however, including all the winning teams, opted for the easy route of instant, guaranteed profit and justified their actions on the grounds that this was part of life—see a loophole, exploit it, and beat the other person. Perhaps we should not be surprised. A press report a few years ago indicated that high-school students maintained they would be prepared to resort to evil and illegal behaviour in the name of business.[16] No doubt the students are right to claim that such is part of life, but the teachers are morally at fault for failing to advise their students that this line of justification is far from adequate. What *could* be objected to if such a defence were allowed? The students are right in another sense too, for it is not just that people are prepared to do whatever it takes to come out on top, but it is also widely held in respected professions that such behaviour is *perfectly appropriate*, as we have seen.

What has happened in such cases is that those involved have lost sight of the central aim and nature of the activity in which they are engaged, and also of the fact that this activity is not somehow hived off from the rest of life. They have forgotten that general moral principles remain *relevant*, and their sense of judgment has succumbed to the pressure to succeed. In competitive games, surely, the aim is to employ one's skills *at the activity* to emerge the winner. Using steroids, as so many athletes have done, shows that the central assumption has been abandoned. Moreover, one takes an unfair advantage. In the case of the stock-market game, the ill-thought-out procedures permitted the loophole to arise, but this could not have been part of the intention because it destroyed the essence of the contest. Many teachers apparently could not see, or did not care, that the justifications offered for exploiting the loophole were no more than self-serving rationalizations, which further encourage a tendency already far too common in society.

They also missed an opportunity to explore with their students the distinction between a move technically permissible under existing rules and a critical evaluation of the rules themselves.

## Unthinking Submergence in the Context of Teaching

Let us look more specifically now at teaching in order to illustrate two kinds of blinkered perspective. First, teachers can be so convinced that the position they personally subscribe to is both true and important that they justify to themselves the use of virtually any tactic which will ensure that their students come to share their views. Second, and at the opposite extreme, teachers can see themselves, in Dewey's apposite phrase, as mere tradesmen[17] routinely relaying officially sanctioned information. To put the point rather starkly, we have on the one hand, the zealot, on the other, the hack. Different as these are, both have lost sight of what they should be about and both are guilty of a similar moral failure as concerns their students.

Jim Keegstra will serve as an example of the zealot in the classroom.[18] Keegstra, as most Canadians by now know, subverted the curriculum to ensure that his own bizarre views about an international Jewish conspiracy would dominate the classroom and seize the minds of his students. Moreover, once the students started to entertain his ideas at all seriously, the trap was set. His theory was so constructed that nothing could emerge as counter-evidence. Anything advanced as such was reinterpreted as further evidence supporting the theory. Thus, the dissenting views of standard authorities were taken not as counter-evidence at all, but as evidence of the conspiracy at work. The case is, I think, a paradigm example of indoctrination, where the intention was to make certain that the students would come to accept a set of ideas irrevocably. Keegstra was so submerged in his own views that teaching became for him a matter of ensuring that particular claims, regarded as incorrigible truths, were passed on to others so as to prevent them from being duped.

Unpleasant as it may be, especially if we would like to tell ourselves that Keegstra was an exceptional case, we must recall that he was *widely* regarded as a good teacher. Much as people were only able to recognize the deficiencies of the van Meegeren forgeries when the deception was

finally revealed at the end of the Second World War, so too an appreciation of the enormity of the Keegstra case came far too late to many
who should have known better, especially his colleagues and superiors,
and certain officials in the Alberta Teachers' Association. An ethical
appraisal was embarrassingly absent, with the notable exception of
several parents and the superintendent who pursued the case. Instead,
utterly superficial comments about classroom management and discipline were allowed to count as establishing that he was a good teacher,
a disturbing indication that this notion is in danger of becoming ethi-
cally bankrupt. When the school board finally moved against Keegstra,
what followed was knee-jerk protectionism on the part of the teachers'
association. Serious ethical questions about his teaching were brushed
aside, sometimes with a spurious appeal to freedom of expression and
tolerance, as if these were absolute principles.

In Keegstra's own case, fanatical zeal led him to engage in outright
propaganda for his views. Keegstra is a man of principle and conviction,
and quite certainly sincere; however, fanaticism—what Russell usefully
characterized as the inclination to think some one thing so overwhelm-
ingly important that everything else pales into insignificance beside
it[19]—meant that critical questions he might otherwise have raised
about his approach to teaching were put on indefinite hold. We may
even admit that Keegstra has a sense of responsibility, that is, he takes
what he sees as his duty seriously, but he has *no* sense of what his
responsibilities as a teacher are.

The classic instance of the hack is Thomas Gradgrind, and since
such teachers rarely reach public notoriety in real life, perhaps we
should prudently confine our illustrations to fiction. What is so glar-
ingly absent in this approach to teaching is any attempt to encourage,
or even permit, the students to think, to question, or to reflect on what
they are learning. Nothing but Facts! Over the past century, leading
philosophers of education have regularly expressed concern about the
sorry condition of intellectual independence and vitality in teaching.
We have Dewey's criticism of the machine teacher, that servant of rule
and routine; Russell's attack on the modern teacher as a civil servant;
and Scheffler's rejection of the conception of the teacher as a minor
technician.[20]  In his most recent collection of essays, Scheffler has

returned to this theme with a warning that notions which are fashion-able in the computer age are liable to confirm the erroneous conviction that education is no more than the acquisition of information.[21]

Both types of teacher fail to respect the independent judgment and potential autonomy of the student. The one seeks to suppress these abilities and rights, the other fails to foster them. Whether through design or default, however, the result is that the student fails to develop a critical attitude with respect to ideas and information. Mindless cramming may seem less offensive from the moral point of view than outright propaganda, but remember that cramming leaves students ill-equipped to deal with propaganda when it appears. Habits of uncrit-ical acceptance will have been inculcated. Moreover, the information conveyed will certainly not be free from assumptions and associations which deserve to be critically examined. Both approaches to teaching seriously misinterpret the nature of teaching. What is missing is any sense of teaching as a rational activity, an open-minded enterprise in which ideas are open to the critical assessment of one's students. And these ideas are central to any serious conception of education.

## Getting On With the Job

Practically-minded teachers express their impatience with the pro-tracted and abstract disputes and arguments of philosophers of educa-tion by pointing out that there is, in fact, a *job* to be done. Come Sep-tember, every teacher will have four or five classes of thirty-five or more students to cope with, and the business of teaching them must proceed. Even if we agree with Dewey that education should not be reduced to "covering the ground", there is a curriculum to be covered, texts to be read, objectives to be met, grades to be assigned, and so on. The daily and weekly responsibilities are time-consuming and exhausting, with energies drained by mundane and routine tasks which, nevertheless, have to be done. Small wonder, then, that efficiency and effectiveness become the watchwords, and notions like enthusiasm, imagination, open-mindedness, and judgment begin to sound like gestures towards an ideal world far removed from the realities of the average school or college.

In the end, however, this point of view is not completely satisfying. The basic problem is that the fundamental concept of "the job" which is to be pursued remains problematic. Our work involves an interpretation of what our function as teachers is, and the conception which guides our practice may be limited and inadequate. Clive Beck makes this point, somewhat dramatically perhaps, when he notes that "it might be argued that in some educational institutions no more good than harm is being done, year in and year out; so that in these institutions *every* person/hour is being wasted, a staggering thought."[22] Put bluntly, there is little point in getting on with the job, if the job we are doing is of dubious educational merit.[23] As John Passmore has pointed out, it is a function of critical reflection that it lead to certain types of performance being *abandoned* rather than pursued more efficiently.[24]

General excellences such as open-mindedness, imagination, a sense of judgment, and enthusiasm do not indicate precise strategies to be followed, nor do they come with a guarantee that greater efficiency will be achieved. It is easy to lose sight of them as we slip into thinking of teaching as covering the ground, getting through the text, providing information, instilling the basics, "time on task" (but which task, and why?), preparing for examinations, and so on. Beyond these routines, which in time distort and trivialize our overall approach, there are *attitudes towards* knowledge and study which must be communicated if our fondest hopes for education are to be attained but which cannot be reduced to a set of "instructible" skills. Such attitudes *are* relatively hard to pin down in concrete, practical terms, and yet it can be absolutely clear that they are present or absent, as we have seen.

The challenge for teachers is to try to maintain a proper perspective on their work as a whole. This ultimately requires having a coherent and defensible conception of education and teaching which provides a justification for all the particular decisions that are made with respect to the curriculum, pedagogical strategies, tests, and so on. The question is not so much what the teacher should do, but rather what sort of person the teacher should be. Teachers, for example, who ask their students "Are you trying to teach me something?"—and my own children have all heard that sarcastic and threatening question at some point—show that they have not adequately thought out the meaning of education, and they communicate to their students a distorted notion of teaching. Presumably, such teachers define their work as a one-way, authoritative transmission of infallible information, where the ideal student is a passive and deferential recipient.

Teaching is inescapably a serious enterprise since both the form and the content of education influence the development of students. Recall that Socrates pointed out that the choice of a teacher for one's children is especially daunting and difficult because, in effect, one is deciding the kind of person the child will become. We dignify the teacher's position by calling it a trust, and indeed it is an enormous responsibility. How we deal with students, with respect or contempt, interest or indifference, impartially or unjustly, will convey by example attitudes they may learn. What we choose to teach more directly—the ideas, theories, principles, and skills which form the content of our teaching—will constitute an important part of the resources they will have available to bring to the problems and issues they will face. How we address these issues, courageously or evasively, showing open-mindedness or dogmatism, displaying judgment or stupidity, will help to shape the future attitudes and responses of our students.

If we were to lift our sights above the immediate and pressing concerns of the daily schedule, what kinds of moral, intellectual and personal qualities would we wish those who teach our children to possess? These have been alluded to in passing, but it is time now to introduce them explicitly. The qualities which are important suggest themselves when we bring to mind complaints that arise about many teachers. They are arrogant and dismissive of the views of their students. They fall in with fashionable trends and fail to challenge the status quo. They are often biased and prejudiced. They are dogmatic. They are indifferent to the concerns of their students. They often seem uninterested in their work. They treat rules as if they were absolute. And they are uninspired and uninspiring. What qualities would serve to correct these failings?

# CHAPTER TWO

# *Excellence: Seeking Ideals*

Everything the teacher does, as well as the manner in which
he does it, incites the child to respond in some way or other,
and each response tends to set the child's attitude in some
way or other.

John Dewey—*How We Think*

## *Humility and Courage: Neglected Virtues*

Reflection on the potentially immense influence teachers may have
on their students for good or evil should induce a sense of humility. A
useful beginning on the path of self-awareness would be made if we were
to disturb the overly sharp dualism of teacher and student. There is, of
course, a distinction in *relative* terms with respect to knowledge and
skills, but teachers need to remember that in another context they
would be, and sometimes are, students themselves. In a general sense,
they need to see themselves as learners as much as teachers. Recognition of this point is not furthered, I think, by the view, enshrined in the
Bill of Rights promulgated by the American Federation of Teachers,[1]
that any further studies following initial qualification as a teacher must
be freely chosen not required. There is a distinction between attaining
and maintaining a level of competency which is somewhat obscured by
thinking of the right to teach as a property right. A certain complacency
associated with the idea that one's status as teacher is determined once
and for all does not bode well for an appreciation of the ethical responsibility of keeping up in one's field, a responsibility which is strikingly
absent from codes of ethics for the teaching profession.[2]

Jacques Maritain echoed Socrates' insight in his comment that "the
educational task is both greater and more mysterious and, in a sense,
humbler than many imagine."[3]  Greater, I think, because of the far-

reaching consequences; more mysterious because of the difficulty in determining the aims of education and how they can possibly be achieved; and humbler than we imagine because the teacher's relative superiority disguises the tenuous grasp we have on knowledge and wisdom. Maritain was right to believe that the point needed making. One will look in vain, for example, in an influential writer like Skinner for any appreciation of this notion. He loftily dismissed the view of Marcus Aurelius that opinions cannot be changed and announced that the techniques of indoctrination, psychotherapy and advertising were at hand.[4] The very distinctions which should give us pause in teaching, such as that between propaganda and education, are simply obliterated by Skinner.

Humility, by contrast, involves a due sense of one's limitations, always in danger of being ignored in a context which encourages deference and invites the abuse of authority. Etienne Gilson told the story of a shop in France displaying the notice: "If it concerns motor cars, ask us. We know it."[5] His sensible advice to anyone encountering such a notice was to steer clear. A *fortiori* for the context of teaching. A healthy development would be a greater willingness than we often find in the context of teaching to admit that one doesn't know or is mistaken, for the idea of the teacher as the omniscient fount of wisdom seems ever likely to take hold. The failing is clear enough in the case of the zealot convinced of his or her own infallibility even where the matter is eminently controversial or where the relevant experts think otherwise. The propagandist, having *found* the truth, is content to neglect the teacher's primary responsibility to engage others in the *pursuit* of truth.

The teacher who "sticks to the facts", however, is also falling short of a responsibility to ask, and to stimulate the students to ask, if what we are inclined to view as facts really are facts at all. Not, I hasten to add, in the manner of the mere iconoclast, for that approach would lack the humility Gilson also speaks of which involves submission to truth from whatever source. And, we may add, however unpalatable. Submission, however, presupposes critical assessment, and precisely this is absent when teaching forgoes the connection with reason and degenerates into the mindless inculcation of information. Dewey reminded us that "there is all the difference in the world whether the acquisition of information is treated as an end in itself, or is made an integral portion of the training of thought."[6] The teacher who communicates an uncritical attitude towards views currently regarded as true has not learned, and is not fostering, that humility which is suggested by Russell's observation that very few opinions current three hundred years ago are thought right today.[7]

Just as an appeal to tolerance and freedom of expression can mask our unwillingness to make difficult judgments, so too humility can become a convenient excuse for avoiding matters which are likely to prove controversial and expose teachers to potentially hostile reactions. Rationalizations are readily available. Who are we to pretend that we can resolve such issues? Are we not likely to influence our students unduly? The line of thought which leads to teacher neutrality comes rather easily. During the Gulf War, the Halifax City School Board circulated to all teachers a one-page list of suggestions as to what they should and should not do. There were some valuable reminders here, such as the need to avoid ridiculing or belittling questions raised by students, but the fundamental message was one Thomas Gradgrind could applaud. Stick to the facts and avoid speculation, personal opinions, philosophical and religious ideas, and any kind of judgment. Proper humility, however, does not require that teachers forbear making any comment when there is less than universal consensus that the claim made is certain; it is shown in the attitude we have towards the claims we make, and in the manner in which we make them.

Paul Weiss once remarked that one virtue alone is not enough to make a person virtuous. The virtues must support each other.[8] In the case of teaching, humility is naturally complemented by moral courage. The zealot, of course, may show courage in facing and enduring the consequences which misguided convictions bring on, but this sort of case shows clearly how courage needs to be tempered with humility. (The example also shows how particular virtues have to be placed in context before any *general* conclusions about the person's character can be drawn.) Conversely, humility needs to be accompanied by courage. We can learn the lesson of humility, recognize the fallible nature of our position, yet still need to find the courage to pursue and defend those ideals and objectives which are central to our work as teachers. Humility must not translate into diffidence, hesitancy or timidity.

It is a forbidding prospect for individual parents to take on the educational establishment, but teachers and administrators face difficulties also. Teachers, for example, are often encouraged to believe that it is unprofessional to criticize the work of a colleague. Codes of ethics rarely emphasize the moral responsibility to expose abuse. The Keegstra case is a sobering reminder that, even when a situation is such that almost everyone will come to condemn it *in the end*, courage is still required to make the first move.[9] The superintendent in question had to face the hostility and bitterness of Keegstra's colleagues, an encounter few would relish. Now, of course, it no longer takes courage to speak out on this case. The criticisms are perceived as valid and have come to gain general acceptance. It has, in effect, become a safe example. This did not happen overnight, however, and there were many unpleasant moments and situations along the way.

Courage is shown not only in attacking an evil but also in refusing to go along with an injustice to which most are prepared to turn a blind eye. Socrates reported at his trial that he was the only member of the executive to oppose the decision to try the ten commanders as a group rather than individually, a proposal which enjoyed popular support but which was unconstitutional. Socrates took his stand on the side of justice.[10] Consider then a contemporary situation in which an author or teacher is accused of racism by a group which sincerely believes the charge is justified. If it is true, it is a serious matter and must be dealt with. But if it is *not* true, our concern to oppose racism must not overshadow the right to a fair hearing. In an emotionally charged atmosphere, how many will be willing to speak up for someone unjustly accused? It is possible that one's objections may be misrepresented as indicating one's own latent racism. One exposes oneself to the same charge with little likelihood of others rallying to one's defence on such a sensitive issue. Educators have often timidly accommodated pressure groups to the point where a crisis is provoked. The California State Department of Education felt obliged in 1985 to reject as seriously inadequate *all* of the elementary-school science textbooks previously approved, which had tried to entertain every objection and demand raised by interest groups until nothing of value remained.[11]

Topics and causes can become *sacred* in the sense that anything short of immediate and unqualified agreement with the dominant view invites suspicion and calls one's integrity into question. Edward Wynne has observed that it may require "considerable moral courage to take public positions contrary to certain popular causes."[12] To raise a critical question about a school programme designed to alert young children to the nature of sexual touching is to run the risk that one's motives will become suspect.[13] To ask for hard evidence about the effectiveness of French immersion programmes is perhaps to lay oneself open to the charge that one's question is a cloak for prejudice. To query the claim that hate literature has a causal influence on behaviour may create the impression that one does not disapprove of the sentiments expressed in such writing. And so on. Twenty-five years ago, John Passmore remarked, somewhat pessimistically, that a teacher will find life less troublesome if he or she permits criticism of what is generally admitted to be a proper subject for criticism, and it is not clear that the situation today is very different.[14]

It was suggested, during the period of student unrest at the end of the 1960s, that what was heralded as "the right to dissent" was no longer being interpreted as the right to advance and defend unorthodox views but as the right to assert certain, approved ideas and to prevent other people from stating contrary ones.[15] Today, such a right seems to be openly claimed by those who see, even if they do not describe, themselves as Politically Correct, and already there is plenty of evidence that resistance to the tactics and demands of this movement will trigger the worst accusations, name-calling and even disruption of one's classes.[16] Let us recall that what was objectionable in Keegstra's approach was not the *consideration* of offensive ideas but the systematic attempt to ensure that these ideas were *accepted* at all costs by the students. Our objection, surely, is to certain aims and methods which subvert the educational process by overriding the critical faculties of the students. If our objection really is to the aim of indoctrination and the methods of propaganda, must we not also object to these aims and methods when they characterize the work of those whose views we happen to share? We need to have the courage of our convictions.

## Impartiality and Open-Mindedness: Vital Attitudes

In trying to meet the demands of humility and courage in our work as teachers, one guiding principle is impartiality. We need to be humble enough to ask awkward questions about our own biases yet courageous enough to challenge bias when we discover it elsewhere. Of course, freedom from bias is an ideal and we would do well to retain a healthy scepticism about our own ability to avoid bias. Relative success demands skill, judgment and self-awareness. There is an ethical dimension in our concern to try to eliminate bias in our teaching, since such a concern indicates respect for students as independent inquirers with a right to honest answers. If truth and genuine understanding are important to our idea of what it is to become educated, then we need to be acutely aware of the way in which our own desires and preferences can bias our inquiries and our teaching. Russell reminded us that "this may seem no more than a trite truism. But to remember it consistently in matters arousing our passionate partisanship is by no means easy, especially where the available evidence is uncertain and inconclusive."[17]

Critical examination of school textbooks over the years reveals a great deal of bias, taking various forms, as well as a view of society which is, in the words of one commentator, non-controversial and conventional.[18] Nowadays, we try harder but it is worth observing that the name Donald Marshall does not appear in the social studies textbook *The Maritimes: Tradition, Challenge and Change* published in 1987.[19] It is not time yet to become complacent. Still, if we can identify in our own work an example of bias, overt or implicit, we are in a position to try to remove it, or to rewrite the offending passage, and this constitutes one more step in the direction of the elusive ideal.

The notion of offense, however, is potentially troublesome. I have referred elsewhere to a disturbing incident in 1988 when an assistant deputy minister at the Department of External Affairs in Ottawa sent a letter to the Ottawa Board of Education in an attempt to alter the historical content of a high-school course. Apparently, the motive was to avoid giving offense to a trading partner, namely Turkey.[20] Whether or not a certain incident occurred, however, and how it is to be characterized, are matters to be determined through historical scholarship, and the serious study of history is *abandoned* if such questions are decided by reference to what is politically expedient. The ethical requirement is plain, and has been succinctly stated by Harvey Siegel in the context of science education: "If we are to meet our moral responsibilities as educators, we cannot wilfully distort the history of science—or anything else—no matter how effective such distortion might be."[21] Such an incident makes it clear why it is important to add the words "however unpalatable" to Gilson's ideal of submission to truth cited earlier.

No one in Canada has addressed this issue more effectively than John Trueman, an historian who has had the experience of seeing one of his own books delisted. It was removed from the list of approved school texts in Ontario. Trueman, very appropriately, entitled his article dealing with the affair "Lest we offend: The search for a perfect past",[22] and his concern was to defend the integrity of history as an independent and disciplined form of inquiry against attempts at rewriting history to accommodate the preferences of pressure groups. Trueman was in trouble for failing to record *as an historical fact* certain theological claims. Diane Ravitch has observed that publishers strive to offend no one as they try to reach the largest market possible.[23] The profit motive, however, is not sufficient to explain the decisions of education authorities. Other factors are at work, as we shall see.

Trueman draws the depressingly accurate conclusion that the principle of offending no one will ensure that serious history will cease to exist in our schools. One qualification to Trueman's excellent critique concerns his reference to Allan Nevins' remark that impartial history in the sense of lacking conviction would be a poor affair.[24] Nevins, of course, is arguing that convictions are as desirable as they are inevitable in writing history, but the point is made in a misleading way. What needs to be said emphatically here, is that impartiality does *not* require the absence of conviction.[25] Impartiality speaks of the way in which our convictions and conclusions are arrived at, and of how we review the case made by others against them. The impartial jury is still required to produce a verdict, and a passionate conviction that justice matters is entirely appropriate.

It is extremely useful for teachers to have access to helpful guidelines as they strive for impartiality, but even relatively sophisticated guidelines fall into confusion over this ideal. Bear in mind that the underlying purpose of guidelines with respect to bias is to enable teachers to avoid discrimination and prejudice against identifiable groups. Thus, in the *Standards* issued by the California State Department of Education in 1986, the purpose of the guidelines which concern male and female roles is "to promote the individual development and self-esteem of each student, regardless of gender."[26] That is a principle or conviction, and eminently defensible, but it does not require that we adopt the view that other cultures cannot be evaluated adversely at all.[27] Here, surely, we see the influence of relativism, the idea that all cultures must be deemed equally worthy in every respect. How is one to respect the principle concerning gender equality if no adverse comment can be made about a culture which not only does not subscribe to this norm, but treats females as second-class citizens or worse? Impartiality requires that we apply our principles without prejudice to all societies, taking into account relevant differences in circumstance. Failure to do so, by ignoring violations of a principle, means that we are *not* being impartial.[28]

Although open-mindedness cannot guarantee that we will succeed in avoiding bias, it is nonetheless the appropriate attitude in this connection just because it involves the attempt to sift the evidence on its merits, to set aside irrelevant considerations, and to take into account whatever has a legitimate bearing on the matter at hand. The open-minded person is prepared to be influenced by reason and evidence in coming to a conclusion, and holds his or her beliefs in such a way that they are subject to modification and even revocation in the light of emerging knowledge. Dewey aptly characterized open-mindedness as that attitude which sought freedom from prejudice, partisanship, and other habits which prevent the mind from considering new ideas.[29]

Teaching is a position of trust because initially children are not really capable of challenging and critically examining the ideas they are presented with. They naturally tend to have confidence in their teachers and must be encouraged gradually to move towards a more independent position of their own. How are we, as parents and citizens, to believe that even such preliminary and tentative confidence in an individual is warranted? John Stuart Mill's general answer to this question is still valuable: "Because he has kept his mind open to criticism of his opinions and conduct. Because it has been his practice to listen to all that could be said against him; to profit by as much of it as was just, and to expound to himself, and upon occasion to others, the fallacy of what was fallacious."[30] Mill was speaking of the grounds which justify confidence in a person's judgment. We can add that reassurance would also come from knowing that a teacher had an open-minded disposition since errors of judgment would be tempered both by an inclination to reconsider and an example to students of an adult whose pronouncements were not dogmatic.

Karen Warren, writing from a feminist perspective, takes the view that open-mindedness is a disposition which persons do or do not exercise *within* a conceptual framework. She gives as an example of a fundamental (and invisible) assumption the belief that science is objective and value-neutral. On this view, she comments, it will be extremely difficult, if not impossible, to entertain certain ideas seriously.[31] The slippery patch, however, from extremely difficult to impossible is absolutely critical, and the casual phrasing makes it tempting to slide on by. It *cannot* be impossible to entertain ideas contrary to this thesis about science if for no other reason than because some people *have* entertained such ideas and subsequently *modified* their original view. There are any number of examples in the history of thought where the once invisible has been rendered visible and subjected to critical scrutiny. Warren is unwilling to admit that one can be open-minded *about* one's fundamental conceptual framework, but she gives us no reason to believe that this is impossible, however difficult it may be.

Her conclusion, namely that feminists who do not take certain arguments seriously should not be dismissed as closed-minded, does not require the view that open-mindedness is only exercised within a certain conceptual framework which is itself, presumably, impervious to criticism. Moreover, Warren's view that open-mindedness does not necessarily require that *all* points of view be given equal consideration is not particularly feminist. All that needs to be said is that certain views *have* been examined and found wanting, and in the absence of further and more compelling grounds of support, they can safely be ignored. Some views and arguments have nothing going for them, and open-mindedness does not impose an obligation on anyone to waste time on fatuous ideas. It would be foolish to take seriously an argument which is clearly deficient.[32]

At the same time, however, we would all do well to remember that assumptions which once seemed solid and beyond question have been shown to be untenable. Stephen Toulmin is right to remind us that what we once termed inconceivable has turned out to be true more often than we care to admit.[33] If we tell ourselves that our open-mindedness is restricted to modifications which leave our fundamental views intact, then we set ourselves to avoid making changes to those basic views *whatever arguments emerge*, and that *is* closed-minded and short-sighted. Moreover, in the context of teaching, it is vitally important to consider rival views so that our students realize that the teacher's own position rests on evidence and argument and that other views are rejected because they fail to withstand critical scrutiny. In this way, teaching fosters long-term dispositions which reach beyond the particular substantive positions being defended. It is not prudent, to say the least, for teachers to tell themselves, following Warren, that their own positions may be biased but *only* in the limited and special sense that they are not value-neutral. *Any* position may turn out to be biased in the more serious and literal sense of being distorted, exaggerated, misleading and so on.[34] It is a mark of open-mindedness to be conscious of this possibility.

## Empathy and Enthusiasm: Potent Forces

If we reflect on some of the earlier examples, it is not difficult to see why many have come to think that some ideal, in addition to impartiality or open-mindedness, must be introduced. The school officials in Oklahoma who lock students in the cafeteria closet very likely apply their discipline policy impartially. There is no suggestion that they discriminate against certain groups. But they seem incapable of *empathizing* with another person's fear and humiliation.[35] The lawyer who can watch with equanimity as an innocent person is convicted may have followed the procedural rules properly but has ceased to care for others as persons with hopes and fears, not to mention rights. The teachers and students who exploit loopholes to secure their own advantage are moving in the same direction. The propagandist has missed the point made by Russell that the teacher who can be trusted must care for the students *on their own account*, not merely as potential allies in a cause.[36] If the propagandist were to care for the students as independent inquirers, this would offset an inclination to care only that whatever he or she views as the truth be accepted. In effect, genuine caring for the students would underline the need for a stronger commitment to impartiality with respect to content.

Impartiality and empathy can and should complement each other, and we should resist any temptation in the direction of either/or reasoning. For example, it is sometimes suggested that impartiality is inimical to empathy. One philosopher observes that a person whose commitment to impartiality led him or her to care no more for his or her own children than for strangers would seem to us a terrifying saint.[37] The idea would seem to be that true impartiality would preclude any *special* feelings for one's own children or students. Should not the impartial teacher care as much about *any* potential learner as about his or her own students? Does not the special caring for *our* children or students violate the universality implicit in impartiality? These alleged implications run counter to our deepest intuitions. It *is* terrifying if a parent lacks those human emotions which would translate into spontaneous action, forgoing impartial deliberation, were his or her own child to be in danger. But does impartiality carry these implications? Should we see such a parent as a saint?

Three basic points need to be made. First, we can subscribe to the principle that *any* parent or teacher ought to care primarily for their own children or students. Since this principle is universalizable, it avoids the criticism that in acting so as to favour one's own children or students, we are following a principle which unfairly builds in a reference to ourselves. Second, this principle can be justified on utilitarian grounds as likely to be more productive of good than diffuse efforts to care for anyone and everyone.[38] The "terrifying saint" is misguided. Third, given this principle, impartiality enters in with respect to the way in which we treat our own children and students. All must be treated impartially, as children themselves quickly remind us in condemning favouritism. Scheffler makes the nice point that care itself requires to be apportioned equitably.[39]

Why *should* empathy be considered so central an ideal in the context of teaching? What is the link between teaching and caring for one's students? If it were simply a matter of empathy in general, we might take our stand with Hume and say that it is a superfluous task to prove that the benevolent affections are estimable.[40] It might be maintained, however, that teachers and other professionals ought to strive for a certain detachment, not allowing themselves to become "personally involved" as it is sometimes put.[41] How is the ideal to be defended against such doubts? Let us set aside, first, the idea that empathy is a necessary condition of any teaching occurring at all. Surely, *some* teaching, not necessarily the best kind perhaps, can occur in a lecture to several hundred students, when talk of empathy would be idle. Second, we need not insist that *at every point* in the teacher's role empathy is central. If a teacher is serving as adjudicator at the annual school science project fair, a certain professional detachment is probably desirable. Having made these qualifications, however, our basic questions remain.

Recall again Socrates' remark to Callias about the momentous consequences implicit in the choice of a teacher for one's children. If we value the benevolent affections in human relationships, and I assume that we do, then we need teachers who can help to foster these dispositions through the very way in which they interact with their students. The caring teacher does not respond out of a sense of duty but in a genuine display of a benevolent disposition. What is needed is not a didactic approach, but an atmosphere or environment which is warm, supportive, tolerant and sensitive. The individuality of our students and circumstances, however, means that teachers cannot learn to show that they care by rehearsing a set of behaviours.[42] We need teachers who do care but who also have the necessary judgment to act in ways which show that they care. There is a tendency in educational theory to reduce these ways to particular arrangements and practices, but in addition to the fact that such restrictions can make one's response seem contrived and inauthentic, they also represent an arbitrary limit on the ways in which people can communicate attitudes.

It is not enough, however, to care for one's students, vital as this may be. It is also important to care both for one's subject and for teaching it, if the students are to be well served. (Perhaps it was a failure to remember consistently that one is never *just* teaching science or history but also participating in the overall upbringing of a human being which allowed some philosophers of education in the recent past to maintain that many excellent teachers remain rather remote figures showing little positive interest in their students as human beings.[43]) At its best, such interest amounts to a vibrant enthusiasm which communicates itself to the students. Perhaps because too often teachers have been found to be less than minimally competent with respect to subject preparation and teaching ability, recent educational theory has emphasized competency-based teacher education in order to meet the demand for accountability. No one can sensibly be opposed to competency with respect to valuable skills and activities, but competency does not preclude being dull and dreary. Dewey made the point that "in urging the need of psychology in the preparation of the teacher there is no question of ignoring personal power or of finding a substitute for personal magnetism."[44]

When one sees genuine enthusiasm for a subject in an individual, it is immediately clear that it has very little to do with a stylized performance where readily identifiable gestures, movements and so on are observed. Sir Isaiah Berlin was interviewed in the 1970s by Bryan Magee in a BBC television programme concerned with philosophy. Their topic was the nature of philosophy itself, and involved the consideration of questions which Berlin must have discussed a thousand times during a long teaching career.[45] The two remain seated throughout the fifty-minute conversation, so there is no opportunity for the kind of dramatic movement about the room so beloved of textbook writers who condemn teachers who are "relatively motionless". It is, in fact, an example of the much despised "talking heads" approach. And yet there is no denying the enthusiasm, excitement, animation, and sense of vital importance evident in the facial expression, tone of voice, and energy which accompany Berlin's remarks. These come naturally to someone who has a passionate interest in the questions, and cannot be rehearsed.

Carl Sagan has called attention to the regrettable fact that the enthusiasm which elementary students display for learning early in their school careers has largely disappeared by the time these students reach high school. Presumably, there are many factors involved here, but one factor surely has to do with the failure of teachers to respond with real enthusiasm to those difficult, often unanswerable, questions which children pose: "Too many teachers and parents answer with irritation or ridicule, or quickly move on to something else. Why adults should pretend to omniscience before a five-year-old, I can't for the life of me understand."[46] No doubt Sagan really does know what is at work here, namely a limited conception of teaching as a process of infallibly imparting information at the cost of ignoring the enthusiastic exploration of ideas.[47]

## Judgment and Imagination: Crucial Talents

In March 1992, the Supreme Court of Canada issued a judgment with respect to its own so-called Askov decision in 1990 which had held that a person's constitutional right to a fair trial could be violated by delays in bringing the case before the courts, and suggested that delays of more than six to eight months were excessive.[48] The result of this decision was that thousands of criminal cases in Canada were simply dropped, including some for very serious offences. The Supreme Court felt it necessary to state explicitly that the Askov guideline is just that, a guideline, not a rigid formula to be applied mechanically. In reaching a decision with respect to a delay in proceeding to trial, the Supreme Court pointed out that many factors have to be taken into consideration and there is no automatic way of determining whether or not the delay is acceptable. The Supreme Court, in effect, said that the lower courts have to use judgment.

Howard Hampton, Attorney-General for Ontario, was quoted as saying that it would have been helpful if the original Askov decision had made it clear that it was *not* prescribing rigid time constraints. This comment is quite revealing. It suggests that, in the absence of explicit instructions to the contrary, what is stated will be taken as a firm rule to be applied to the letter. Kim Campbell, Federal Justice Minister, was reported as being delighted that it was now clear that judges have to use common sense in deciding when to throw out a case. But how could it be otherwise? How could it have been thought that judges should *not* use common sense in these matters? Since it is plain that many factors enter into such cases and that cases have unique features, why would it be automatically assumed that the Askov decision laid down an inflexible time limit?

The general problem addressed here is a familiar one in virtually every profession and context where decisions are made. We read with a mixture of amusement and despair of an individual who has lived in Canada for sixty years, with a Canadian spouse and children, being refused entry by Immigration Canada on her return from a trip outside the country, and classified as an illegal alien. But the rules were followed, we are told, as no doubt they are when members of terrorist organizations are given security clearance and admitted to the country as refugees. Immigration Canada makes decisions about landed immigrant status on the basis of a points system, designed to promote fairness, but which in practice means that arithmetical calculation often overrides judgment.

Another government agency which abjures judgment is the Social Services Department of the Northwest Territories which has banned its drug and alcohol counsellors from consuming *any* alcohol at *any* time. (Presumably, then, communicants are prevented from taking the sacrament in those churches where alcoholic wine is used.) Andrew Langford, director of alcohol, drug and community mental health services in the Social Services Department, favours the slippery slope argument: "Where do you draw the line? If one drink is okay, why are two drinks not okay, or three drinks?"[49] Or twenty perhaps? In other words, the Department cannot or will not distinguish between those who exercise judgment in consuming alcohol in a responsible and moderate fashion, and those whose lives are being ruined by reckless consumption of alcohol. Such judgments, sometimes involving borderline cases, will not be made, and the Department will not recognize that there are those who can make them for themselves.

A review of the media in any given week will yield a rich supply of examples. A man is stabbed outside a hospital but taken to another hospital six kilometres away where he is dead on arrival. The ambulance workers are praised for "following procedures". (Is there, one wonders, in fact a procedure which holds that *a dying person outside a hospital must, regardless of the person's condition, be taken to another, specified hospital?* Rather, one suspects, a certain hospital is generally indicated as appropriate for particular injuries. It would be remarkable if the regulations covered this particular incident in all its specificity. In fact, regulations *cannot* anticipate every contingency, hence the in-eliminable need for intelligent judgment in the application of regula-tions.) Other cases abound. Homicidal persons are given day release from hospital or prison only to kill again; children are removed from caring homes by zealous social workers who cannot tell the difference between birthmarks and bruises; academics seriously propound absurd theses which effectively thwart intelligent judgment (such as the view that you *are* a racist if someone of colour *says* you are); forensic experts prove unable to distinguish blood from spray paint (as happened in the Lindy Chamberlain case in Australia); an Olympic Games' judge en-sures that the gold medal is awarded to someone who clearly has not gained the highest score rather than correct a human error. And so on. Readers will quickly draw up their own choice list.

Naturally, the field of education is not exempt. In one recent Canadian case, a fifteen-year-old received a month's detentions to be served at lunchtime when a school board official heard him singing the rap song "Let's talk about sex" outside school grounds on the main street of the town. School-board lawyers claimed the boy was punished for purposely offending a school-division official, but even so the ques-tion remains as to whether the reaction stands in any sensible relation to the alleged offense.[50] (Incidentally, who judged that the offense was intentional?) In a case with more sinister implications, a fifteen-year-old Edmonton youth was jailed for truancy. The boy spent more than five weeks in the Edmonton Young Offenders Centre. Leo Hansen, Assistant Superintendent of the Fort McMurray School Board, de-fended the action, asserted that he would do the same thing again, and protested that schools are forever being criticized for high dropout rates.[51] Mr. Hansen and the other officials involved, like those men-tioned in the earlier case of the cafeteria closet, have lost all perspective, forgetting that jail is the most serious penalty we impose on anyone in a democratic society. They would be well advised to reflect on why students are reluctant to attend school and to ask if such draconian measures are likely to promote an atmosphere conducive to productive learning. It would seem that a low dropout rate has started to replace education as the goal of schooling.

It is also fair, I think, to charge that there is a serious failure of imagination here. Instead of looking for ways in which school might be made more interesting and valuable to students, our officials resort to force and intimidation to compel students to attend. Surely, too, it takes little imagination to see that these tactics are likely to be counterproductive. The rules, however, make provision for such penalties in the wake of truancy, and if they are available they are to be used. Can implies ought. The jail case above is an extreme one, but many teachers are obsessive about attendance. Consider the high-school math teacher who took it as a personal affront, an incident to be harped on constantly, when two sixteen year olds, with parental permission, absented themselves from one class to attend the annual computer show in town. What is needed, however, are teachers and administrators who can see beyond the existing framework and imagine other possibilities; teachers who can imagine that valuable learning can occur outside their own classroom. One would not have thought that a connection between mathematics and computers was difficult to grasp.

In setting out some aspects of imagination in teaching, I will not be concerned with gimmicks. University teachers have lately been roundly criticized for putting their best efforts into research rather than teaching, and the media has carried a number of reports of professors who, in the course of a renewed attention to teaching, have "set fires, donned costumes and hurled filthy garbage cans across lecture halls".[52] Doubtless it does take some imagination to think of these tactics, but there is a real danger that imagination will not be recognized, or admitted, in the context of more conventional approaches if our notion of "imaginative teaching" is too closely associated with these entertaining gambits. Moreover, we need to bear in mind that the imaginative is not the merely bizarre. Fanciful behaviour in the classroom needs to be critically assessed in terms of its value in actually promoting worthwhile learning.

The case of the teacher who staged a mock attack and hostage-taking situation in her classroom also suggests the need for imagination coupled with judgment.[53] This dramatic event might initially commend itself as at least imaginative if lacking in judgment; but on reflection it is clear that a little imagination would have readily suggested a number of ways in which this strategy might easily have had most unfortunate results. That it did not was mainly a matter of luck.

To have a talent for imaginative work is not to possess a unitary or generic ability which can be developed in isolation from particular contexts and applied across a range of different activities. We speak of a person as having imagination, but this does not mean that he or she possesses a general talent which can be drawn on whatever the context may be. To say that a person has imagination is, in effect, to say that he or she can do certain things imaginatively, and not to say that the person is capable of being imaginative in any and every area.[54] Imaginative solutions to problems presuppose an understanding of what the problem is, and a person's understanding in one area is not matched in every other.

Similarly, in providing a general characterization of imaginative teaching, indicating the sorts of things imaginative teachers do, there is no implication that a talent for imaginative teaching carries over from one context to another. Imaginative teachers have certain features in common which make the ascription "imaginative" appropriate in each case, but this is not to say that there is a generic ability which each possesses. In Dearden's words, the assumption that there is "confuses conditions for the application of a concept with the presence of a unitary psychological ability".[55]

We are now ready to turn to a more detailed examination of the excellences which have been introduced. The general conclusion is that we cannot sensibly formulate rules or recipes for fostering ethical, intelligent, and sensitive behaviour in teachers, and any such formulae we encounter need to be treated with the utmost caution. Dewey brought out with great clarity the confusion which enters the teacher's mind with respect to general principles and practical suggestions. The latter turn into eternal laws and the former are wrongly supposed to offer specific direction in particular circumstances.[56] The general ideals, qualities and pedagogical principles we have met in this overview have an impact which, again echoing Dewey, can only be indirect. They affect us at the level of attitude and sensitivity, not offering definite answers to practical problems but altering our perception of alleged problems and suggested answers. This may seem like a poor offering when compared with rules and recipes which promise immediate and direct application. We can become preoccupied, however, with techniques, skills, rules, routines and measurable results, and lose sight of that richer conception of teaching and education which philosophers from Socrates to Scheffler have articulated. Let us turn first to the virtue of humility.

# CHAPTER THREE

# Humility: Recognizing Limits

Humility is the most difficult of all virtues to achieve; nothing dies harder than the desire to think well of oneself.
T.S. Eliot, "Shakespeare and the stoicism of Seneca"

## The Unaccountable Virtue

In his book *Government and the Mind*, Joseph Tussman has given voice to a doubt which others have surely felt even if, in the end, they decided in favour of discretion. Put bluntly, it is the fear that in the context of teaching, eagerness for the role is more likely to be a sign of unfitness than of fitness.[1] In view of the pious declarations of generations of applicants to teacher-education programmes to the effect that they have always and only wanted to teach, Tussman rightly notes that his observation is heretical. Heresy or not, however, the underlying concern is that very different motives can attract people to the teaching profession, and at one end of the spectrum there is "a dangerous disposition to impose oneself upon others, an eagerness to shape the malleable, a confident egoism, far removed from the spiritual condition of the true teacher".[2] As if to drive home the point, my writing of this very paragraph was rudely interrupted by two doorstep preachers who wanted to "share a message" with me. Canadian society as a whole had a rude awakening in the 1980s, with the Keegstra scandal[3] revealing not only that preachers and pitchmen were busy in our classrooms but that many were quite incapable of distinguishing their activities from those of genuine teachers. Painful as it may be, we need to remind ourselves that Keegstra was widely heralded as a good teacher.

In speaking here of genuine teaching or, as Tussman does, of true teaching, a certain ideal of teaching is being implied. There are many aspects to such an ideal characterization, but our focus at this point is on the virtue of humility. There is a danger that reference to such a quality will appear platitudinous, and yet it is not difficult to see that reflection on the idea of teaching suggests a certain puzzle concerning the alleged need for humility. The problem is that in order to have something to teach, the teacher must be something of an authority on the subject or topic in question. The teacher's superior knowledge has led some to deny that a teacher should manifest humility towards his or her students.[4] The authority in question, of course, is a relative one. In another context, the same person might find that he or she is a relative novice with respect to the same subject matter. Nevertheless, with respect to his or her own students, the teacher will generally be more familiar with the material than the students, a familiarity which enables the teacher to introduce others intelligently to the subject.

It was the unavoidable element of authority in education which prompted Russell to formulate the problem in the following way for the teacher who wants to treat the child with reverence:

> In the presence of a child [the teacher] feels an unaccountable humility—a humility not easily defensible on any rational ground, and yet somehow nearer to wisdom than the easy self-confidence of many parents and teachers.[5]

Given the teacher's superior command of the subject matter, it is all too easy to think so well of oneself that one expects uncritical deference from the student. I think of the elementary teacher who was adamant that division by zero was a viable operation. And of another who obstinately maintained that there are fifty-two states in the American union: "Class, how many of us think there are only fifty?" These teachers had forgotten Dewey's point that a teacher, although learned, should still be a learner. This contrast, he urged, is relative, not absolute, and perhaps Dewey himself erred in adding that in the earlier stages of education the contrast is practically all-important.[6]

Notice that it is not confidence itself which Russell and Tussman are warning against. Russell speaks of *easy* self-confidence, and we can understand him to mean slipping into that comfortable delusion that our position is perfectly secure, overlooking the fact that teachers of an earlier generation had the very same attitude towards beliefs which now provoke in us only a condescending smile.[7] The point in question was also made memorably by Russell's colleague, Alfred North Whitehead, who observed in the mid-1930s that every single generalization about mathematical physics he had learned as an undergraduate fifty years earlier had now been abandoned in the sense in which it was then held.[8] Notice also that it is confident *egoism* which Tussman warns against—the attitude that our own views are so clearly important and right that they can and must be impressed on others.

None of this is a general argument for diffidence and hesitancy in the classroom. It would be equally misleading to suggest to students that we have grounds for being uncertain, other than the general ground of human fallibility, when we do not. Teachers cannot hope to convey Whitehead's cautionary advice by simply deleting, as some have urged, words such as "proof" from their vocabulary. This is a cosmetic approach which seems more likely to foster scepticism than a critical tentativeness. This distinction itself, however, is one which causes many to stumble. Jean Ruddock quotes with emphatic approval a commentator in *New Statesman* who remarks that school should give students scepticism so that they leave with the ability to doubt rather than the inclination to believe.[9] The over-simplified contrast invoked here cannot but remind one of Dewey's perceptive observation about the human tendency to think in terms of hard-and-fast alternatives.[10] It is ironic that, a few paragraphs on, Ruddock bemoans the difficulty students experience in moving away from "dualistic reasoning" where they assume that an answer must be right or wrong.[11]

The particular dualism of ability to doubt versus inclination to believe tends to blind us to Hume's insight that belief can be proportioned to the evidence.[12] Being proportioned to the evidence, belief can be readjusted as appropriate. Students and teachers need to recognize the *vulnerability* of their beliefs to counter-evidence and counter-argument. Such recognition means that although we are inclined to believe something, we can also preserve our ability to come to doubt it should the weight of evidence shift. This is not to say, of course, that we can regard beliefs which are incompatible with our present views as equally acceptable, but our present belief does not mean that we must hold that incompatible beliefs could never turn out to be true. Belief and doubt *are* at odds with each other, though we may, of course, believe something *to some extent*. The *ability* to doubt, however, remains if we are able to entertain criticisms of our beliefs. Objections which we consider may in time become doubts of our own.

## Three Examples

One strategy which has been much employed in recent years to counteract a tendency to assume that there is one correct answer is to ask students so-called *divergent* questions which invite a multiplicity of responses. The questions are sufficiently open-ended that they preclude the possibility of the one, predetermined, correct response. The teacher who heeds Russell's advice will certainly want to raise some such questions and to listen carefully and with respect to the students' responses. Two lessons about humility might be taught in this way: one, that it is not assumed that all the answers are in; two, that it is not suggested that the teacher's own answers are obviously the best. Some commentators, however, have seen the need for the following rule in this situation, namely that if the teacher elicits diverse responses from the students, *the teacher has the professional obligation to accept* the students' responses.[13]

Once again, however, either-or reasoning is leading us astray. That there is no single, correct response does not mean that any and every answer is acceptable. Criticism of answers offered does not mean, as suggested in the text, that the teacher engages in "putdown" tactics. There is a third lesson about humility, applicable to teacher and student alike, which this strategy is not likely to teach, namely a willingness to submit to *standards of assessment* in the consideration of suggested answers. Relevance, plausibility and truth are standards which can be applied to student responses. Even if a variety of responses is acceptable, some may be irrelevant, implausible or simply mistaken. These lines of criticism do not mean that the students are not being shown respect, for this turns on *how* the criticisms are made. (Incidentally, it is far from clear to me that one advantage claimed for the acceptance strategy, that disadvantaged students get to become "stars" in the classroom, is either plausible or compatible with real respect.) These confusions take on an added urgency when we learn from a recent survey of some one hundred classrooms in the United States that in two-thirds of these teachers *never* clearly indicated that a student answer was incorrect, and in the other classrooms criticism only amounted to about five percent of teacher-student interactions.[14]

If the policy of blanket acceptance represents one extreme, it is not difficult to find an example of a very different attitude towards teaching. Here, for example, is a philosopher reflecting on classroom teaching:

> What I present in the classroom is a compendium of my work on a problem, not the work itself. To initiate them into the activity of philosophizing about a problem, I give a mock performance of the way in which I pursue the truth concerning it. When I present material in the classroom, I am never surprised to find what I find.[15]

The contrast at work here is between teaching and research, and it is only in the context of research that the writer encounters surprise. Yet the subject is philosophy and the students undergraduates! Has the philosophical research reported to the students been so successful that the teacher *never* encounters an objection he has not anticipated and dealt with? It sounds too as if this teacher never *expects* to be surprised, that it is in the nature of teaching to be a straightforward transmission of results. We need not, of course, deny that there is a difference between the context of research and the context of teaching. It would be foolish to maintain that every class can be a cooperative pursuit of pure philosophical truth. Nor need we get too excited about the reference to a "mock performance", despite the connotation of pretence. After all, the students may be in on the act. I take this in much the same spirit as Jay Rosenberg's description of his own philosophy classes as elementary dancing lessons.[16] It is never being surprised which is both surprising and disturbing, for this turns the performance into a *mere rehearsal* of ideas. What is missing in the account of teaching free of surprises is any sense of intellectual humility which would suggest an acknowledgement that one's well-thought-out compendium of ideas might not be as clear or compelling to one's students as it is to oneself. If philosophy teachers can hold this attitude towards undergraduate teaching, how confident can we be that elementary-school teachers will feel that they might have something to learn from their students?

Some teachers, then, seem so assured of their own authority that humility is completely absent from their perspective on teaching, while others seem to have translated humility into a denial of their right to critically assess a student's response. Some, however, manage to hit the mark exactly and capture the delicate balance between authority and humility which teachers must strive to attain. Dennis Gunning puts it this way in his admirable discussion concerning the teaching of history:

> However often it is pointed out, though, it is hard for a teacher not to feel uneasy when faced with a fourteen-year-old giving an unorthodox interpretation of a piece of source material. We really have to school ourselves not to 'put him right', not to sweep his interpretation aside (or, equally bad, apparently accept it, but in such a way that everybody knows that we are just humouring the student).[17]

Here, Gunning recognizes the temptation Russell called attention to, that of allowing the student's relative inferiority to justify a heavy-handed approach which would pronounce with finality on the question at hand. Faced with this temptation, it is useful for teachers to recall the *pedagogical fallacy*, the belief that this is our Last Chance to correct what we take to be an error. We forget that the discussion can continue, and that the students have not said their final word on the subject.[18] Gunning associates his recommendation with two central aims: first, to observe the tentativeness of knowledge, and second, to respect the student's own interpretation.

## Revision of Ideas and Respect For Students

In the context of teaching, the ideas which we present to students as *true* are capable of revision, the point made dramatically by White-head reflecting on his own education. Claims to knowledge, theories, interpretations and arguments may be revised and rejected as we advance our understanding. Not only is our own personal grasp tentative, but what is universally regarded by all the experts as established truth is itself open to revision and falsification. Fallibilism recognizes that our claims to knowledge rest on reasons and evidence, and our awareness and understanding of the latter can change. This view, then, is incompatible with the kind of scepticism which regards all claims and interpretations as equally dubious. If, however, those who advocate scepticism as an aim of education really mean to emphasize the point that the last word has never been said, that our assessment of reasons and evidence may in time lead us to a new view, then this is in fact a way of making the point that knowledge *is* tentative. Clearly this interpretation of scepticism leaves intact the legitimacy of appeals to reasons and evidence, since it is in terms of the latter that a new view will be framed. Teachers who embrace fallibilism recognize the possibility of improving their present knowledge and understanding. Their humility takes the form, not of despair with respect to knowledge, but of deference to reason and evidence. It is not the view that they have nothing worth offering their students, but rather the Deweyan view that the learned can still learn.

Such deference to reasons and evidence helps to explain why respect for the student's interpretation is also an ideal the teacher needs to strive towards. The teacher can demonstrate his or her commitment to the principle of a reasoned and evidential basis for beliefs, theories and so on by taking *seriously* reasons and evidence which students bring forward. Respect will be shown by trying to decide if such and such is a good reason, or a relevant and accurate piece of evidence, not by "accepting" whatever the student presents. In this way, despite the fact that the teacher may well have claimed that something is true, the teacher will demonstrate that his or her primary allegiance is to reason and evidence, not to some particular truth which is exempted from further critical scrutiny. Russell's maxim, that "education ought to foster the wish for truth, not the conviction that some particular creed is the truth",[19] is relevant here, though we should not interpret this as meaning that conviction *as such* is undesirable. The question is not whether or not the teacher should take a stand on issues, but rather how the teacher can communicate the point that the stand is tentative though based on reason and evidence. In fostering the student's own orientation to a reasoned and evidential approach, we show that what we value is the student's attempt to provide good reasons, not simply the correctness of the position taken.[20]

## Humility, Ideals and Progress

These thoughts suggest a connection between humility and *ideals* which was first brought out clearly in the work of Henry Sidgwick. If a person's merits are comparatively high, Sidgwick noted, it seems strange that humility would prescribe that one have a *low* opinion of oneself.[21] Is it not just as irrational to underrate ourselves as to have an exaggerated estimate of our abilities? Should we not simply aim for an accurate self-appraisal? Now, we might say, if one deserves to be called a teacher at all, a person must have some merits such as possession of knowledge and ability to bring others to share it. A certain self-esteem, then, is appropriate and, as others have pointed out, essential if teachers are to avoid apathy and a sense of powerlessness.[22] Sidgwick suggested that the value of humility lay in its ability to temper the emotion of self-admiration, and to prevent appropriate self-esteem—what he called self-approbation—from turning into self-complacency. Contemporary writers are following Sidgwick when they point out that humility does not require a *false* low opinion of oneself nor an absence of self-esteem.[23] It serves rather to offset the kind of self-satisfaction which interferes with a recognition of the possibility of, and need for, *improvement*. The absence of humility, Sidgwick thought, would impede progress.

The notion of ideals, however, might be thought to introduce a paradox if associated with humility. Is there not something pretentious and arrogant involved in setting for oneself goals which, by their nature, cannot be completely achieved? Ideals would seem to demand saints and heroes, and might seem, therefore, to involve a certain self-conceit.[24] Humility itself is also an ideal and its pursuit may seem inconsistent with the idea of humility. Certainly, humility would destroy itself if a person were to become proud of his or her humility. We can admit this danger but there is no contradiction involved in associating humility and ideals. The objection would be valid if the recognition and pursuit of ideals entailed the presumption that we ourselves possessed the extraordinary and superhuman abilities required to achieve them. But this is not so. To believe that something is worth striving for is not to believe that one can attain it. We may believe that we can go on indefinitely approaching the ideal, and that its pursuit will bring various benefits which otherwise would not arise. One can have appropriate humility about one's chances of success. As for humility itself, it need not be worn on one's sleeve. An ideal can serve to give our actions direction and to remind us that present achievements remain inadequate. Teachers who agree with Gunning that the tentativeness of ideas and respect for the student's interpretation are worthy principles in education need not assume that they themselves will invariably resist the temptation to violate these norms in practice.

## Socrates As Exemplar

There are echoes of Socratic thought in what has been said thus far, and it is time to bring the connection into the open. Socrates reacted sharply against what he viewed as the arrogance of Protagoras' boast: "Young man, if you come to me, your gain will be this. The very day you join me, you will go home a better man, and the same the next day. Each day you will make progress towards a better state."[25] Although teachers do see their efforts directed at improving the student's condition in some way, what was lacking here was a proper sense of one's limitations, and a recognition of the many difficult and vexed questions about virtue and value. In the *Apology*, Socrates presents his own view of the nature of wisdom as an appreciation of our own extensive ignorance.[26] He did not think he knew what he did not know. When in the *Apology* Socrates reports having asked Callias to tell him who is an expert in perfecting the human and social qualities, he is driving home the point that many who set themselves up as teachers pretend to a wisdom which they do not possess, or are self-deceived. In particular, they do not have final and authoritative answers on the question of what constitutes the good life. Not surprisingly, then, Socrates calls attention to the importance of the individual trying to *decide* whether or not advice offered by friends ought to be followed.[27]

These ideas are closely related to Russell's remark quoted earlier about that unaccountable humility which is somehow closer to wisdom. A teacher ought to be struck by the momentous and incalculable consequences of his or her influence on the student, a matter which makes the concept of trust so appropriate in characterizing the teacher's position.[28] Lacking such humility, and devoid of reverence for the child, the teacher "thinks it his duty to 'mould' the child; in imagination he is the potter with the clay."[29] The teacher, of course, need not think that the student is presently his or her equal, but does need to see the student as potentially an equal. Humility in teaching involves admitting that the student can grow into an adult capable of critically and independently assessing what he or she has been taught, and education needs to keep this option open. The child's right, in Feinberg's words, is to have "future options kept open until he is a fully formed self-determining adult capable of deciding among them."[30] R.M. Hare captured the appropriate attitude very well when he spoke of the teacher working himself or herself out of a job, being ready to retire gracefully.[31]

Some who grasp the Socratic insight manage, nevertheless, to misrepresent it so badly that the central point is virtually lost. Neil Postman, for example, contributing a "professional viewpoint" to a recent text for teachers, echoes Socrates in saying that "a learned person knows how ignorant he is and, in teaching, simply gives more prominence and emphasis to what he does not know than to what he does."[32] Even this errs to some extent in making the point in terms of more and less rather than, following Sidgwick, in terms of an appropriate balance between what we do and do not know. Moreover, Postman could not resist expressing the Socratic idea in the kind of mindless slogan which seems *de rigueur* in texts for teachers: The dumber the teacher, the better the student. Although Postman goes on immediately to point out that he is not, in fact, arguing that teachers should be ignorant, one wonders if the damage has not been done and why such an inane slogan needed to appear at all. Will the retraction be remembered or the misleading slogan, when the latter has the dubious distinction of being just the kind of trite catch-phrase which tends to stick in the mind? I am bound to say that it strikes me as a patronizing simplification. It is *not* the teacher's knowledge as such which is an obstacle to the students becoming independent and critical learners. It is the teacher's *attitude* towards knowledge, especially the view that claims to knowledge are beyond criticism. A good teacher recognizes that there is much that he or she does not know, but it is a fallacy to think that one will be a better teacher if one knows less!

Some remarks attributed to Socrates, of course, do suggest a more far-reaching view than simply the idea that our ignorance is *extensive*.

In the *Apology*, for example, Socrates comments that "the wisest of you is he who has realized, like Socrates, that in respect of wisdom he is really worthless."[33] And Diogenes Laertius is responsible for associating Socrates' name with the aphorism, "I know nothing except the fact of my own ignorance."[34] This is the view that our ignorance is *complete*, except for our own awareness of that fact, and popularly this epitomizes the Socratic outlook. It is by no means clear, however, that Socrates himself really subscribed to this extreme view. There are passages, for example, where he urges his friends to go on searching for knowledge as if the search were not in vain.[35] Humility does not require that we adopt the extreme view; and if the extreme view is false, as I think it is, then we slip into a false humility in asserting it. We only need to recognize our extensive ignorance and general fallibility. Socrates, I suppose, presents the extreme view to *balance* the equally extreme, and readily misunderstood, view that he is the wisest of all people. Other things being equal, humility calls for an accurate appraisal of one's merits. But faced with praise couched in such superlatives, the humble person will not want to be seen as being attracted by these flattering descriptions. Socrates also has the task of undermining the facile thinking which leads to false assessments and misunderstandings of human wisdom, and exaggeration can play a role in this deflationary process.

A second strand to the Socratic ideal of recognizing one's limited knowledge involves knowing where one's expertise lies and when one is getting out of one's depth. Socrates discovered that those who possessed knowledge in one area tended to assume that they were *generally* knowledgeable, and were happy to pronounce on matters far removed from their own special area. The poets and craftsmen came in for particularly severe criticism in this respect. In our own day, scientists have often been singled out for criticism along these same lines. Perhaps the spectacular achievements of science have encouraged the belief that a scientific training can be brought to bear successfully on any question. Robert Gilpin, for example, has suggested that "the scientist believes that he carries with him into the political arena certain unique habits of mind which lend him advantage in understanding politics."[36] When the scientist is called in, however, as expert adviser to policy-makers, the advice tendered is seldom purely technical in nature, and the scientist is not an expert with respect to the non-technical assumptions—moral, political or otherwise—which enter in. The point is not that the habits of mind associated with the scientific attitude—impartiality, open-mindedness, respect for evidence and so on—are unimportant in the context of moral and political questions. There is, in Scheffler's words, "a strong analogy between the moral and the scientific points of view, and it is no accident that we speak of reasons in both cases. We can be reasonable in matters of practice as well as in theory."[37] Being able to meet these standards in one area, however, is no assurance that one will succeed in some other. Often, a person will have no idea of the traps which lie waiting in areas beyond his or her expertise. Everyone knows by now how distinguished scientists have made fools of themselves pronouncing the deceptions of pseudo-science merchants authentic, falling for tricks which trained magicians easily detect.[38]

## The Context of Teaching

These have been sobering lessons. The question is how to apply them to the teaching context. Schoolteachers, in particular, are often required to teach outside their own area of expertise. This can lead to desperate efforts to stay one step, or one chapter, ahead of the students, hoping that the moment of humiliation will not arrive too soon.[39] In many jurisdictions, moreover, specialist teaching licences have all but disappeared with the result, and to some extent reflecting the view, that a teacher is a teacher. (No doubt, tired slogans about teaching students not subjects are implicated in this error.) This is the educational equivalent of, and no more plausible than, the view that there are "ball-handling" skills, and therefore someone good at soccer will be good at tennis. Faced with the unenviable task of "teaching" an unfamiliar subject, and prior to gaining the necessary level of competency, a teacher should surely advise the students in all honesty that in these circumstances he or she can only be a co-inquirer. It may be, of course, that the teacher will prove to be a faster learner and will be able to draw on general teaching skills to help others master the material. But these fortunate outcomes should not deceive us into thinking, like the poets and the craftsmen, that our abilities know no bounds.

We should not be sidetracked here by whatever our views might be on the desirability of a curriculum differentiated along subject lines versus a more holistic, theme-oriented approach. If we favour the latter, there will presumably be topics, issues and materials with which we are less familiar and less comfortable. We still need a sense of our limitations. If, on the other hand, we are teaching a clearly defined subject, our discussions will almost certainly stray into other fields. The appropriate conclusion, however, is not necessarily for teachers to resolve to abstain from comment on the grounds that they are outside their speciality. The tendency of analytical philosophers in the recent past to avoid being drawn on questions of practical ethics ultimately led to the charge of sterility.[40] In the context of teaching, the constant retreat to one's area of expertise can be simply boring. Students expect their teachers to be able and willing to join an intelligent general discussion even if it lies beyond the teacher's special expertise. An opinion can surely be offered "for what it is worth". Humility does not translate into a *rule* prescribing a policy of "no comment", but has to be captured in the spirit in which the comment is made. Carl Sagan is probably wise not to be drawn out whenever the popular press asks him for his "gut feeling" on an issue where he has no compelling evidence—"I try not to think with my gut."[41] Equally important for the teacher, however, is the reminder that tentativeness comes in degrees, and there will be times when we want our students to understand that our remarks are very tentative indeed.

A complication with respect to humility in the context of teaching arises simply because the teacher is not just personally striving to exemplify this virtue but is also trying to encourage others in the same direction. As Oakeshott has pointed out, however, the teacher cannot promote the intellectual virtues explicitly without appearing priggish, and this would obviously run counter to any attempt to set an example of humility. The intellectual virtues are "implanted unobtrusively in the manner in which information is conveyed, in a tone of voice, in the gesture which accompanies instruction, in asides and oblique utterances, and by example."[42] Kant stressed the latter in the context of humility, and suggested that one could not help but respect the humble person because such an example serves to undermine our own self-conceit.[43]

At times in teaching, however, the teacher may need to show the student that the position the student has taken is untenable, and the student has the direct, sometimes uncomfortable, experience of being challenged to accept criticism and concede that his or her position is mistaken. Ideally, the aim would be to have the student appreciate the lesson taught by Epicurus, that to be defeated in argument is better in that one learns more.[44] But to show that the student is wrong, must not the teacher be claiming a more secure position for himself or herself? How is this compatible with setting an example of humility?

There is no ready rule to offer teachers here, hence Oakeshott's emphasis on manner, tone of voice and gesture. The teacher cannot just proclaim that he or she remains humble about the position he or she is defending. Students may feel that the teacher is simply imposing a view deemed to be correct and which the teacher is not prepared to think critically about. This impression will not necessarily be corrected just because the teacher, in rejecting the student's view, has no positive answer to propose. We can, of course, be confident at times that such and such is wrong without knowing what is right. This will help to play down the suspicion that the teacher is infallible, but the teacher is still taking the *objections* to the student's position as decisive, and the student may see this assumption as unwarranted. The teacher's task is to find a way of conveying the point that the objections themselves are not beyond the bounds of critical challenge *while defending them.*[45] Success here will depend upon a number of factors, including: previous evidence that the teacher is the sort of person who is prepared to concede positions he or she had once defended; a sense among the students that the teacher is more concerned with finding out what is true than with scoring a point; and an indication that the teacher's objections rest on reason and evidence and remain open to discussion. These qualities require courage.

# CHAPTER FOUR

# *Courage: Steadfast Principles*

>
> It may be said that reasonable people will respect us all the more for having the courage of our convictions, and that, no doubt, is true. But the trouble is that the world is filled with unreasonable people....
>
> Brand Blanshard—*The Uses of a Liberal Education*

## *The Virtue of Courage*

Examples of courage are often taken from such contexts as military action, heroic rescue, daring exploits and so on, where there is a dramatic and inspiring display of fearlessness in dangerous and difficult circumstances. Such episodes are singled out for mention and celebration, and awards and honours await those cited for bravery, gallantry and valour.[1] We can all recognize courage in the actions of Boris Yeltsin during the abortive Soviet coup in the summer of 1991. Since it is unlikely that anyone will question such examples, it is natural to refer to these striking and extraordinary cases when we wish to illustrate courage, but the result is that superhuman efforts in desperate situations come to dominate our conception of this virtue and eclipse other possibilities. It is easy then to wonder what courage has to do with teaching.

Of course, the media occasionally report inspiring acts of heroism by teachers when deranged persons enter schools or classrooms, or when teachers are physically attacked by irate parents or students. And these acts resemble those which serve as paradigms. It so happens in such cases that a teacher is called upon to display courage, but it might just as easily have been a doctor, store owner or bank clerk. Is there any reason to think that courage deserves *special* consideration in the context of teaching? Probably not, if we confine our attention to physical courage despite the alarming statistics indicating just how many students carry weapons to school in our larger cities.[2] There are, certainly, schools where teachers and students alike need courage just to show up, and I would not want to trivialize this serious and growing problem, but these schools, thankfully, are not as yet typical.[3] If this trend, however, is to be reversed, we will need teachers and school administrators with the courage to speak out about the problem of violence.

It is a different matter if we turn to moral courage. Courage in this sense is important in teaching just because many of the truly central aims of education, and the principles which ought to guide teachers in their work, are rarely honoured, even in relatively democratic societies, in any serious way. Consider, for example, the aim of instilling a critical spirit in one's classroom. There is a good deal of rhetorical support for this ideal, but it is also clear that being critical, which ought to involve something like the Socratic ideal of following the argument where it leads, often comes to mean no more than accepting those criticisms which happen to be fashionable at the time.[4] Ironically, this very often involves going along *uncritically* with currently popular ideologies.

Courage would hardly be necessary in teaching if society welcomed and applauded the teacher who, for example, pursues the ideal of critical thinking. Humility is a virtue in teachers just because the attainment of knowledge is so elusive. It is an appropriate acknowledgment of human fallibility. Moral courage in teaching, however, is a virtue whose need turns on the predictable reactions of others and their ability to make life unpleasant for anyone whose inquiries seem threatening.[5] Having said this, however, it is worth reminding ourselves that the enemy may be within, and that teachers need to confront their own fears of seeing cherished beliefs crumble.[6] This kind of courage in facing uncertainty is necessary if an open-minded disposition is to be sustained, even if one's views remain private.

In speaking as we have been doing just now of courage as a virtue, it is important to note the point made by Philippa Foot that "courage is not operating as a virtue when the murderer turns his courage, which is a virtue, to bad ends".[7] The idea is not that a courageous disposition is *never* a virtue on any occasion for the man or woman who is also a murderer; rather that courage is not acting *as a virtue* when one draws on one's courage to commit murder. David Solway makes a related point when he comments that traits such as modesty and disinterestedness are not sufficient virtues in themselves. One may, he observes, be disinterested "without possessing the convictions that make impartiality or self-distrust an ornament of character".[8] Similarly, we need to know what an individual is courageously doing before we can praise his or her courage unreservedly.

The familiar point from Aristotle that courage can turn into recklessness or foolhardiness shows that courage has to be guided by judgment.[9] It takes courage, as we shall see, to deal with certain topics or to adopt certain strategies in teaching, but such seeming courage can easily suffer the fate mentioned by Aristotle. It was reported in the Canadian press, in the aftermath of the massacre of fourteen women at the *École Polytechnique* in Montreal in December 1989, that a teacher at a junior college in Jonquière had staged a mock attack and hostage-taking situation in her class, apparently to simulate a crisis situation so that the students would experience the kinds of emotions generated in such circumstances.[10] A hooded man carrying a gun burst into a classroom making threatening remarks about women reminiscent of the remarks made by mass murderer Marc Lépine. Meanwhile, police cars arrived on the scene having been notified by a student who had witnessed the events unfolding. Common sense would indicate that such a strategy could easily lead to tragic consequences, and the decision to implement this strategy, regardless of one's motives, reveals itself as foolhardy, not courageous. This teacher had forgotten the advice of Epictetus that we must be at once cautious and courageous.[11]

Consider again the case of Jim Keegstra.[12] We have seen earlier that it took courage for the parents and the superintendent to pursue the case. Now, however, the unpalatable fact to be acknowledged is that Keegstra too showed courage in doing what he believed his own principles demanded. Let us be clear here. It did *not* take courage to proselytize in the relatively secure confines of his own classroom where he could depend on his authority status to silence dissent and where he was generally safe from adult observation. When the truth began to trickle out, however, and serious scrutiny of his teaching was initiated, he might have then agreed to observe the official curriculum and almost certainly his position would have been secure. Surely it took some courage to face possible dismissal, criminal proceedings and public revilement. I take it, however, that courage was not operating as a *virtue* in this case because it was associated with the practice of indoctrination and in the service of fanaticism. Keegstra's conception of intellectual and academic freedom was fundamentally flawed. His was not the determination to follow the argument where it leads, but the determination to lead others to follow his own "argument" blindly. So we cannot *admire* his courage as we admire that of Socrates or of a genuine champion of academic freedom like George Grant.[13]

## Courage and Cowardice: The Cannizzo Case

The situation with respect to moral courage is complicated by the fact that a teacher may be genuinely uncertain as to what a certain principle requires in a given situation. We speak of "having the courage of one's convictions", but the problem is that teachers may be unclear whether a particular action violates one of their principles or not, and thus be unclear about what their convictions require. For example, is the proposed removal of a book from the curriculum illegitimate censorship or a belated recognition of bigotry? Teachers who say nothing may not necessarily reveal a lack of courage, only an inability to sort out the complexities involved in these disputes. Recently, for example, New Brunswick School District 20 referred complaints of racism it had received about Harper Lee's novel, *To Kill a Mockingbird*, to the Minister of Education for resolution. It is good to note that at least one high-school English teacher in that province was prepared to be interviewed for CBC Radio's 'Arts Report' and state firmly that he believed the charge of racism to be misguided, as indeed it is.[14] His more reticent colleagues may simply not know what to think. Still, one would expect the teaching profession, and especially the association of English teachers, to be courageous enough to *debate* these issues, so that false accusations do not gain legitimacy by default.

In Toronto in 1988, a petition organized by black students succeeded in having William Golding's *Lord of the Flies* removed from the English curriculum of a certain school. Deanne Bogdan, referring to the role of the English department in this case, comments:

> What it did *not* do was evade the lived experience of the students under the cloak of an abstract principle. This took courage, especially in the face of the enormous sway of liberal beliefs about the unfettered right to know regardless of its cost in human sensibility, or of the opprobrium borne by those who risk challenging the blanket application of the principle that knowledge is inviolate and inviolable.[15]

I do not find this at all persuasive. Certainly, liberal beliefs ought to have enormous sway in education. Not the *unfettered* right to know, of course, as Bogdan's prejudicial account puts it, but rather liberal principles concerning open discussion, the pursuit of truth, and fair criticism.[16] It is not clear, however, that such principles do have enormous sway when educational decisions are dictated by petitions and protests.[17] Surely, courage would be shown in *defending* the book and facing the predictable charge that one is fanatically wedded to abstract principles which pay no heed to human emotions.

Teachers who ordinarily have the courage to come to the defence of good literature when censorship rears its head might well hesitate in such cases even if they were personally convinced that these particular novels are not racist. The present climate, in Canada at least, is such that to question whether or not a charge of racism is well-founded is to invite the accusation that one is a covert racist oneself. (This is similar to the way in which honest criticism of some particular policy of the government of Israel is taken by some as revealing one's covert anti-semitism.[18]) Of course, this is the method of attacking the person rather than the merits of the case, itself ironically a tactic regularly associated with racism, but a distinction of this sort will provide little protection once the mud-slinging starts. R.M. Hare has well remarked that people can try to be more courageous than they have it in them to be, and it is sensible to know something of one's own capabilities to prevent one's pursuit or defence of an ideal from creating personal tragedy.[19] Of course, one's limits, and the repercussions of one's actions, often only become clear too late. Moreover, many teachers had not realized that their institutions would abandon them and the principles which are supposed to govern liberal education.[20]

The now notorious events surrounding the recent exhibition at the

Royal Ontario Museum in Toronto entitled "Into the Heart of Africa" dramatically illustrates the quagmire that the issue of racism has become. This case is as sordid and depressing as any reported by Dinesh D'Souza in his detailed exposé of political correctness in the United States.[21] The exhibition, which opened in November 1989, was designed to reveal the attitudes and behaviour of nineteenth-century Canadian missionaries in Africa through the various artifacts which the Museum has in its collection. Thus, for example, there was a large drawing of one Lord Beresford stabbing a Zulu warrior, a photograph of a white woman giving African women "a lesson in how to wash clothes", and a slide show with the spoken words of missionaries very clearly illustrating their patronizing and racist views. By all reports, favourable and unfavourable, the displays had a powerful impact on museum visitors. Though there can be no serious doubt that the intention of the curator in charge of the exhibition was to *expose* the racism espoused by the missionaries,[22] the exhibition itself and those who organized it were denounced as racist.[23] By March 1990 there were noisy and angry demonstrations outside the Museum led by a group calling itself the Coalition for the Truth About Africa, demonstrations which lasted throughout the summer until the exhibition closed in August. This hostile reaction no doubt helped persuade other museums which had agreed to carry the exhibition to revoke their commitment.[24]

To dwell for a moment on the photograph mentioned above of African women washing clothes, the caption on this exhibit read: "Mrs. Thomas Titcombe offering 'a lesson in how to wash clothes' to Yagba women in Northern Nigeria in 1915." Susan Crean observes: "Tell me this is how you would explain the cultural bias and racial arrogance of that image to school children."[25] Very well, I *do* say that I would have children come to an understanding of these matters in this way, though Crean's use of the word "explain" reveals the problem she is having in grasping what is going on. Unlike Susan Crean, I believe in children seeing, and drawing conclusions, *for themselves*, learning through practice to formulate *their* own judgments, not having a correct view *imposed* on them. And unlike Susan Crean, apparently, I also believe that children *can* think these matters through for themselves if given the opportunity.[26] This point is absolutely fundamental since, in many of the debates about books which deal with sensitive themes, the idea seems to be that unless the book comes with *Officially Correct View* as imprimatur, the students will not know what to think.

Personal tragedy was indeed to be involved in this case. Of immediate concern in the context of a discussion of teaching is the fact that Jeanne Cannizzo, curator of the exhibition, was subjected to intimidation and harassment in her anthropology class at Scarborough campus of the University of Toronto in September 1990 by several students who, it appears, registered with the express intention of disrupting the class and denouncing her as a racist. Some of these students had been active participants in the demonstrations, and evidently did not enroll in the class with any serious intention of studying with their professor. The final confrontation came, according to the report of one student present, when Jeanne Cannizzo was called a "white supremacist, racist, [obscenity] bitch" in class.[27] Some have professed to be surprised that she did not remain in the class to discuss the issue.

Cannizzo had shown moral courage in putting on a challenging exhibition, but now it was hardly a matter of standing one's moral ground. The circumstances were threatening and frightening.[28] The norms of civilized discourse had obviously been flouted, as University of Toronto professor, Ron Blair, pointed out on W5 when he aptly summed up the whole episode as "sheer harassment". The general university community, however, did *not* come to her defence. Faculty Council endorsed a resolution expressing "equal sympathy" for all parties, but equal treatment, as Aristotle pointed out, does not necessarily mean just treatment;[29] and it was never made clear what Cannizzo had done to the activists who made the class unteachable that called for an expression of sympathy towards them. Cannizzo took sick leave, no students were disciplined, and the class was simply cancelled. She was indeed "hounded out", and Robert Fulford described it as "an occasion of great shame for the University of Toronto".[30]

It is, therefore, passing strange for Canadian commentators to ridicule the suggestion that censorship on the basis of political orthodoxy is an issue of concern in universities in this country. Michael Keefer, to his credit, does allow that what he calls the harassment of Jeanne Cannizzo by activists was "genuinely disturbing", although he rejects the idea that there is a pattern of repression.[31]  Thelma McCormack, on the other hand, makes no reference to the Cannizzo affair as she charges that American debates are simply imported into Canada.[32] Representatives from the University of Toronto who are involved with developing a policy on discriminatory harassment—interviewed on CBC's Morningside on May 15, 1991, at the end of the same academic year when Cannizzo was forced out—denied that censorship and repression was a problem in Canada.[33]  One case, of course, does not constitute a *wave* of repression, but the failure of the University of Toronto to find the courage to defend a beleaguered faculty member in such a glaring instance sends a chilling message to other teachers who believe in the traditional principles of liberal education.[34]  As the Philosophy of Education Society pointed out during an earlier period of intellectual repression, "mature minds cannot be developed where ideas deemed dangerous are kept out of our common life."[35]

## Fundamental Principles and Distinctions

In the late nineteenth century, Thomas Henry Huxley set out to challenge the assertion that it is, and it ought to be, an unpleasant thing for a person to say plainly that he does not believe in Christ. Hiding under the label of agnostic, such a person is really an infidel.  My own first-year philosophy students are rather bemused by the passionate defence which Huxley presents for honest disbelief: "A thousand times, no!  It ought *not* to be unpleasant to say that which one honestly believes or disbelieves."[36]  These students, however, live at a time and in a culture where the label "infidel" would only excite amusement, and it takes an effort of the imagination to enter into the cultural climate that made Huxley's work an act of moral courage.

If the issues have changed since Huxley's day, the general principle he laboured to defend is still relevant and vital in education and elsewhere.  Huxley defended the view that there are no propositions we ought to believe in the absence of logically satisfactory evidence.[37]  This principle seems perhaps innocuous, one that will readily be granted, but cases arise where we are expected to believe something even though the necessary evidence is not provided.  To suspend judgment in accordance with Huxley's principle is interpreted as indicating that one is unwilling to condemn certain moral offenses or that one is clearly biased.

Consider, for example, the 1991 U.S. Senate Judiciary Committee hearings involving Anita Hill and Clarence Thomas, where Thomas faced charges of sexual harassment. Barbara Ehrenreich, in an essay entitled "Women would have known", observes that of course fourteen male senators "didn't get it". Her conclusion is that "on some subjects, for reasons both historic and tragic, women know best."[38] One can agree with every observation that Ehrenreich makes about the offensive nature and prevalence of sexual harassment, but none of that can alter the fact that in this case there was simply no corroborating evidence on either side. One can agree that women know better than men what it is like to experience sexual harassment, but it does not follow that women senators would have *known* that Thomas was guilty. To any such suggestion, the question must arise, *how?* In the absence of evidence, one can only suspend judgment.[39] Principles of justice also require that guilt be proven.

Huxley himself offered an example which bears closely on this case:

> I may have the most absolute faith that a friend has not committed the crime of which he is accused....At the present day, if I tendered myself as a witness on that score, the judge would tell me to stand down, and the youngest barrister would smile at my simplicity. Miserable indeed is the man who has not such faith in some of his fellow-men—only less miserable than the man who allows himself to forget that such faith is not, strictly speaking, evidence.[40]

The point is not that one does not believe strongly in one's friend, nor that one does not champion a particular cause, only that one continues to recognize the distinction between belief, even to the point of feeling certain, and knowledge. Does this matter?

Surely it does. Racism is a moral outrage and, therefore, constitutes one of the most serious offenses with which a person or an institution can be charged. It deserves moral opprobrium because it involves trampling on the rights of individuals who are adversely treated on the wholly irrelevant ground that they belong to a particular racial group. The same concern for the rights of individuals, however, means that the charge of racism must be properly substantiated. If we can develop anti-racist approaches in education, that is much to be desired. We have already seen, however, that racism is *sometimes* alleged with no justification, and there are further examples to come. Our concern to root out a moral evil must not persuade us to take a short cut on the matter of evidence. D'Souza reports that policy guidelines on discrimination by students, issued by the University of Michigan in 1988, contained the comment: "Experience at the university has been that people almost never make false complaints about discrimination."[41] This truly astounding statement would effectively mean, I suppose, that evidence is unnecessary. To be charged is to be guilty, and it is hardly surprising that this university has not detected false complaints. Given this assumption, Stephan Thernstrom is right—the charge *is* unanswerable. In this instance, the university has abandoned its commitment to the *pursuit* of truth. Similar assumptions in Canadian society about the presumed guilt of anyone charged with sexual abuse have already led to notorious cases of injustice and suffering, such as the case of children's entertainer, Eric Nagler.[42] Transferred to the context of literature, exhibitions and so on, the implication is that a complaint is sufficient. At this point, the distinction between belief and knowledge has been obliterated.

## Permission to Speak

Some years ago, Karl Popper remarked on the existence of false philosophies, i.e. uncritical philosophical ideas whose influential character demanded a critical, philosophical response. He identified one such uncritical thesis as the view that a person's opinions are always determined by economic or political interests, and he deplored the fact that this view eliminated serious discussion. Instead of asking about the truth of the matter, Popper observed, people merely ask about the person's motives, and this is of little significance.[43]

Two decades on, uncritical views closely related to Popper's own example are, if anything, even more influential and constitute a serious threat to fundamental principles of education. Part of the undercurrent in the Cannizzo affair was the assumption that members of one racial group cannot understand, and are not entitled to interpret, the culture of another group. One's understanding, it would seem, is determined and limited by one's racial or cultural origins, and this assumption leads away from a consideration of the merits of one's interpretation to unsupported allegations of bias. One would have thought this assumption was itself racist, but paradoxically the charge is levelled at those who challenge such gross generalizations about human beings.

Early in 1992, Concordia University Women's Centre rejected a work submitted by artist Lyn Robichaud for an exhibition devoted to art by women. The painting is of a black woman carrying bananas on her head. Robichaud was informed by the organizers that her painting showed "condescending stereotypes about women of colour, and about all women".[44] She was also told that, being white, she ought not to paint women of colour at all. One of the organizers, Shira Spector, herself an artist, is quoted as saying: "We feel that this is racist....It reminds us of colonialism and the noble savage who is happy with her life and smiling....I couldn't imagine a black woman having painted that image."[45]

It is embarrassing to reproduce these absurdities, and it is a pity that they cannot be consigned to the oblivion they deserve. Unfortunately, to echo Popper, views which are false and pernicious can be extremely influential, making critical comment necessary no matter how fatuous and contemptible the views happen to be.[46] First, then, if the organizers are concerned to present an exhibition of works of *artistic* merit, they need to judge the aesthetic quality of the work itself, not inquire into the skin colour of the artist. They might profitably reflect on the point that "the only coherent way in which to view creativity is in terms of the production of valuable products."[47] Shira Spector and her colleagues are committed to the absurd view that they can judge a work of art without even seeing it, simply by being informed as to its content and the racial background of the artist. Second, the view that this cannot be a worthwhile painting because the artist is white is itself a racist view because it appeals to racial background in a context where that is irrelevant to pass an adverse judgment on an individual. There *are* wrong reasons for disliking a work of art, as E.H. Gombrich remarks,[48] and the Concordia University organizers have appealed to one of the worst. Third, it ought to be obvious to anyone who knows anything at all about art or literature that a certain theme can lend itself to stereotypical treatment *and* to sensitive, artistic portrayal. The same point applies to words and phrases in literature. It takes judgment to tell the difference. Serious criticism and judgment cannot proceed by pulling a phrase, or image, out of context and condemning the work in which it appears because in some other context that phrase or image would have racist connotations.[49] We need artists and critics who will not shy away from this point, abandoning art at the first sign that a work might be misinterpreted. And we need teachers who will continue to meet their responsibility to help students to think critically about art and literature.

At this point, we can usefully turn to the general issue of what is now known as cultural, or voice, appropriation, though the euphemism found in ordinary usage where the term "appropriation" implies theft is hardly calculated to foster an impartial discussion. Unfortunately, a number of different concerns are run together under this label, creating further confusion. Let us, then, set certain issues aside. First, it is a matter of simple justice that government funding programmes be accessible to artists and writers from all cultural and racial backgrounds. I am not aware that there is any serious dispute about this as a matter of principle in Canada. Second, special provisions should be in place to attempt to ensure that deep-seated bias does not lead in practice to applicants from certain groups being passed over. Juries for the Canada Council, for example, should be broadly representative of the various artistic communities in the country. Third, with respect to cultural designs and artifacts which others exploit commercially, protection ought to be provided by the law and redress available. These are important matters, but they do not, in my view, capture what is now controversial about the issue of appropriation.

Allan Hutchinson of the Osgoode Hall Law School believes that Canadian authors "remain free to write about whom or what they choose....[Such] writers can speak in any or all cultural voices and identities."[50] His reference is to the policies of the Canada Council, which provides financial assistance to artists and writers, and one can only hope that Hutchinson is correct in his interpretation. Certainly, Joyce Zemans, Director of the Canada Council at the time the debate erupted in early 1992, has gone on record as affirming that the Council will never impose limits on artistic imagination. The issue, as she sees it, is one of *access*.[51] Unfortunately, as we are about to see, these views are not shared by everyone. The proper and essential view that juries must decide on *merit* can provide little reassurance if the notion of merit is distorted to include racial origin as a relevant factor.

Thomas Hurka, for example, allows that in some egalitarian future whites might write about natives, but in present circumstances they should exercise self-restraint. This, he claims, is only to be socially responsible; it is not a question of censorship. Hurka stops short of the claim that it is *impossible* for a non-native to understand native culture, but he makes what he calls the realistic claim that such understanding is "very difficult"; so much so that "if a white addresses a native subject he is likely to get it wrong". Hurka supports the use of the word "appropriation" since theft is involved in the following way: white writers distort native symbols, and white readers accept the distortion; hence, the native writer cannot reach his or her audience with an authentic voice—the audience has been stolen.[52]

Some writers too have joined with philosophers and taken similar positions. Lenore Keeshig-Tobias, an Ojibway, takes the view that natives know best about their culture, and native culture should not be filtered through the eyes of, in her words, the white man; native sensibility is going to be *white* washed. In her culture, individuals, families and tribes *own* stories, and no one else may tell them. She herself comes from a storytelling family and is, therefore, entitled to tell stories. She is also on record as holding that white Canadians want to tell native stories because they, the whites, have a poor self-image and find their own lives boring.[53]

The one encouraging aspect of this depressing trend is that many of Canada's distinguished writers have spoken out clearly and eloquently about the sinister element in these proposals. Timothy Findley, Alberto Manguel, Richard Outram and many others have condemned the drift towards censorship, none more powerfully than Neil Bissoondath.[54] Many of the central points have been made by these writers, so let me concentrate on some matters which have not yet been given sufficient attention.

Suppose Hurka were right to hold that self-imposed restraints should not count as censorship. Even so, the spectre of censorship would still be present in the context of *education*. If writing about other cultures is socially irresponsible when done by whites, how could schools and teachers responsibly decide to include such writing in the curriculum? *To Kill a Mockingbird*, *The Slave Dancer* and many other titles would have to go, and the decision to exclude them would not reflect any judgment about their *actual merits*, only an assumption about their presumed lack of merit given their authorship. It is beside the point to observe that the issue of censorship is constantly in the offing in debates about the curriculum. What is at issue here is the attempt to legitimize exclusion without reference to actual literary or artistic merit. This attempt undermines a central feature of education itself, namely the development in students of the ability to evaluate the merits of ideas, theories and claims. Incidentally, Hurka speaks of whites *addressing* a native subject, so presumably white teachers should not even *discuss* these topics in their classes.

Suppose, further, that we agree with Hurka that it is "very difficult" for whites to understand native culture. How are we to decide if a particular white author has managed to achieve some understanding? When individual cases are introduced as counter-examples, apologists for the cultural appropriation thesis backtrack and talk about exceptions and differences. The concession, however, precisely shows that it is the *work* which must reveal whether or not there is insight and understanding, not the author's background.[55] The latter is irrelevant. Moreover, why should the fact that something is very difficult mean that it should not be attempted? Is it any easier to get things right when philosophers write about abortion, euthanasia or justice? In trying to understand we increase our understanding, and if critical commentary flourishes, our shortcomings can be pointed out. Hurka's point about stolen audiences should be addressed by resolving the problem of access. Then critical readers must sort out for themselves, making whatever use they can of advice from critics, the authentic voices from the inauthentic. Hurka seems at one point to support his position on the ground of protecting natives from the inauthentic voices of white writers but this seems offensively paternalistic.

The different claim, by Lenore Keeshig-Tobias, that individuals and families *own* stories raises separate issues. First, however, this claim does not affect the more general matter of writing about other cultures. Her view on this issue is that "natives know best". It is only necessary to repeat that it is the stories, poems and novels themselves which will show where merit is to be found. Any other approach will inevitably lead us away from the work. Second, stories can be told in many different ways and we introduce an arbitrary barrier to artistic and literary imagination if we say that a certain story cannot be retold because it belongs to someone else. Of course, the laws with respect to credit and acknowledgement would apply, and in some cases the charge of plagiarism will arise.

Finally, the claim may be that in a certain culture, certain stories may only be told by certain people. When this point is made, the implication seems to be that disagreement would entail lack of respect for that culture. The reply to this must be that while it may be appropriate and useful in certain cultures to have designated families and individuals who are storytellers, that does not seem to be appropriate and useful in general. There is no evidence to suggest that storytelling ability is passed on from generation to generation. We do not typically find that sons and daughters of great novelists and poets have the creative talents of their mothers or fathers. Stories and poems must be written by those who can write.

Canadian writers have, to their great credit, spoken out on these issues, but many voices have been silent. Where are the superintendents, directors of education, principals, heads of departments, and teachers in this debate? Where are the university presidents and professoriate? Alberto Manguel comments: "There are times when raising one's voice is imperative....our much vaunted soft-spokenness begins to sound suspiciously like cowardice."[56]

## Concluding Comment

Much of the discussion about these issues has been bedevilled by seemingly intractable problems with allegations of bias and how that notion is to be understood. Racism is clearly a vicious and virulent form of bias, and yet it is equally clear that a great deal of confusion surrounds its ascription in particular cases. A person who is concerned to avoid or diminish bias will strive to be impartial, so it will be helpful to give this ideal close attention.

# CHAPTER FIVE

# *Impartiality: Confronting Bias*

And it was wonderful to hear him: such a completely dedi-
cated, biased but tolerant man.

Bernard Crick—"On Bias"

## *Learning About Bias*

Teachers do not necessarily require a sophisticated philosophical
account of bias in order to recognize a particular case as an example of
bias. As Peter Geach has reminded us, there are many things we can
recognize and identify which we would be hard pressed to define or
analyze.[1] Children's books setting out possible careers for girls and boys
but which see the girls heading for nursing school while the boys become
doctors are now embarrassingly obvious examples.[2] It is sobering to
recall, however, that they were not always so obvious. Still, there needs
no philosopher come from the ivory tower to tell teachers this is bias.
Over the past two decades, we have witnessed a powerful campaign of
consciousness-raising concerning bias, especially racism and sexism;
and a proliferation of practical guidelines for teachers, librarians and
publishers designed to put the spotlight on more subtle cases. What
remains to be done other than to keep up the good work? Apparently
very little. The basic lessons, it would seem, have been learned, and
there is any amount of practical guidance at hand for those who are
unsure.

Perhaps with justification, the emphasis in recent years has been
on expunging bias from materials used in the classroom, and on teachers
and schools learning to recognize and counter their own biases. For
example, the curriculum may suggest that only subjects which have
utilitarian value of a definite kind are important. The meagre time
devoted to art may itself undermine the art teacher's efforts to interest

students in this area. Many otherwise well-educated people cannot grasp the value or point of a subject such as philosophy whose relevance to practical problems is not direct and immediate. The bias here is that one kind of value is dismissed without proper consideration. Clearly then, efforts are needed to remove bias from the teaching context so that teaching itself will not be infected.

In addition to prevention, however, students also need an adequate preparation to cope with the bias they will almost certainly encounter in other contexts, always supposing that teaching itself could be made bias-free. Consider the bias they will meet elsewhere concerning the subjects they have studied in school, a bias which may lead them to adopt a cynical attitude towards those subjects. One does not have to look far, for example, to discover a powerful bias against science in the media:

> Now it is scientific theories such as Darwinian evolution which are given the status of revealed truths and to maintain one's sensible scepticism in the face of the claims of science is to invite ridicule.[3]

It would be a great pity if the way in which science is taught in school helped to make this jaundiced view seem plausible. Education needs to equip the student with the ability to distinguish between a revealed truth in the traditional and dubious sense of one proclaimed by infallible authority, and a truth revealed and confirmed through experience. Further, the student needs to learn that the claims of science, no matter how confidently advanced and defended, are revisable, and critical comment on them cannot be ruled out of order. What constitutes "sensible scepticism" requires discussion if open-mindedness and critical thinking are not to degenerate into general scepticism. The claim, appearing in the same source, that science demands "a suspension of one's critical and rational faculties in loyalty to defined truths" is evidently a biased view of science but one which emotionally-charged rhetoric and conceptual sleight-of-hand can encourage.

## Bias and Opinion

Attempting to teach in an unbiased and critical manner oneself may not be sufficient to prepare one's students adequately. Some direct *exposure* to biased views is needed, together with a philosophical perspective on the subject being studied. It is not difficult to see how a failure to reflect on the nature of scientific theories, for example, invites both the accusation that the theory of evolution is "only a theory" and the demand that other "theories" such as creationism be given equal time in the science classroom if balance is to be achieved.[4] Bias *does* call for balance, but equal time for evolutionary theory and creation science cannot remove bias because it can only create a distorted and misleading impression of the current state of scientific thinking.

One line of thought which serves to fuel such confused policies is the fashionable notion that having a point of view at all, but especially a strong point of view, actually *amounts* to being biased. On this assumption, a teacher strongly endorsing the theory of evolution is bound to seem suspicious. Consider the following advice to teachers of history and social studies:

> The teacher should be impartial in the classroom and where he knows he is strongly committed to a viewpoint, do everything possible to compensate for his bias by giving alternatives a fair run.[5]

The assumption here, however, is mistaken, and the teacher's first task is to recognize that having and defending a point of view does not, as such, amount to bias, even if the point of view expressed represents a value judgment.

Certainly, the avoidance of bias will call for impartiality and a fair review of alternatives, but the advice above manages to confuse bias with opinion. Even strong commitment to a viewpoint does not automatically involve bias. Consider, for example, the report of an inquiry into an air disaster which concludes *decisively* that pilot error was to blame. It is nonsense to suggest that the conclusion *alone* makes for a biased report. Such a judgment could only be based on a careful review of the report and the evidence available to the inquiry team. The inquiry was expected to reach an *impartial judgment* and such an expectation is not incoherent. What is true, of course, is that in the case of strong commitment especially, we should guard against potential bias in presenting or reviewing our position or in forming a view on related matters, since we know how easy it is to suppress, or minimize, considerations favourable to an alternative conclusion. Still, guarding against one's potential bias is not the same as compensating for actual bias, a bias which is supposed to exist just because we have a point of view.

## Compensating For One's Bias

Let us pause for a moment, however, to consider more fully the notion of compensating for one's bias. We might wonder if this is *ever* really appropriate on the grounds that one ought to *remove* one's bias rather than *compensate* for it. If one can recognize that one's view is biased, should one not revise it accordingly, especially if one is in the role of educating others? Indeed, if we begin to regard our own position as biased, in that central sense of concern here which links bias with distortion, have we not *already* begun to revise it just by recognizing those very places where it is faulty? And if we do not recognize a bias in our view, how can we compensate for it?

Despite these considerations, some sense can be made of compensating for one's bias even in the context of teaching. A person might know that in a certain area he or she has a tendency to be biased in favour of or against a particular group, theory, or whatever. Experience indicates that he or she is not good at avoiding bias in this area though there is no attempt to deliberately distort the account. (Subsequently, the individual can often see that he or she had been biased but at that point, after the fact, one must try to modify one's position.) Here is a case then where an individual can reasonably expect to fall into bias, and one might compensate in advance by calling *special* attention to sources where a rival view can be found, or by advising students about one's track record. A second kind of case is that in which others charge one with bias. Of course, to be accused of bias is not thereby to be guilty of bias, but where matters are controversial we cannot be certain that our account is free from bias. Here, we cannot modify our view to remove a bias which we do not yet admit or recognize, and which may not even be present, but we can compensate for the bias which may well be there by ensuring that our students do not neglect views which we ourselves are said by others to underestimate.

A few years ago, a Committee of Inquiry in Canada, established to review a controversial case in which a professor's contract had not been renewed because of alleged political bias in her teaching, determined that the professor had alerted her students to the bias which, as it was put, was bound to affect her presentation. The Committee added that "every conscientious teacher should do no less, and beyond ensuring by reading assignments or in other ways that students encounter opposed positions as presented by opponents, need do no more to guard against indoctrination."[6] Essentially, then, the recommendation was to compensate for her bias, and it certainly seems that compensatory action was warranted.

It is not at all clear, however, why this is all that a teacher needs to do in such circumstances. There is, in fact, something else any teacher *could* do, namely attempt to discover and then remove or reduce one's biases. If it were learned that the consequences of one's teaching were miseducative, that despite one's intentions students were uncritically accepting just one side of a controversial matter, presumably one ought to take such further steps. Of course, the sense of obligation here is blunted once we speak of bias being *bound* to affect our teaching. This suggests that the teacher is helpless with respect to his or her own biases, and if there is nothing one can do, any obligation will founder. But if others can detect bias in our work, why is it *impossible* for us to recognize this, and make suitable amendments, if we are genuinely trying to arrive at, and present, a balanced view? It will not do to give as the reason that we are biased, since the question is why we must continue to be biased.

One confusion which can push us into scepticism here is the idea that we would need a perfect conception of a bias-free position before we could begin to recognize and remove any bias we might have, a requirement which would leave our efforts stillborn. There is a fallacy at work here which derives from Plato, but it is alive and well today.[7] It arises when we forget that we can make our view *less* biased by attacking those biased aspects which we do recognize. We may well discover, of course, that there are further improvements to be made. Our view may still be biased even though we have modified it. We may also discover that certain revisions were themselves unfortunate, but that is not a reason to conclude that *any* new view is just as biased as before.

## Relativism and Bias

Compensatory action is, then, often desirable, though not a *substitute* for trying to identify and remove one's biases. Some recent suggestions for teachers in areas where bias is alleged, however, seem unhelpful. David Layton has concluded, in connection with the issue of creationism in the science classroom and the concerns of those who see science as challenging beliefs which are sanctioned by religion, that:

> The demand on science teachers here is not for some dramatic recasting of material or syllabus reconstruction. Rather the need is for an extension and sharpening of existing sensitivities to the range of value positions in any classroom and the fostering of styles of teaching which convey respect for them.[8]

Layton does not elaborate on these vague remarks, but presumably by ruling out a dramatic recasting of material, he is denying, quite properly, that the present emphasis on evolutionary theory is necessarily biased. But what are we to understand by the need for styles of teaching which convey respect for the range of values present? One can respect someone's right to hold that the earth is no more than a few thousand years old. This is a form of tolerance. A science teacher cannot, however, respect that view as one would respect an alternative theory which had scientific merit. Certainly a teacher should be sensitive to the values of his or her students, but this cannot be translated into a demand that their opinions be regarded as plausible or persuasive. In the prevailing climate of relativism, a vague call for respect is potentially misleading.

Relativism is perhaps most commonly invoked in the case of value questions, so we should consider carefully the charge of bias where the teacher's commitment is to some substantive *value* judgment. The popular view seems to be that any such commitment *necessarily* amounts to bias, with the result that alternative views must be no more than rival biases.[9] It is not difficult to illustrate how this sort of view leads to problems. Consider the recent suggestion that the view that one's own culture is superior to that of another is racist.[10] This is an instance of the general idea that a substantive evaluation involves bias, in this case a particularly virulent kind. This, however, would have the absurd consequence that any sincere condemnation of racism in another society would itself be racist unless the person judged his or her own society to be equally racist. *Is* every culture *equally* racist? Contemporary Sweden and Nazi Germany? More generally, the point is that we must examine a value judgment and how it has been reached before we can usefully apply the notion of bias. If every value judgment is said to be biased, the charge loses its sting. We are concerned about bias because it involves distortion, and there is an implication in the charge of bias that there is an *improved* view to be found. These connotations evaporate if value judgments are beyond any kind of reasoned assessment, as the relativist holds.

Relativism about values, the view that rival value judgments are equally acceptable, lies behind the view that all value judgments are biased. Nothing is to count as arriving at an improved view, though it is not clear what remains of the charge that value judgments are distorted. Taken seriously, this would mean an end to reasoned discussion about values. On this view, there is no chance of improving our judgments, nor of deciding which of the rival views is preferable, and even the possible increase of tolerance through the promotion of sympathetic understanding resulting from discussion cannot consistently be regarded as an improvement over intolerance. Why prefer tolerance? More to the point, why be concerned *at all* about racism and sexism if value judgments are all of a piece? Relativism actually cuts the ground from under a concern over bias. There is clearly no point, on this view, in developing guidelines on bias in school materials at all.

Nevertheless, it is easy to show that guidelines on bias for teachers often do inconsistently build relativism into the framework. Consider, for example, a specific criterion from the 1981 guidelines issued by the California State Department of Education which reads:

> When diverse ethnic or cultural groups are portrayed, such portrayal must not depict differences in customs or lifestyle as undesirable and must not reflect an adverse value judgment of such differences.[11]

The explanatory note accompanying this remark reveals that it covers two points: (i) that differences as such are to be prized; (ii) that particular differences must not be deemed inferior. The crucial objection can be stated quite simply, and seems to me unanswerable. What are we to say of another culture which does *not* subscribe to the value of pluralism which is evidently implicit in the guideline? Is that other position just as acceptable as our own and beyond legitimate criticism? If so, it is not clear what our norm amounts to. If not, we have made an adverse judgment.

More generally, however, the relativism involved in this criterion is ultimately inconsistent with the overall stated purpose of these guidelines which is to *promote* certain values such as self-esteem, and to combat others such as racism. The California guidelines maintain that when material in the curriculum depicts an attitude towards women or minority groups which was prevalent at an earlier time, or is prevalent today in another culture, an editorial comment in the student edition of the text must explain that "that attitude has changed or does not occur in the contemporary United States."[12] (Potential cases might include the practice of female circumcision, the execution of females for adultery, and the forced marriage of women, not to mention many other examples where the freedom of women to exercise choice is denied.) Such editorial comments, however, can only be interpreted as criticism, albeit polite criticism, of the attitudes which lie behind certain practices. The reference to what "does not occur" *is* a value judgment, barely disguised in sociological trappings. The purpose of the comment is not to provide information, but to ensure that in this case, in the words of the guidelines, the students will not pattern their ideas after what they see and hear. The authors of these guidelines and standards have been intimidated by the dogma of relativism to the point where they are afraid to stand behind the very values they have put their efforts into promoting. The matter of courage arises again.

In taking a stand against certain attitudes and practices, the California State Department is *not*, as it at times seems paradoxically to fear, thereby falling into a bias of its own. What is crucial is the extent to which rival views are given a full and fair hearing, and whether or not attempts are made to justify the positions taken. A teacher who argues for or against a certain cultural practice, arranged marriages say, may or may not present a biased view. We can distinguish between the teacher who distorts the situation by failing to present a defence of the practice as it would be presented by those who favour it, and the teacher who considers the matter sympathetically and impartially, taking into account the relevant cultural context, but nevertheless comes out against the practice.

It is a separate question whether or not the students will be capable of attending to the teacher's reasons rather than being influenced by the teacher's position of authority. And if it is the latter which dominates, then bias enters in again because the play of evidence and argument is distorted by an irrational factor. David Bridges favours teacher neutrality on controversial value questions as a "useful transitionary stage in weaning pupils from dependence on her authority".[13] It is important, however, to realize that there is no suggestion here that non-neutrality *as such* amounts to falling short of impartiality; moreover, neutrality is seen as a temporary measure designed to produce a subsequent stage where students will be expected to cope with an argument which seeks to convince them. David Bridges' point simply recognizes that there is a difference between the real world of the classroom, with its potential for a hidden curriculum of deference and authority, and the ideal world of free and impartial discussion and controversy.

## Reporting and Recommending

The distinction between the real and the ideal is relevant in another way to the problem of bias. The California guidelines, for example, reveal that a large part of their concern is to widen the child's horizons, to show him or her what is possible:

> Children dream of and aspire to those goals they are encouraged to attain. Their world can be expansive and filled with exciting and infinite possibilities, or frustrating in its limitations, depending on their exposure.[14]

It follows, as my earlier example of doctors and nurses shows, that curriculum materials which *arbitrarily* restrict possibilities for certain people are biased. They do not present an accurate picture of what one can aspire to, and they actually serve to close off possibilities, thus helping to make their arbitrary picture a reality. It is sensible and important then for teachers to insist on materials which, for example, portray women in creative, problem-solving roles and members of minority groups in professional and executive positions. All of this is part of a process of undermining that bias which persists because traditional practices and beliefs are taken for granted.

There are traps, however, for the unwary. Serious efforts to change a situation for the better presuppose that we understand what the present situation is. If children are to grow up into adults capable of challenging bias, they need to become acquainted with the forms bias takes in society. Education includes not only opening our eyes to possibilities but also rubbing our noses in reality. Both points suggest the need for a realistic treatment of bias. Obvious as this may appear, however, we are told that "socioeconomic characteristics should not be portrayed as correlated to race or ethnicity".[15] Here we are surely in danger of blurring the vital distinction between the ideal and the real. Socioeconomic characteristics *are* frequently correlated with race, ethnicity and other factors, and an accurate portrayal of society cannot pretend otherwise however much we deplore the fact. A novel which aims at realism simply cannot present certain characters in certain roles however much we might want to see such possibilities open up. The criticism unfairly directed at novelists who have tried to capture realistically biases which pervade society is akin to shooting the messenger.[16] If indeed society has restricted certain groups to menial occupations in laundries and garment factories, such association in history books and stories is not an example of stereotyping but merely an accurate portrayal. If we show men and women in equal numbers in our accounts of the Canadian, British or Australian parliaments, we are in serious danger of failing to alert our students to the actual situation. We need to remember that the possibilities we hold out for children are *less* likely to become live options if they underestimate the efforts they will need to make to overcome the bias in society working against their success.

Clarity in this area demands that we hang on to the distinction between what we report and what we recommend. Without this, realistic novels and accurate history can only be misinterpreted. We constantly meet the view, however, that what we report is irredeemably contaminated with our preferences.[17] It is not at all clear how, on this view, there can be any confidence that there is a genuine problem of bias at all, for any allegation of bias is itself a report which presumably then is only a preferred way of looking at the world. David Layton, however, cites the notorious dispute in the late 1950s between Linus Pauling and Edward Teller on the consequences of radioactive fallout from nuclear tests as an illustration of the problem:

> Pauling expressed his conclusion as the absolute number of deaths likely to occur. Teller, in contrast, gave the expected shortening of average life expectancy compared to shortening due to smoking. Each statement embodied a value judgment on the desirability of continued testing of nuclear weapons; indeed it would be difficult to think of a way of reporting in this case which was not similarly value laden.[18]

The implication would seem to be that we must conclude that both Pauling and Teller were biased and, worse, that they were *inevitably* biased because their political preferences determined the selection of "facts" which each made.

Such a case raises interesting points, from which various implications for impartiality in teaching may be drawn. It is widely agreed that Pauling and Teller remained within the bounds of the available scientific evidence, employing indeed the very same data. It is also clear that this would not be sufficient to avoid the charge of bias. Bias is not the same as outright fabrication of data even though a biased recommendation may make use of claims known to be false. Bias concerns the way in which the data has been dealt with, in particular whether or not one's report does justice to the whole body of evidence. The facts reported may be accurate enough while not the only relevant facts; and those suppressed or minimized might place the issue in a very different light. Similarly, brevity is not the central issue though it may cause problems. A report which is brief may nevertheless be "on the right lines", requiring the details to be filled in. The notion of "relevant facts" implies that the legitimacy of the charge of bias depends upon the question or issue involved. Pauling's report, for example, was not biased if the issue is agreed to be the number of deaths likely to occur. But it becomes a case of bias if he has unfairly made this out to be *the* issue.

For the teacher struggling to be impartial, the moral here is that bias may enter in *as the issue is characterized and delineated*. Open discussion with the students on this matter is vitally important. Moreover, it is not enough for the teacher to find evidence which supports his or her preferred interpretation. To avoid bias, one needs to follow the Popperian model of falsification, i.e. seeing if there is evidence which runs counter to one's own view. A teacher with this approach may slip into bias but is taking appropriate steps to guard against it.

It is worth reminding ourselves, in response to Layton's somewhat despairing conclusion, that a report *incorporating* the two perspectives, and other relevant interpretations, could have been drawn up for policymakers to consider. Subsequently they would have to decide what weight to attach to each view. Human fallibility means, of course, that some important perspective might be omitted, but until this is shown to have occurred we cannot know that the report *is* biased. When bias is shown to be present, remedial action in the form of a revised report can be taken. Even if a particular report does not remain neutral, but argues ultimately for the greater significance of one set of statistics or the preferability of one course of action over another, it is conceivable that we might agree that this followed a judicious and impartial review of all the relevant evidence and did not simply proceed from a partisan position held dogmatically. These points apply *pari passu* in the context of teaching.

Both Pauling and Teller were accused of intellectual dishonesty in allegedly tailoring their selection of facts from the common data to accommodate their own political preferences. Teller and Pauling, so the accusation runs, *would* argue as they did because of their respective political differences. Here, however, we are in danger of assuming deviousness without taking the trouble to critically examine their reports. It is possible to find, after a fair review of the evidence, that the view one initially and instinctively favoured is supported; and possible also to change one's view as the evidence begins to weigh against it. Once we judge a report as biased on the sheer basis of the author's real or alleged motives or preferences, we ourselves introduce a bias against the author, for we are inclined to consider his or her view discredited before we have seriously reviewed it.[19]

## Fashionable Confusions

The matter raised here has been a source of great confusion in education in recent years, and the confusion has found its way into influential guidelines for teachers.[20] It is commonly argued, for example, that one's race, gender or class necessarily prevents one from teaching certain courses or issues in an appropriate way.[21] There has been a fashionable view that certain people, because of their background, simply *cannot* understand certain issues, and cannot remedy the deficiency. They cannot, therefore, present anything other than a distorted account no matter how sympathetic or well-intentioned they may be. Whites, for example, cannot understand the problems faced by blacks, and thus cannot write or teach about blacks in an unbiased way. The same objection is raised when men attempt to address the situation of women. In these cases, however, where a person cannot normally move from one group to another, the claims seem self-defeating. Their truth would preclude the possibility of their being known. The claim that those across the divide—white/black, male/female—cannot understand each other's situation is a claim that the thesis cannot allow, since the claim purports to cross the divide. The view that whites cannot understand the situation of blacks cannot be coherently advanced by a white person. How could he or she know? Similarly, how can it be made by a black person without claiming the kind of knowledge, this time of whites, said to be impossible?

Besides this logical problem, how plausible is it to say, for example, that John Howard Griffin gained *no* understanding of the condition of blacks in the American Deep South when, in 1959, he darkened his skin and passed as a black man for several weeks in Mississippi, Alabama, Louisiana and Georgia?[22] Those who read his powerful account are able to experience vicariously his ordeal and gain *some* insight into an oppression they may never have personally had to suffer. Often, of course, although a person may not have experienced the precise form of suffering of some other group, there may be sufficiently analogous experiences in his or her own background to permit an empathetic response to arise.

Setting aside one's own bias, or finding an impartial arbiter, is such a difficult matter, however, that many have favoured an approach in the area of public policy which tries to ensure that advice is received from a committee of experts who have, and defend, opposed biases.[23] Something like this approach is favoured also by current affairs programmes on television where it no doubt is thought to make the sparks fly and the ratings soar. Occasionally it is proposed in the area of education,[24] and it may have the merit of bringing in the very important dimension of realism discussed earlier. The hidden curriculum of opposed biases, however, may teach that the best we can hope for is an exchange of biases, and this may serve to further fuel relativism. This approach, useful on occasion and as a basis for subsequent reflection, is not a substitute for the example of the teacher struggling to formulate and present an *unbiased* account of an issue.

A concern to combat bias, like other concerns which become causes, can cloud our judgment. Occasionally, perhaps as a result of a sincere desire to raise consciousness, commentators exaggerate claims. Although Godfrey Brandt, for example, criticizes research findings reporting the respective achievements of West Indian and Asian children in Britain on the grounds that a whole community has been treated as an undifferentiated mass and "gross generalizations" have resulted, he is nevertheless ready to assert that "Britain is a racist state in that racism is not only an endemic part of the personal perceptions, attitudes and actions of white people, but it is an institutionalized part of both governmental and non-governmental organizations."[25] This comes from a book whose stated purpose is to challenge students and teachers to struggle against racism. But if gross generalizations are the breeding ground of bias, can it be helpful to indulge in and encourage this kind of thinking oneself, even if it is directed against the despised group? Ways of thinking can spill over into areas outside the original context. Notice that Brandt speaks of white people, not of many or even most white people, a thesis which is falsified by a single counter-example. If white people can be captured as a whole in this way, may not the student begin to suspect that the same is true of blacks or Asians? Thus, even as a tactic designed to "even the score", it seems fraught with danger and likely to perpetuate the problem it claims to be anxious to eliminate. A teacher would be well advised not to emulate Brandt.

The opposition to certain reports being presented in school textbooks reflects the recognition of the fact that even true statements in certain contexts can mislead the reader and distort the situation. This admission, however, does not justify the numerous efforts in recent years to delete from history texts true statements which some particular group finds offensive.[26] Clearly, certain episodes in history can hardly reflect well on certain nations, but the distinction between writing history and rewriting it is a precious one. The fashionable criterion of what "tends to demean" should not be invoked to distort the serious study of history. Gratuitous offense must be avoided, of course, and sensitive treatment is required. The historical record must not be altered to accommodate preferences; when it is, we must give up talk of studying history. The general point here was made memorably by Bertrand Russell in his first published paper on education when he characterized the scientific outlook as "the refusal to regard our own desires, tastes, and interests as affording a key to the understanding of the world".[27]

Some philosophers, I believe, allow the difficulties involved in the critical process to engender an unwarranted cynicism. Richard Pring, for example, considers the way in which political bias can influence school subjects and remarks on the accusation that peace studies is politically partisan. He continues:

> The assumption is, however, that so much of what has been taught in history is not politically partisan—the selection of heroes, the focus upon particular eras and events, the interpretation of events through textbooks. To some extent (although thanks to the resilience of young people, only to *some* extent) the control of the curriculum is the control of young people's minds, and then the control over the future shape of society.[28]

It would be a pity if the opening remark here were to encourage the view that since all subjects are biased we need not be surprised about peace studies. This view is unfortunately fostered by the ambiguous reference immediately following to the "control of young people's minds". This is calculated, I think, to suggest a process of indoctrination in which reasoned discussion loses out to manipulation. Pring is no doubt correct to conclude as he does that there will always be political problems to face in promoting values in school, but his remarks do not contribute to a balanced judgment.

We can admit that other traditional subjects have been biased though long regarded as objective. But just as these subjects have at last come in for critical scrutiny, so too peace studies needs to be examined for bias. Suggesting that it is no worse than other subjects is a rather desperate defence. Reference to mind control is not likely to promote a more rational critique. Control, however, can have weak and strong interpretations. In its strong form, it tends to imply that the student's beliefs, attitudes and values will be determined by someone else—the state or curriculum planners. In its weak form, however, it means that the student will be influenced to develop his or her critical ability so that self-control, or autonomy, develops. Obviously, it cannot be pretended that a curriculum does not seek to influence a student in any way whatsoever. It is not a necessary truth, however, that it must seek to exclude independent thought and autonomous judgment. On the strong view, bias enters in in at least two ways. First, whoever controls the curriculum determines that a particular set of beliefs, which may be controversial, is inculcated. Second, the student will not be able to review his or her position critically and will, therefore, be biased against counter-evidence. Fortunately, teaching need not degenerate into the strong form of control.

## What Is Wrong With Bias?

Bias undermines teaching and education because it interferes with an impartial review of evidence and argument. If our approach is biased, we fail to do justice to the overall account. Our interpretation is distorted because certain aspects have been played up and others comparatively neglected. If we are biased, we are inclined to accept some position or account more readily than an impartial consideration would warrant, or we are disposed to reject an idea before it has been given proper consideration. Many underlying factors may be at work, including pride, favouritism, ignorance, tradition, loyalty, hope and corruption.

In some of these cases, we may not be aware of our biases. It is something we have slipped into as we are swept up in, for example, national pride or blind loyalty. We judge one performance superior because a fellow Canadian is the performer and the occasion is one where national honour is at stake. Our judgment has suffered, but if it is a slip arising from emotional fervour, we may be able to show our open-mindedness by revising our judgment when we are challenged.

At other times, however, our biases run deep. Biased views in the form of gross generalizations about other groups may have become so much a part of our outlook that we are immune to obvious counter-examples to our view. We are not willing to see these as counter-examples, and our bias helps to explain them away. The spectacles we have put on distort what we see including that which might put us right. Bernard Crick says that biased opinions by themselves do no harm: what matters is how we hold our opinions.[29] This certainly recognizes that an individual may indeed revise the biased opinion he or she has slipped into, but it underestimates the potential harmfulness of a one-sided view on even a reasonable person. There remains a strong case for trying to reduce, even if we cannot remove, our biases.

In teaching, bias can translate into propaganda and experience suggests that it is all too easy to succumb. The propagandist engages in a one-sided, characteristically emotional, tirade in an attempt to persuade.[30] It is not at all the same as reasoned persuasion and the two should not be confused. One factor which causes confusion here is that with propaganda, as distinct from persecution, there is some semblance of free choice.[31] Those who are won over believe that they have chosen freely, not realizing that they have been manipulated and harmed. Someone has set out to close their minds to the reasoned consideration of alternatives, and they have cooperated. Unfortunately, their willingness to listen was not balanced by an ability to critically evaluate what they have heard.

People can also engage in deliberate bias out of self-interest, or in order to win converts, or for some other reason. Of course, such people know that they are distorting the case to serve their ends, so they are not blind to what they are doing though they will not admit it. Typically, such flagrant bias is in the service of what they regard as a higher end about which they have a closed mind, an attitude which helps them to overlook the moral offensiveness of their conscious bias, and to control those normal feelings of care and concern for others which might otherwise have tempered their actions. It will be useful then to examine the virtue of open-mindedness.

# CHAPTER SIX

## *Open-Mindedness: Against Finality*

In the case of any person whose judgment is really deserving of confidence, how has it become so? Because he has kept his mind open to criticism of his opinions and conduct.

John Stuart Mill—*On Liberty*

### *The Ideal in Question*

God, for all His virtues, is not open-minded. Omniscience precludes the possibility of such a trait. No occasion can arise in which doubts or fresh evidence need to be taken into account. There is no point in reconsidering an opinion which cannot be in error; no reason to wonder about the merits of an alternative point of view. Since an omniscient being makes no inquiries, there is no sense in recommending that inquiry be conducted free from prejudice and bias. Open-mindedness is a virtue for fallible and limited human beings whose attempts to achieve knowledge are often frustrated and always open to challenge. It is an important virtue for teachers.

Open-mindedness exists when we are willing to have our views influenced by evidence and argument, and it can be shown both in the process of inquiry which leads to the initial formation of a view, and in the process of reconsideration which leads to a view being modified or abandoned.[1] Concerning the former, it will require among other things that we attempt to avoid any bias which would lead us to exclude the consideration of relevant matters. Subsequently, it will require that we attempt to deal impartially with difficulties which arise for whatever views we have formed. The difficulties will have to be dealt with reasonably and fairly, not shunted aside or dismissed in cavalier fashion.

Open-mindedness will reveal itself in a disposition to engage in a wide variety of practices which support the underlying aim of holding views—whether they concern facts, values, theories or policies—which have been critically considered in the light of evidence and argument. Such practices will include: considering seriously rival points of view; subjecting one's own view to critical tests; taking into account evidence newly emerging; attempting to identify and counter one's own biases and prejudices; supporting a climate which tolerates free inquiry; suspending judgment when the available evidence and arguments are inadequate, and so on. We often make mistakes in judgment in applying the notion of open-mindedness to people, including ourselves, but this is because it is not always easy to tell if these practices are being genuinely followed, not because open-mindedness is a particularly mysterious notion.

One succinct formula for open-mindedness is the Socratic maxim to follow the argument where it leads.[2] It is the means we employ to examine our ideas, discard faulty ones and replace them with more adequate views. But if it is a *means* we use to arrive at truth and wisdom, in what sense is it an ideal? Certainly, it is common enough to hear open-mindedness referred to as an ideal, not simply as a useful tool or technique. Introducing the notion of ideals satisfies two important conditions. First, it emphasizes the practical impossibility of fully displaying the disposition in question. There will always be blind spots, biases and unexamined assumptions which make us less open-minded than we might be. Open-mindedness, like other ideals, is to be approached but rarely, if ever, fully attained.[3] Nevertheless, it is properly applied to those whose relative success is noteworthy. Second, although it is a means to other ends such as knowledge, it is not a means we can ever expect to dispense with. We are never going to achieve an omniscient state where open-mindedness is redundant. It will, given our fallibility, remain the appropriate attitude to have with respect to our ideas. It is, indeed, part of our insight into the human condition, an aspect of human wisdom.

There is no suggestion that open-mindedness is our only ideal, or all we need. This is not because, as some assume, open-mindedness provides no direction for action. A number of associated practices have been outlined above indicating that open-mindedness does not involve irresolution. But we also need ideals, concerning justice, education, freedom and so on, which capture specific principles to guide our actions and decisions in particular spheres. Open-mindedness itself is no substitute for these, but rather co-exists with them and invigorates them as they are continually revised and reinterpreted.

Ideals of any kind are given short shrift by practitioners, in teaching and elsewhere, because their practical value is questioned. Certainly, mere lip-service can be paid to ideals breeding a cynical attitude in those who see through the charade. Ideals can be subverted, and can wear a false face, as when open-minded inquiry is permitted in certain areas while other issues are declared off-limits.[4] A preoccupation with ideals can blind us to shocking realities, and modest improvements can be postponed while the perfect blueprint is forever refined. Ideals are often couched in vague, ambiguous rhetoric permitting almost any interpretation and proving useless as concerns practical direction.

All this is undeniable but does not constitute a reason for teachers to neglect ideals. Our ideals can give us a sense of direction and help us to determine whether or not more immediate and practical aims are on track. Ideals help to keep possibilities before our minds, possibilities which go beyond present achievements with which they must not be confused. The particular ideal of concern here, namely open-mindedness, is invaluable if any of our ideals are to be really useful. It can serve to keep alive that on-going reinterpretation of other ideals which prevents them from degenerating into empty slogans; and it can expose our fond belief in the perfect blueprint which inhibits action. A critical review of ideals is indispensable if false versions are to be detected. Open-mindedness itself can be misunderstood and it is no idle paradox to suggest that the interpretation of open-mindedness is itself something about which we should remain open-minded.

Ideals need to be brought down to earth by being translated into practices which serve to advance them. This means, of course, that they must first be understood so that inappropriate and misleading strategies can be avoided. The temptation here will be to try to find secure, general rules to guide practice, and yet the actual context will demand variation on what are in effect guidelines. Inevitably, there will be no simple formula to adopt, and those who seek teacher-proof strategies are destined to fail. Ideals are by their nature at the edge of the attainable, and one of their besetting difficulties is the context-bound character of appropriate strategies. Teachers will have to live with advice which is often but not invariably useful. Open-mindedness will sometimes take the form of suspending judgment, for example, but not always. This is one reason why we properly speak of ideals *inspiring* our actions. A direct calculation of means is not always possible.

Consider another example. The person who is open-minded will have to be prepared on any particular occasion to change his or her mind. But the ideal cannot be captured in a rule which would require us to change our minds every time our view is challenged or an alternative presented. That way lies the confusion with empty-mindedness.[5] Such a theory would make us mindless victims of whatever contrary view happened along. The ideal, rather, is to be prepared to change our minds whenever there is good reason to do so, a principle which requires intelligent and flexible judgment.

One danger with ideals is that they mark out a path which may lead to fanaticism. An ideal comes to be seen as of all-consuming importance, and in its pursuit other values are trodden underfoot. (We have earlier noted the view that someone whose commitment to impartiality led him or her to care no more for his or her own children than for strangers would seem to us a terrifying saint.[6]) Open-mindedness is an ideal for ideals: it confronts fanaticism and forces us to consider if one ideal should balance another in a given context. It may itself have to be balanced! Odysseus had himself bound to the mast and the ears of his men shut up with wax so that the Sirens could not lure them to destruction.[7] We should remember, however, that this was a temporary and desperate remedy if life itself was to be preserved. A fanatic would have insisted on facing the music.

## Misunderstandings in the Family

A recently published glossary of concepts and terms relevant to critical thinking makes only passing mention of open-mindedness.[8] This may reflect the view that the term is no longer serviceable because usage has rendered it irredeemably confused and confusing. For Dewey and Russell it was a key term which captured a central educational ideal, though both had to warn against common misunderstandings.[9] And these typically involved a failure to distinguish open-mindedness from related notions. Difficult as it may be to pin down, we cannot really afford to omit open-mindedness from any glossary for teachers. First, it is still used frequently to identify a certain ideal, and some important contributions to the debate on critical thinking list open-mindedness as one of the dispositions a critical thinker must possess. Robert Ennis' taxonomy is a case in point.[10] Second, moreover, all of our concepts in the area of critical thinking, including critical thinking itself, are inter-related, and an understanding of one contributes to an understanding of the others. We are dealing with the members of an extended family, and it is not easy to get the connections sorted out, but a gap anywhere reduces our overall grasp.

What are the confusions with respect to open-mindedness which have perhaps persuaded some educators to drop the term from their working vocabulary? Possibly the openness in open-mindedness en-courages the view that open-mindedness is uncritical, the ever-open door with no one at home, the open sink into which anything and everything is poured. For many people, too, there is a problem in seeing how the open-minded person can possibly have any convictions: thus open-mindedness comes to be associated with suspended judgment, hardly an ideal to guide one's life or one's teaching. Certainly, when we hear of someone having or keeping an open mind on something, we infer that they have formed no settled opinion. A further difficulty arises when we recall that the dogmatic individual insulates himself or herself against doubts. The open-minded person by contrast must entertain doubts, and imperceptibly we slide from genuine open-mind-edness towards scepticism.

Let us see if open-mindedness can be rehabilitated, given a stable interpretation, and generally freed from confusion. First, consider the view that open-mindedness represents an "anything goes" outlook. The key to exposing this error lies in recognizing that open-mindedness requires a generous attitude with respect to what can be advanced for consideration, but a stern attitude with respect to what should be adopted. Certainly, the open-minded person must be relatively tolerant with respect to speech and behaviour, otherwise he or she would be in the odd position of professing a willingness in principle to be influenced by views and practices which they were closing off from their experience. Of course, some practices cannot be tolerated. They deeply offend our moral convictions, or they are presently illegal. There remains some room for open-mindedness, however, since we can continue to ask ourselves if our moral norms and laws are defensible. Our tolerance is not unlimited but we can continue to review the limits we impose.[11]

Although open-mindedness presupposes a measure of tolerance, this does not indicate that open-mindedness is uncritical. Tolerance itself, as we have seen, need not be uncritical. Moreover, open-mindedness cannot be equated with our acceptance of all of the views whose expression we tolerate. The tolerant person, of course, may be quite closed-minded because he or she refuses to entertain seriously any of the views which they are not willing to suppress. The open-minded person, however, will entertain them without necessarily accepting them. Many of them will be incompatible, and "accepting" them could only mean adopting a relativistic attitude in which rival views were considered equally worthy. Relativism undermines open-mindedness. If no view is superior to another, why consider new ideas at all? Alternatively, a person could "accept" whatever idea comes along, adopting and abandoning ideas as they drift in. But it is only as a bad joke that we call a person open-minded—How very open-minded!— who takes on board an obviously foolish idea. Russell's example of the eminent psychiatrist who constructed a new logic on the basis of the advice of the lunatics in his care serves to make the point.[12]

A person who subjects a new idea to stringent critical scrutiny does nothing thereby to endanger his or her claim to be open-minded. The false charge of closed-mindedness is often made, of course, by those who would wish to see such critical scrutiny curtailed with respect to their pet beliefs. Hence the frequency with which the charge is made in such areas as parapsychology when claims are reviewed critically. We have other words to describe those whose acceptance of ideas is uncritical— for example, gullible and credulous. We should not abandon the valuable notion of open-mindedness and debase its meaning. The open-minded person is generally tolerant and the tolerant person is accepting of ideas and practices. To tolerate, however, contrary to Nathaniel Ward, is not to doubt one's own view nor to be insincere.[13]

Tolerance is a kind of acceptance, but the idea of acceptance conceals a slippery patch. What we, as tolerant persons, accept is others holding and expressing certain ideas.[14] As open-minded individuals we also accept the responsibility of *considering* those ideas, assuming their foolish character is not immediately apparent. But we do not have to accept (as true, worthy, valid, significant) the ideas as such.

Sometimes, we simply don't know what to make of certain ideas, and open-mindedness demands neutrality or suspended judgment. A view is controversial, perhaps, and we cannot decide which side is correct or how a compromise view capturing the truth in the various positions can be achieved. We remain neutral while reflection continues. Or an unexpected and serious difficulty arises for a view which once seemed certain. The difficulty cannot be resolved, yet the earlier view retains considerable plausibility. We suspend judgment while further evidence or clarification is sought. We say that we have or are keeping an open mind. We don't quite know what to think, and we are willing to be persuaded. It may be that some questions seem to us so problematic that we adopt a more or less permanent stance of neutrality. The difficulties involved in proving or disproving the existence of God, for example, have led many into agnosticism. Some agnostics like Huxley, however, have hesitated to say that we *cannot* know the answer to this question.[15] We *do* not know, but would do well to keep an open mind as to the possibility of knowledge even here. Whether or not something is *unknowable*, to paraphrase Huxley, is itself beyond our knowledge. Neutrality, then, is often appropriate, but when we do take a position our open-mindedness is not immediately lost. We can go on to show that we are ready and willing to think again as new ideas about the position emerge. We may even develop such ideas ourselves.

This rather obvious truth is concealed from those who have difficulty seeing what it means for someone to remain open-minded about a position which he or she has deemed to be false.[16] Once one forms a view and understands what that view excludes, how can one be committed to that view *and* be open-minded about those ideas which conflict with it? We have made up our minds. How can we be open-minded? As a result, the abandonment of neutrality seems to sound the death knell of open-mindedness. The way out of this dilemma is to recall that we are aware of our fallibility. We believe such and such to be true, but we also know that we make mistakes. The position now rejected may start to command new supporting evidence. Will we dismiss this out of hand, or will we look at it sympathetically? It is the answer to such questions which will determine our open-mindedness, not the mere fact that we have a view of our own.

Those who recognize that open-mindedness is compatible with having a point of view if it is held in a certain way, often suggest that it must be held as doubtful, or held with doubt. And this idea opens the way to a confusion of open-mindedness with scepticism. Many people, for example, hold that the chief lesson to be learned from science is scepticism, but a careful review of their position indicates, I believe, that they really mean to advocate open-mindedness.[17] What is the difference?

Scepticism in general is the view that sure knowledge is not attainable, a position which is taken seriously not only by many philosophers but also by popular writers on education. If, however, one holds that knowledge is unattainable, that one cannot hope to replace ignorance with knowledge—save perhaps for the knowledge that knowledge is impossible—open-mindedness in general becomes pointless as in the case of relativism. On the other hand, a sceptical attitude can be adopted as a *technique*, much as Descartes adopted it, in order to see how far apparently proven claims can be called into question. This is obviously a useful practice, for in discovering grounds for doubt we make our position, as Russell put it, less cocksure.[18] We recognize that many of our prized opinions are by no means as certain as we had thought, and we become more tentative with respect to them. We begin to see them as subject to revision.

Nevertheless, this line of thought can be pushed too far. If a person is quite confident that a view is correct, it does not follow that the absence of doubt implies closed-mindedness. We need to know how the person will respond when serious questions or doubts about the view begin to emerge. At this point, the open-minded person will need to consider such doubts. Earlier, however, he or she may have no doubts whatever, and even subsequently may be able to show that the doubts do not succeed in undermining the view. Being certain is a state which is perfectly compatible with the disposition to consider fresh evidence, evidence which may well produce a change in one's state.

## The Fixed and Final Point of View

When we describe people as closed-minded, we are primarily saying something about their present attitudes. Here and now, it seems to us, they are unwilling or perhaps unable to accept that their view is even conceivably vulnerable. Sometimes, as with those who claim divine inspiration for their beliefs, this unwillingness is admitted. We cannot be wrong because this is the word of God, and apparent difficulties are to be explained away. Thus Henry Morris, of creationist notoriety, admits that his view is that there is not the slightest possibility that the facts of science can contradict the Bible. At other times, we must infer a person's unwillingness from particular reactions. They profess open-mindedness but refuse to consider an objection to their view, suggesting that their real attitude is that their view is beyond the reach of criticism. Our assessment then is of their present attitude. It is not, primarily at least, a prediction about their future behaviour, since even Henry Morris might be overwhelmed by the evidence. Clearly, however, there is a predictive element because if we are right about the present attitude, it will colour their future responses.

We are not always right, however, in our assessment of closed-mindedness. Sometimes we think that someone will not consider an objection or piece of evidence when he or she has *already* considered and rejected it. A piece of evidence is so telling to us that we assume that only closed-mindedness explains the refusal of someone else to accept it. Some were quicker than others to recognize the Van Meegeren paintings as fakes when the story began to unfold, but the slower ones were not necessarily closed-minded. It required some skill and insight to see the difference, and an ability to reconstruct a conception of a genuine Vermeer free from the influence of false examples previously admitted.[19] The charge of closed-mindedness is employed quite casually very often, which undoubtedly weakens its practical value as a critical term, but on occasion its use is as justifiable as any other ascription which reaches behind our behaviour to capture a mental state.

Why would anyone set themselves to ignore potentially relevant evidence and argument? Closed-mindedness is surely foolish. If, however, you believe that you have received a special, divine revelation as to the truth, then the idea of further evidence or counter-evidence can seem absurd. God, after all, has always had all the relevant evidence. This attitude, however, faces two major difficulties. First, *is* the belief you hold divinely sanctioned? If it is, you are safe—but it is not clear how you can know that you are. Second, the belief in question, the age of the earth for example, certainly seems to be such that empirical evidence *is* relevant and cannot be discounted in advance.

Some may be unable to question certain beliefs because it would be psychologically traumatic to do so. If all that we have ever heard has encouraged us to think that our own country has a glorious and unsullied past, and our own sense of worth is intimately connected with this idea, then all the evidence to the contrary amassed in the museums of other countries may fail to reach us though we wander through. We cannot and do not take the evidence seriously because it is capable of undermining a belief to which we are emotionally attached at the deepest level. There may well be the feeling that if this belief were undermined, we would be all at sea.

Some philosophers have proposed cases where future evidence can be discounted now. Leave aside as genuinely special those peculiar statements, such as "I exist", whose truth is a condition of their being uttered. (Unless I exist, I can make no utterance.) But what of other cases such as the claim that there is a pen in my hand right now. (There is. The word processor comes later.) Could future evidence conceivably count against this? Some philosophers have boldly excluded this possibility, and denied that their attitude is unreasonable.[20] If the pen suddenly vanishes, they say, we are not bound to concede that it never existed, that our earlier claim was false. No, we could say that a miracle had occurred, or that we are hallucinating at that later moment. No doubt, these are possible escape routes, but how can we know *now*, in advance, that they will be available? Until we assess the character of that later experience, how can we know that that assessment will not force a revision of the judgment we so confidently make now? The possible escape route may begin to seem quite implausible if, for example, signs of a clever illusion were revealed. The present attitude of refusing to *allow* that anything could count against our belief is unreasonable and dogmatic. What we can say is that we cannot see how any reasonable person could be seriously expected to believe that any such future evidence would occur.[21]

For many, the trouble with this conclusion is that it seems to entail that conviction and certainty can never characterize the open-minded person; indeed that these are the marks of closed-mindedness. Others more willingly embrace what they see as the same implication, and hold that it is the pretence of certainty which invites the charge of closed-mindedness. Scientists, therefore, should abandon the misconception that science proves things. But whether we welcome or fear these implications, we should first ask if they hold.

First, there is empirical evidence that absolute conviction does not make for closed-mindedness in practice. A powerful example is found in the work of Michael Ventris who eventually showed that Linear B is written in Greek although the notion that it was in Etruscan possessed him, in the words of a close collaborator, as a *fixation*. Nor was this a case of a closed-minded view changing over time into an open-minded one. The brilliant account of Ventris' work given by John Chadwick shows that *all along* Ventris was willing to entertain possibilities which ran counter to his Etruscan hypothesis.[22] He suspected that the Greek hypothesis would end in absurdity, but he pursued the stubborn clues which seemed to support it until its final vindication.

In the absence of such actual cases, we could argue that there is no necessary connection between conviction and closed-mindedness. We are certain when all the evidence supports a particular conclusion and there are no grounds for doubt. The fact that we can state conditions which, *if* they were satisfied, would mean that the conclusion would have to be revised does not mean that it is less than certain. When we have done what is necessary to make certain, it would be misleading to refuse to say so.

Other philosophers make similar assertions about what follows from knowledge.[23] Once we know that something is the case, they say, we are in a position to disregard any evidence that seems to tell against it because it is bound to be misleading. Thus, even knowledge seems to warrant closed-mindedness. Of course, we all know that what we thought we knew turns out very often to be mistaken, and this needs to be a constant reminder. But suppose we do know, and know that we know? There remains a number of reasons why we should not be closed-minded in the sense of disregarding what purports to be counter-evidence, especially in the context of teaching. We can explain why it appears to be counter-evidence but actually is not. We can show that our view is rationally grounded by refuting the case presented against it. We may discover that what purports to be counter-evidence is really evidence for something else which we did not know. We can forestall incipient doubts which may overtake us if we simply disregard the evidence presented. We may come to a fuller understanding of what we already know to be true by looking at it again in the light of criticism. And, finally, we help to keep alive the spirit of discussion which will be invaluable in other cases when it transpires that we only thought we knew. It seems then that there is a convincing case against closed-mindedness even when we know that something is true.

## The Ever Present Dangers

Probably few people think of themselves as closed-minded, and even those who say that they are about some issue do not normally mean to suggest that they are wilfully ignoring potentially relevant evidence and argument. They would no doubt feel that they have already taken into account whatever can be said against them and have rejected it for good and sufficient reason. If their minds are "closed", they would insist, it is because they do not expect ever to have to change their minds. But not everyone who denies being closed-minded, or who concedes it but only in this weaker, colloquial sense, is making an accurate assessment. Factors can be at work which produce closed-mindedness despite the individual's protestations and disclaimers.

If an individual is the victim of deliberate indoctrination, he or she has been brought to hold certain beliefs as true regardless of any evidence and argument which might be presented, or might arise, against them. Even if they are willing to listen, and though they may think themselves open-minded, they are incapable of conceiving that their position might be false or uncertain. Here we often find a façade of open-mindedness, especially an apparent openness to discussion, but the central assumptions in the position are inviolable. Avid religious canvassers are perhaps the best-known examples. Typically, there is a protective mechanism which shields the central assumptions or which provides reassurance. For example, the very existence of opposition will be interpreted, not as a reason to question one's view, but as further and decisive evidence that one's view is correct. Political and religious movements which see their position as one combatting evil forces, or which outline conspiracy theories, have ready-made, but question-begging, explanations at hand. Alternatively, there will be divine or infallible authority to reassure the faithful. Here we find examples of what Chesterton called the thought that stops thought.[24] In being accepted as a fundamental truth, its role in closing the mind is not recognized.

If we escape indoctrination, however, few can escape the dangers which come with socialization. Consider, first, those insidious beliefs labelled common sense. The label alone tends to protect them, since what is common sense can hardly be in error. And most people, Descartes observed, seem to feel that they have an abundance of common sense.[25] It takes an effort of mind to register the point, and greater effort to recall it on appropriate occasions, that what was once viewed as common sense is now viewed as nonsense; and what was once dismissed as absurd has now entered our common-sense framework.

Second, there are assumptions and beliefs we acquire which come to seem so natural that we scarcely recognize that we have them, and consequently do not see that they require justification. Closed-mindedness operates successfully because the beliefs are barely available for consideration. They escape examination because they are buried deep in the language we speak or the way in which we look at the world. Hegemony succeeds just by keeping ideas away from our scrutiny. What would now be regarded as examples of racism and sexism in textbooks, so obvious as to be themselves textbook examples, were not recognized at all just a few years ago. Aristotle did not worry much over the justification of slavery because the distinction between citizen and slave seemed perfectly natural to him. Some writers identify what they call visceral racism,[26] those unacknowledged and submerged attitudes towards other groups which prevent us from confronting our own beliefs by camouflaging them. We do not notice that our own noticing is selective. It is this phenomenon which makes consciousness-raising necessary, a process we ourselves can initiate by trying to expose those assumptions which would otherwise lie concealed. This cannot be impossible because we know that sometimes it succeeds.

Our prejudices, however, work against us. A prejudice is literally a prejudgment, but it is not the same as a suspicion, hunch or hypothesis. None of these, although formed in advance of all the necessary evidence, need suggest that the view in question will resist modification as the evidence emerges. But this *is* suggested by the notion of prejudice, which is also used when beliefs are held in defiance of evidence. The detectives may have their suspicions as they begin to gather evidence, but if they are open-minded these will be confirmed or discounted in the light of the facts. They are prejudiced when they are disposed to accept or reject the evidence in terms of their prior view, allowing to stand as evidence only what confirms that view. The prejudice colours their investigation. Defence lawyers who question prospective jurors to screen out those who have formed any view about the guilt or innocence of their client do so not because those who have some prior view *must* be closed-minded, but because such views *may* interfere with open-minded deliberation. Defence lawyers take no chances, but we should not transfer the "clean slate" model to other contexts and conclude that any advance view, however tentative, constitutes prejudice. A suspicion may be fuelled by prejudice but this would need to be shown. Sometimes, of course, such a charge is plausible. Why, for example, do your suspicions invariably fall on one particular group when a crime occurs?

## The Marketplace of Ideas

The classroom is one place where we can confront our prejudices and discover that other people hold very different views from our own. From the image of Socrates busy in the agora to the words of Justice Holmes in 1919, the notion of ideas competing with each other in the open marketplace has claimed a powerful hold on liberal thought. In the marketplace of ideas, we take what we will after comparing and considering rival views. The central conviction here is that the most effective method for pursuing truth, by no means an infallible method, is to allow claims to be challenged and contested. It appears in the Socratic ideal of following the argument where it leads; we see it also in the role of the *advocatus diaboli* of the Roman Catholic Church; it is very much part of Popper's view that claims should face critical tests. Its most memorable formulation is Holmes' declaration that the best test of truth is the power of the thought to get itself accepted in the competition of the market. Sceptics will scoff at the ideal in question, but will welcome the freedom to undermine various claims.

Censorship threatens this high ideal. In seeking to keep certain ideas out of circulation, it abandons the objective of having those ideas rejected by those who meet them and substitutes the method of suppression. Almost everyone will agree that the ideal of free expression must be limited in certain circumstances. In wartime, for example, it will almost certainly be necessary to impose some constraints on the free exchange of ideas which might pass unchallenged in ordinary circumstances. There is much less agreement, however, when we turn to other cases. Many claim, for example, that while John Stuart Mill recognized that truth could be crushed by persecution, he underestimated the way in which it could be destroyed by false opinions advanced by rabble-rousers. Is it not naive to think that people are able to eschew the nonsense advanced in the marketplace when it is persuasively packaged? And cannot such nonsense cause harm?[27] Should the open marketplace take care of such statements, or should their publication be suppressed?

The Canadian Criminal Code recognized these concerns when it proscribed the publication of a statement known to be false by the one who utters it and which causes or is likely to cause injury or mischief to a public interest.[28] A notorious case in Canada in recent years has concerned the publication of statements denying that the Holocaust occurred. The injury in question is clearly the danger of anti-Semitic attitudes spreading. It was commonly alleged, and apparently claimed by the defendant himself, that the prosecution and trial in this case provided the defendant with a platform for his obnoxious views, a million dollars worth of free publicity. Subsequent surveys by social scientists, however, suggest that very few people were persuaded to alter their attitude towards Jewish people despite the extensive coverage of the trial.[29]

It is not clear how we should react to this finding. Typically, it is introduced to counter the views of civil libertarians who opposed the trial, and who warned of the opportunities it afforded the defendant to address the general public via the media. But the finding surely cuts both ways. It *also* suggests that the public is not likely to be impressed by such claims when it meets them, and therefore the causal argument linking publication and injury is undermined. Of course, decent people will be offended when they encounter such publications, should they be permitted to circulate, but here we can appeal to the criterion of reasonable avoidability.[30] Unless such pamphlets are stuffed in our mail boxes or otherwise forced on our attention, we need not attend to them.

Often, there is genuine uncertainty about the likelihood of harm or injury, and in these cases we should persist with the marketplace conception until we have compelling evidence to abandon it. Justice Holmes' criterion of a clear and present danger is still a useful guide despite the fact that familiarity has almost caused it to sound trite. It is extremely difficult to predict definite and demonstrable harm from publications. Mordecai Richler recounts the anecdote about the kindly old lady who drowns her grandson in the bathtub because, having read *1984*, she suddenly realized that he was going to become Big Brother.[31] Similar stories are in circulation about the effects of certain movies. Clarence Darrow made much of the influence of crime stories on Dickie Loeb in his defence plea at the Leopold-Loeb murder trial. These cases, however, seem too tenuous a basis on which to impose censorship. We might recall Socrates' advice not to do what we have solid reason to regard as evil in order to prevent a possible evil.[32]

Currently the most difficult cases concern the publication of pornographic material which, it is claimed, may give rise to violence against women, and the publication of racist material which may provoke racial attacks. In the latter case, the problem is exacerbated because of the inability of many to identify genuinely racist material. Thus, even if it were agreed by the experts that racist material provokes racist behaviour, this would demand a proper identification of material falling into this category. And there have been numerous examples of material unjustly classified. Here we encounter one of the perennial problems with censorship—the way in which the censor's net catches innocent and worthwhile material. This forces one to place the onus firmly on the would-be censor to justify the proposed suppression. In the case of racism and pornography, we should demand clear evidence that the work in question is likely to cause real harm, not just offense, to identifiable groups. Vague possibilities will not suffice.[33] Our main focus here, however, is on the school classroom. Is this a forum protected by the marketplace ideal? Judging from historical and current experience, it has rarely been seen as such. School teaching has been dominated by the concept of information at the expense of inquiry. At a recent In-service for teachers, a provocative paper was delivered in a vain attempt to stimulate discussion. It was strikingly incongruous when the teacher-chairperson thanked the keynote speaker for the "information" presented. Schools have typically presented a rather bland and innocuous version of generally accepted findings as information to be digested: witness blackboard notes to be copied down and quizzes to test recall. The marketplace conception is one of a learning environment where inquiry is the dominant idea, and no more than lip-service is paid to this ideal in schools. Even civil libertarians, who might have been expected to champion inquiry, make apologetic noises about the not yet fully fledged minds of children.[34]

This is surely a spurious move. When students complete high school, they are adults. Most will have also completed all the formal education they will ever receive. The marketplace conception is not applied to schools out of some romantic conception that children can unerringly pursue truth, but because school represents an opportunity for inquiry to be *practised*. If material is banned, as in the total ban in Nova Scotia schools on "Restricted" movies, this must be an admission that the schools are unable to bring children to the point where they are capable, as young adults, of deciding what movies they will view. When the word "evolution" is deleted from grade-12 science textbooks, out of deference to the ignorance of creationists, such censorship means that the school is preventing access to significant ideas. The theory of evolution, as such, is not even controversial in science, though there are controversies about the details.

Why, however, should we agree with those who want to impose censorship with respect to controversial material? If it is pointed out that students can hardly be expected to resolve issues which divide society, we can respond that it is vital that students recognize that there *are* such issues and appreciate what stands in the way of their resolution. Of course, we can always find enough non-controversial material to fill the curriculum, and anyone who wants to argue that there is no time to do other things could have an easy victory—except that the position begs the question about the best way to spend our time in schools. Students will, at some point in their lives, have to assess their own views in the light of doubts raised by others, and to do this effectively they will need the skills and habits of reasoning. They need to interpret and deploy information, not simply amass it.

Can we ourselves condemn the censorship activities of others if we, for example, fail to include creation science accounts in our teaching? Certainly, such omission has often been portrayed as censorship by those who resent the exclusion. The response here must be that a failure to include something does not always warrant the charge of censorship, since the teacher's intention is all-important. Relevance, for example, is a criterion which can exclude material, and any coherent subject must have a sense of what is relevant. We also have to have some sense of what is fatuous if we are not to waste the time of our students. Nevertheless, it is surely advisable, when the charge of censorship is raised, to find a way of including the previously omitted material to some extent. The reason for this is simply that it is preferable not to leave any *impression* of censorship in case that should weaken the marketplace conception. This policy emphatically does not endorse equal time for such alternatives—that would be a mindless concession to vocal opposition. Nor does it require that we withhold criticism of such alternatives and studiously steer a neutral course. We should indeed capitalize on the inclusion, and show why it is an alternative which the relevant experts, with good reason, ignore.

There have been celebrated cases in Canada and elsewhere when certain speakers have been prevented from addressing audiences at universities. This is a form of censorship since it seeks to prevent the dissemination of ideas and access to them. Those who oppose such speeches hold, quite sincerely, that the views to be presented—for example, in defence of apartheid—are morally offensive and dangerous. It is argued that a university should not dignify outrageous views by providing a forum for their expression. What is missed here is the point that the university respects the principle of open inquiry not the particular views in question, so there is no question of dignifying the views as such. If the nature of the university were understood, the fear would dissipate. Another point is that the occasion also provides one with the opportunity to *counter* fallacious arguments and false claims. Totalitarian regimes also tend to practise censorship to ensure that their own citizens do not have access to dangerous ideas. In our concern to combat such regimes, we should be careful not to adopt their illiberal practices.

We are speaking here of showing intellectual respect for others and their opinions. This is vital in the context of teaching and education where students need to know that their ideas are taken seriously, and that they are at liberty to raise issues which concern them and to adopt positions which their teachers may not favour. It is also important, however, for students to know that their teachers care for them as persons, and this brings us to the matter of empathy.

# CHAPTER SEVEN

# Empathy: Who Cares?

Caring is the antithesis of simply using the other person to satisfy one's own needs.

Milton Mayeroff—*On Caring*

## The Caring Person

A caring person contrasts with one who is indifferent. The latter is someone who is aware of the problems and struggles of others yet remains untouched by sympathy or compassion. Hume refused to believe that anyone could be absolutely indifferent to the misery of others and regarded fellow-feeling as a principle of human nature.[1] Nevertheless, it is clear that there are significant relative differences among people in this regard. The care of the not indifferent[2] covers a wide range from minimal sympathy to the kind of fellow-feeling which approaches saintliness. The caring person is not merely not indifferent, but someone whose response to others is admirable as far as this virtue is concerned. Reference to non-indifference is only a preliminary way of marking off this sense of care from others.

Not every absence of indifference, moreover, indicates caring. Many motives may be involved besides a felt concern for the other person's welfare, interests and development. We are not indifferent, perhaps, but only because what happens to the other person will reflect somehow on our own performance, or on our own self-assessment, so that prudence, pride or personal gain become the determining factors. We may be actively involved in efforts to relieve another person's suffering, but what drives us is a strong sense of duty and not any emotional identification with those we try to help. We do not ignore their plight, and it would be too much to say that we are indifferent, but we hardly care for them in the sense of vicariously entering into their condition and responding because we are moved. Even when our emotions are engaged, it may be a matter of pity rather than of care. We see the other person as helpless, entirely dependent on our efforts, incapable of dealing with his or her own misfortune. Needless to say, such an attitude is typically resented when, by contrast, a caring response which left one's dignity intact would be welcomed.[3]

To be placed in someone's care, and even to be cared for by that person in the sense of being looked after, is not necessarily to encounter a caring person in the sense suggested above. One who is charged with the care of another person may, of course, behave irresponsibly and improperly. Children in care have often been abused. But even if cared for in strict compliance with whatever terms and understandings may apply in the situation, there may still be lacking that genuine human emotion which would reveal that the caregiver is personally moved by the needs and aspirations of the one who is at the moment dependent. There may be a total absence of any fellow-feeling. Those in charge may take care to provide instruction, protection, medication or whatever, but we are not bound to agree that these same persons are caring individuals.

It is not easy to say how individuals who genuinely care for others are to be recognized. The difficulty is the familiar one of trying to determine internal states from external clues. We know that we sometimes discover that someone we had thought of as a caring person is after all insincere, perhaps using us for some selfish purpose. Typically, we sense that someone cares or does not care for our well-being, but this sense is not infallible and we can misjudge people and be misjudged ourselves. Benevolence cannot be seen with certainty in a person's eyes.[4] Certainly, there are actions, gestures and words we conventionally expect from someone who cares, expressions of pleasure, sympathy, support, interest and the like. Even within a given culture, however, unless these matters are highly ritualized, there is great variation in the ways in which people show that they care. We need to resist the temptation to identify caring with particular forms.

Those who have written about caring have often made the point that the caring person will take the features of the particular situation into account rather than relying on rules and generalizations from other situations.[5] The obvious trap is that we would offer a stock response, one which would not really make a connection with the unique individual before us. Given this insight, it is puzzling that so often we encounter in the literature on caring a remark to the effect that a caring person would not say or do such and such in a certain situation.[6] Adding "might" as a qualification does not avoid the difficulty, since we still tend to set up a generalization which encourages a formulaic response to certain problems. Nor is it clear why what needs to be said must be said gently, as is typically proposed.[7] It is not difficult at all to imagine or recall situations where what is proposed as a caring response would be viewed by the other person as condescending, trite or pointless circumlocution. What needs to be said depends so much on the person being addressed and the relationship which exists between the persons involved. The tone in which remarks need to be made varies greatly depending upon context, so that particular suggestions can only be misleading.

The existence of a conventional form, for example a ritual expression of one's condolences, tells us what is expected in society but does not reliably identify genuine caring. Of course, to the extent that these particular outward forms matter very much to those concerned, we will not want to offend or insult people by flouting them. To do so might well indicate that we do not care. We cannot, however, make ourselves caring individuals, or ensure that we are seen as caring, by simply mastering these conventional forms.[8] There may also come a time when the convention has to be challenged on the grounds that it is not compatible with caring for others.

Some of the Stoics urged that we *limit* our response to someone else's sorrow to outward expressions of sympathy, not permitting ourselves to experience that sorrow vicariously in our own emotional experience.[9] This is the Stoic ideal of equanimity, accepting that which cannot be changed. Of course, it was part of this ideal that we adopt towards our own misfortunes the same indifference we often have towards the misfortunes of others.[10] Nevertheless, to recommend indifference to the sufferings of others who have not personally attained the Stoic attitude of calm resignation is surely an overly zealous commitment to an ideal. The fact that Epictetus warns us to take care not to go beyond the outward form of sympathy indicates that he too recognizes the force of the natural inclination to put ourselves in someone else's situation and vicariously experience what that person feels. If we were to follow his advice, however, our show of sympathy would be just that, a mere appearance, and it is hard to see how it could succeed in giving any comfort at all if its disingenuous nature were suspected.

## A Human Virtue

Most philosophers, and people generally, have not adopted the outlook of the Stoics but, like Hume, have thought it abundantly clear that sympathetic caring is part of our make-up as human beings and that such feelings are admirable. Adam Smith echoed Hume in thinking it "a matter of fact too obvious to require any instances to prove it", that sympathy is a basic and meritorious aspect of human nature: "How amiable does he appear to be, whose sympathetic heart seems to re-echo all the sentiments of those with whom he converses, who grieves for their calamities, who resents their injuries, and who rejoices at their good fortune!"[11] It is worth bringing Hume, Smith, Butler and many others to mind, and worth re-reading their impassioned defence of sympathy and the benevolent virtues, in order to offset the impression that moral philosophy written by men, and reflecting male views, has abandoned these virtues in favour of rules, principles and a quasi-mathematical approach to moral problems.

Caring is a virtue for everyone, men, women and children alike. There is no reason to believe that it cannot be an excellence characteristic of either sex. Some influential writers assert that they are making no attempt to answer the empirical question whether this virtue is more typical of women than of men, and that they do not intend to divide men and women into opposing camps with respect to this issue. These disclaimers and cautions, however, are lost sight of in the body of their work where the impression emerges that both words and actions reveal a clear and obvious difference between men and women in the moral realm. For example, no sooner has Nel Noddings made the disclaimer mentioned above than she asserts that women, in particular, seem to approach moral problems through a caring response.[12] (Indeed, this is how they are said to define themselves.) This, of course, is the very empirical question which was to have been left open. Subsequently, she assumes that "it is well known that many women—perhaps most women—do not approach moral problems as problems of principle, reasoning, and judgment."[13] It is hard *not* to conclude that opposing camps are being drawn up.

The responses of Jake and Amy, two eleven-year-old children attending the same sixth-grade class, have come to epitomize for many the difference between male and female approaches to moral issues.[14] Faced with the same moral dilemma, whether or not a man should steal a drug which he cannot afford to buy, in order to save his dying wife, Jake argues that he should because a human life is worth more than money. Amy, by contrast, rejects the dilemma as constructed and takes the view that the rapacious druggist needs to become more concerned about the dying woman. Carol Gilligan is right to resist the conventional scoring of these responses which neatly places Amy's level of moral development behind that of Jake. The point is well taken that we need to consider Amy's response in its own right. Does any of this, however, justify a conclusion to the effect that Jake cares less for others than Amy, not to mention any more general conclusions about boys and girls, males and females?

Surely not. We can find a useful clue in a remark made by Noddings: "I would not want to choose, but if I had to choose whether my child would be a reader or a loving human being, I would choose the latter with alacrity."[15] The same move is available to Jake who can also say that he would not want to be faced with the sort of choice which is involved in this moral dilemma, but *given* such a situation he would choose as he does. In saying sincerely how he would choose *on the assumption that he has to choose*, we cannot infer that he sees moral problems as nothing more than math problems where feelings can be set aside in favour of logic. We can no more conclude that Jake does not care about those involved in such a case than we can conclude that Amy is not able to weigh competing claims because she chooses not to. Decisions can be made with regret and compassion.

If it is objected that Jake does not *say* these things, we can ask why he should have to. Caring is not to be identified with saying that we care, and in a certain context things do not need to be said for others to know that we feel a certain way. Moreover, in taking the view that the man should steal the drug, Jake is influenced by the fact that the husband cares for his wife. He "can't get his wife again" because she is unique and irreplaceable. There is no plausibility in the interpretation that Jake casts the dilemma as an *impersonal* conflict of claims.[16] The personal relationship between the husband and wife is *one* of the factors which persuades the boy that stealing is justified in this case where the druggist only stands to lose property. (The fact that Jake would favour stealing the drug *even if* the husband did not love his wife does nothing to show that the loving relationship is not an important consideration.) If Jake reveals a sophisticated understanding of the logic of justification, as he does, this does not mean that he is blind to interpersonal considerations. What is normally unjustified he sees as justified in this situation *because* his sympathy for the husband and the dying woman outweighs sympathy for the druggist.

## Caring and Principles

Caring and justice need not, indeed must not, be seen as forming rival ethical positions but rather as complementary. A caring *component* in one's ethical orientation is quite different from an ethic of caring.[17] A just decision can be arrived at and conveyed in a heartless manner, certainly, but care may not be apportioned in a just way.[18] The alleged opposition between caring and principles, which surfaces in much recent writing, represents another dualism of the sort which Dewey warned against. We are told that the violent deeds which are omnipresent in the world around us are so often done in the name of principle. Having established certain principles, the argument goes, we believe that we can do violence to those who do not share them.[19] An ethic of caring is advanced as an attractive alternative to a hidebound morality which has scant regard for human foibles. The either/or we are being invited to accept, however, is made superficially plausible just because having principles is portrayed in the worst possible light.

There are numerous objections to the alleged link between principles and violence. First, it is falsely suggested that principles must be held fanatically and rigidly.[20] (Subsequently, we discover that a caring person may indeed have principles but he or she will treat them warily.[21] Assuming this means they will not be held blindly nor viewed as absolute, however, it surely characterizes any reasonably sophisticated attitude towards principles. Which moral philosopher would object to this? This concession shows that an exaggerated contrast had been drawn earlier.) Second, it fails to point out that there are principles available to temper any inclination to hold that an infraction by others of one's principles merits aggression. One has only to mention the principle of tolerance to see that the criticism collapses. Third, it conveniently overlooks the obvious fact that a commitment to caring can also have deleterious consequences. Suppose, for example, we torture heretics because we care deeply for their immortal souls. Here, reflection on justice and rights might well put our caring into perspective. Finally, why should there be any more danger of self-righteousness with respect to our principles than with respect to our consciousness of being caring persons?

A further obstacle to the view that caring and principles, including the principle of justice, are complementary is thought to be the idea of universalizability, which Noddings says simply that she will *reject*.[22] She tells us that she wants to preserve the uniqueness of human encounters, and that conditions are rarely sufficiently similar to justify requiring that one person do what another person must do. Universalizability, however, does not threaten the uniqueness of situations since it allows that *relevant* differences do make a difference, and we are entitled to say what is different about our circumstances if we wish to avoid the very criticism we ourselves were willing to make of others. If situations were as different as Noddings claims, what could we learn from experience?

Universalizability requires us to consider what might be importantly different in some other person's situation, and those who have written on the role of universalizability in ethics have not neglected the need for empathy. R.M. Hare remarks, for example, that "in putting oneself in this way into other people's shoes, one has to put oneself completely into their shoes, including the places where the shoes pinch *them*."[23] Noddings rejects the notion of "putting oneself in the other's shoes" on the grounds that caring involves reception rather than projection.[24] But this is a distinction without a difference. Whether we step into the shoes or have them placed on our feet, the central truth is that we have to understand how the other person sees the situation and feel how it feels to him or her. We cannot care for someone without trying to understand their situation and their reactions.

Moreover, we need to show *why* our attitude and response to one person, one of our children say, differs from that shown to another with respect to actions which certainly seem comparable. A disposition towards caring untempered by considerations of justice would soon entail the kind of favouritism which children dislike so intensely. Without the constraint of universalizability, the capriciousness which Noddings is anxious to avoid will soon emerge. This is simply because universalizability is the principle which opposes arbitrariness in the ethical life. It has been said that when the vicarious affections come in, impartiality flies out the window.[25] The truth in this remark is that we care more for our own children than for suffering children in some remote country. It is equally true, however, that impartiality remains as important as ever concerning our treatment of our own children.

Caring and justice are not rival ethical views between which we must choose, because we cannot live a moral life without attending to both. The numerous Irish men and women who have been imprisoned in Britain in recent years on the basis of evidence fabricated by the police certainly deserve our compassion, but they also rightly demanded justice.[26] A seriously ill criminal released on compassionate grounds might well feel gratitude, but an innocent person wrongly convicted wants to clear his or her name. It is not a question of gratitude, save to those who worked to expose the corruption which led to their conviction, but a question of rights and justice. If we are to care for these people, we *must* care for justice also.

## Three Teachers

Despite the controversy which surrounds the philosophical analysis of caring, it is often possible to be justifiably confident that someone is a caring teacher. We can point to examples in fiction where there can be little doubt that the teacher merits the description, and not because the writer pronounces authoritatively on the matter. These examples also serve to confirm some of the ideas advanced above. Peter

McGlynn, for example, the school teacher in rural Ireland in Val Mulkerns' story "The World Outside", is surely such a teacher.[27] The setting is the annual visitation to the one-room school by the inspector and there is considerable apprehension in the air. It is in McGlynn's light-hearted exchange with the children just before the inspector arrives that we see his concern for their well-being. There is a deep affection here which all the bantering and pretend threats cannot disguise. McGlynn is no saint and the children know it, though he is a gifted teacher who can fill their imagination with the world outside. They respond to his humour, and the affection is mutual, because they rightly sense that his concern is that they do well for *their* sake and not because any purely personal ambition of his own is riding on the outcome of the inspection.[28]

Consider also the portrait of Miss Totten sketched for us by Hortense Calisher.[29] The word for Elizabeth Totten is austere, a stiff, straitlaced, no-nonsense teacher, the very stereotype of the stern, distant schoolmistress of lore, "neither admired nor loathed but simply ignored". But quietly, Miss Totten coaches young 'Mooley' Davis, the young girl with a cleft palate who has thus far remained silent in the classroom, mocked by fellow-students and ignored by other teachers. There are no rewards in this for Miss Totten beyond the satisfaction which comes from trying to address someone else's difficulties. Her efforts generally go unrecognized and probably are not even fully appreciated, it is suggested, by the student who is helped. But the reader is left in no doubt that we have encountered a remarkable example of empathy.

Dewey's warning about the danger of recipes and models in teaching must not be forgotten, however, for what can be learned from these stories is clearly not readily translated into behavioural recommendations. Nothing, Dewey thought, had brought educational theory into greater disrepute than the attempt to concoct a recipe.[30] The context teachers find themselves in, and the cultural assumptions at work, vary enormously. Peter McGlynn and Elizabeth Totten are, like all of us, trapped to some extent within conventional expectations, and the resulting outward behaviour can give a misleading impression when judged from another perspective. But there remains something valuable to be learned if we can get behind the superficial aspects which might lead to such stories being labelled irrelevant at best and possibly even inappropriate on a casual perusal.

Especially important is the lesson that genuine caring and the appearance of caring are easily mistaken. To appreciate this point more fully, consider the teacher in Richard Yates' powerful short story, "Doctor Jack-O'-Lantern".[31] Miss Price rises to the challenge presented when Vincent Sabella joins her fourth-grade class part way through the year. Vincent is an orphan, supported by the Welfare Department of the City of New York, and instantly a social outcast in this middle-class school. It would not be fair to say that Miss Price is indifferent to Vincent's plight, and this points up the need to qualify the notion of the care of the not-indifferent. Her interest and concern, however, are governed by a sense of mission, and pity all too clearly replaces caring. Not surprisingly, "her campaign to build him up was painfully obvious, and never more so than when she tried to make it subtle."[32] Indeed, subtlety is not her strong suit, and zeal blinds her to the lack of tact she displays in her doomed efforts to help. Her actions are rather too calculated to bear the mark of a caring response. As she is at pains to point out, she does not get angry when Vincent scribbles obscenities on the school wall, and we cannot help but think that things might have gone very differently if her anger had shown itself rather than being suppressed in deference, no doubt, to expert opinion.[33]

Fiction is valuable not only because it shows the rich variety which attitudes can take, but also because it can make us feel the force of an emotion on those who experience it. In making us care for Vincent Sabella, the writer at the same time allows us to feel what is absent in the teacher's response. We hear her say "the right words" but they don't carry the authentic power of genuine emotion. She cannot communicate what she does not feel. In other cases, a caring response cannot be disguised by a tough exterior. These general lessons, of course, can be summarized and conveyed in philosophical terms, as I try to do here, but literature can reach us at the level of our own feelings as we vicariously experience the emotions depicted. If we are asked what it is to be a caring teacher, we can begin by asking in turn if those who ask are acquainted with these fictional characters and others.[34]

## The Caring Teacher

What kind of attitude should we look for in caring teachers? Russell, as we have seen, described the trustworthy teacher as one who cares for the students *on their own account,*[35] but what does this mean? Immediately, of course, it serves to distinguish a caring teacher from a propagandist despite the latter's commitment and zeal. The propagandist cares primarily for the cause, the party and the sacred doctrines, and looks upon the students, in Russell's words, as potential soldiers in the struggle. They are a means to the propagandist's ends, and the camaraderie and esprit de corps are merely devices to foster and consolidate that sense of identity which will ensure allegiance. It is easy also to treat individuals in morally offensive ways, disregarding considerations of justice and humanity, when such actions are seen as furthering a greater objective to which we are fanatically wedded. This shows that open-mindedness can help caring to flourish, and should not be seen as a rival and incompatible intellectual ideal.

Suppose, however, that the propagandist in the classroom sees his or her efforts as directed at benefiting the students themselves, perhaps protecting them from tempting but false ideas, saving their immortal souls or whatever. Surely, this individual *does* care for the students? After all, extraordinary efforts are made in order to preserve and promote their interests, and the propagandist may be prepared to pay a heavy personal price. The students are not primarily thought of as soldiers in the campaign, though they may in turn become fellow soldiers working to save others. They are themselves the object of the exercise. The propagandist acts with their good in mind.

This line of thought forces us to characterize more precisely the kind of caring desirable in teaching. If we ask how the teacher just described is different from another teacher who also wants his or her students to believe what is true rather than false, one important difference is that other teachers may want their students to accept the ideas *only if* the students are personally convinced that the ideas are true after independent consideration. The caring teacher, we can say, is anxious for the student to develop *as a student and person*, becoming capable of autonomous and critical reflection, someone who cares for other people and for certain ideas and ideals because their worth is appreciated, rather than as a result of blind allegiance to a code or creed. A caring teacher has respect for others, in this case respect for the student as potentially an equal, capable of independent thought and human responses.

Russell was right to associate the idea of being trustworthy with this conception of the teacher. Such a teacher will not abuse his or her authority, turning students into disciples. The claim is not that the teacher can be counted on to succeed with respect to the high ideals of autonomy and maturity, but that the teacher's attitude, intentions, and conception of his or her role are appropriate. Having said this, however, the point must be made that the actual consequences of one's teaching *are* fundamentally relevant to our assessment of the teacher in that the caring teacher will monitor the results of his or her work and make appropriate changes in the light of experience.[36] We can hardly claim to care for others if we do not take care to act in ways which actually serve their interests. Miss Price fails because she does not ask these hard questions about her own approach. She blindly follows conventional wisdom and is not responding to Vincent as an individual.

Many who would agree with the general point made here about evaluation would nevertheless maintain that *grading* (reporting to others on the student's standing) is incompatible with being a caring teacher.[37] The concern is that the student is treated as an object, and the process is demeaning. The special relationship which exists between teacher and student, where the two are united in a battle against ignorance, is ruined:

> ...the caring teacher does not shrink from evaluating her student's work along all the dimensions proper to the field she is teaching; but she feels no need, and no right, to sum it up with a report to the world. At this point the relationship crumbles; it is altered. In many cases it is utterly destroyed.[38]

It is suggested that if grading must be done at all, it should be done by external examiners, not by teachers.

One might argue, however, that if the relationship crumbles so easily, the perception of the teacher as a caring individual must have been slight indeed. What is missing in this line of criticism is any recognition of the way in which that trust which grows out of a caring relationship can surmount the tensions involved when one person is called upon to judge another. The fact that the time arrives when the teacher, required to submit a grade, must say that this is his or her final assessment of the student's work *here and now* need not violate the relationship if the student sees that the teacher does care and is attempting to make a fair assessment.

If grading itself is demeaning and objectionable, it is no solution to pass the task over to another group. If the task is to be done, there is no reason why students cannot understand that teachers perform different roles, now teaching, now examining. It is utterly condescending to suggest that students cannot draw this distinction. There are, in fact, reasons for thinking that grading is important. Entry into certain courses and institutions is limited, and it is reasonable to select those who are most likely to succeed and who have demonstrated excellence. Admissions committees need to know the assessments which have been made on the students. A report is made to the world, so to speak, but it is not distributed to all and sundry, and students could choose not to have their grades submitted.

As a teacher, sincerely concerned to further the student's development, it will often be necessary to take the student's comments and efforts to task. R.M. Hare reports that an Oxford student can expect his or her tutor to be a merciless critic.[39] No one, I imagine, would want to invoke that image as a suitable model at every level or in every context, but it serves to make the point, albeit dramatically, that the teacher's role will require reactions which potentially threaten the student's self-esteem. A clear sense that the teacher cares for the student as a human being and is acting in his or her best interests is indispensable. Humility on the part of the teacher will help make the criticism more palatable, and will in itself indicate that the teacher is not simply interested in his or her own opinions.

Occasionally, during the process of evaluation, teachers discover that a student has cheated or is guilty of plagiarism. How is a caring teacher to respond? Some take the view that a caring teacher will not directly accuse the student of cheating, will not explicitly reject the student's protestations of innocence.[40] Noddings, for example, does not believe that children grow best morally through accusation and exposure, but this is a generalization which would have to be applied intelligently in particular circumstances.[41] Students can readily deceive themselves into thinking that they have not been cheating or committing plagiarism, a deception which is reinforced when teachers hesitate to name the act explicitly. Many students are shocked when confronted for the first time, sometimes well into their undergraduate years, with the fact that an essay is plagiarized, and quite sincerely protest that other teachers and professors have not taken that view when similar work has been submitted. These students have not been well served by teachers who evaded the issue. To cheat on one's assignments is simply not to be studying seriously, and to care for one's students *as students* requires that the standards of serious study be respected and upheld.[42]

Noddings also asserts that the caring teacher does not need to resort to punishment in such cases because the rules are not sacred.[43] This is clearly a prejudicial way of describing the situation and creates the impression that punishment is incompatible with caring. The words "resort to" and "sacred" are calculated to create the impression that the use of punishment reflects a mindless following of rules which takes no account of the particular individuals involved. There are, however, many reasons why the use of some appropriate punishment might be justified. It may, for example, be necessary in order to show that the offense is taken seriously, that the rule with respect to cheating is no arbitrary or minor matter but fundamental to any serious conception of honest inquiry. There are no grounds for concluding that the use of punishment necessarily indicates that the teacher is uncaring.

A certain style or approach has come to be thought of as *typical* of the caring teacher, but there seems no reason to believe that caring can be limited in this way. A fashionable view holds that when a student responds in class, "what he says matters, whether it is right or wrong, and she (the teacher) probes gently for clarification, interpretation, contribution. She is not seeking the answer but the involvement of the cared-for....The student is infinitely more important than the subject matter."[44] It is worth recalling here the documented finding that teachers are reluctant to challenge their students on assertions they make and are inclined to accept student answers uncritically.[45] In such a climate, it is clear that these suggestions for caring teachers are quite misguided.

Some years ago, Ryle denounced what he called the popular, sentimental view that "teachers should never be strict, demanding, peremptory or uncondoning....It is not the chocolates and the sponge-cakes that strengthen the child's jaw-muscles."[46] The point is that whether or not what is required at a given moment with a particular student is gentle probing or tough criticism requires *judgment*. The teacher's caring attitude is shown in choosing an approach which will work well with this student. Noddings, moreover, sets up a false dichotomy between student and subject matter, for the teacher shows that he or she cares for the student *by* showing that it matters whether the student is making progress with the subject or not. We cannot be concerned about the student *as a student* if, as teachers, we are not concerned with the quality of the student's answers. Of course, what the student says matters, whether it is right or wrong, because we have to respond to what is said. But whether it is right or wrong *also* matters, and we can involve our students in the inquiry by showing them that we take it seriously enough to try to distinguish error and truth. To involve the student—the cared-for—is to involve him or her in the search for better answers.

How, then, is this search to be conducted? Teachers may be open-minded and caring, yet fail to show or generate any great enthusiasm for their work. A sense of duty may be more apparent than a sense of excitement. Why have so many educational theorists taken the view that enthusiasm is of vital importance in teaching? Are they right to do so?

# CHAPTER EIGHT

## *Enthusiasm: Genuine Interest*

~~~~~~~~~~~~~~~~~~~~~~~~~~~~~~~~~~~~~~~~~~~~~~~~~~~~~~~~~~~~~~

> Every great and commanding moment in the annals of the
> world is the triumph of some enthusiasm.
> > Ralph Waldo Emerson—"Man the Reformer"

### *Enthusiasm on the Wane*

It is all too common to hear students complain that their teachers
are simply not enthusiastic. Has anyone ever heard this complaint
made about a dentist? Enthusiasm in that particular department might
be cause for alarm, and it will be worth asking later why the idea of
enthusiasm comes up so naturally in some contexts but not in others.
The complaints about teachers, which may concern their apparent lack
of interest in the subject or in teaching it, reflect the commonly held
view that enthusiasm is a vital aspect of good teaching. Recently, thirty
well-known Canadian public figures from various walks of life were
asked to name the qualities of a good teacher, and about half explicitly
mentioned enthusiasm, many of these putting it at or near the top of
their list of admirable qualities, while several others clearly had enthusiasm in mind when, like John Polanyi and Lorna Marsden, they spoke
of teachers who were excited by what they taught.[1]

John Dewey agreed, and held that a genuine enthusiasm is an
attitude that operates as an intellectual force.[2] Bertrand Russell took
a similar view when he spoke of teachers having a genuine desire to
impart what they themselves believe to be of value.[3] Indeed, the
conventional wisdom in the profession endorses a favourable assessment of enthusiasm. Often the writing is basically inspirational, taking
the value of enthusiasm as a given. Gilbert Highet serves as a typical
example when he asserts that "the good teacher believes in his subject
and is genuinely, unashamedly enthusiastic about it."[4] These views find

117

their way into those ubiquitous, all-purpose texts for student teachers, full of tactics, strategies, and summary rules, which typically offer an obligatory though perfunctory reference to the self-evident value of enthusiasm in teaching.

This dominant view is not, however, without its critics. Edward Hickcox has suggested that "maybe we shouldn't talk too much about enthusiasm as a criterion for measuring good teaching."[5] He draws this tentative conclusion on the basis of what, he claims, we now *know*, namely that there isn't much relationship between enthusiasm and amount of learning. Conservative critics too have often cast a sceptical eye on enthusiasm as a virtue in teaching, fearing perhaps that it serves to cover up a deficiency in standards.[6] Is then the view which has virtually been regarded as a matter of plain common sense now to be discarded? What are we to say about enthusiasm in teaching? Should we be less enthusiastic than heretofore?

## Recognizing Enthusiasm

It is often remarkably easy in practice to recognize enthusiasm or its absence. On one memorable occasion, it took Jay Ingram less than half a minute to see that it was missing. In what proved to be a vain attempt, the former host of CBC Radio's science programme "Quirks and Quarks", began by asking his would-be guest what it was he found *interesting* about a certain structure. There ensued the kind of silence which is excruciating on radio, culminating in a foolish laugh and some barely audible mumbling from the scientist to the effect that he just didn't think of things as interesting! The word "interesting" had stumped him.[7] The scientist in question remains anonymous, so it is not clear if he is a pure researcher or perhaps a university scientist with teaching responsibilities. In any event, on the occasion in question he was about to be cast in an informal teaching role before a radio audience, presumably because the producers of the show had found his work sufficiently important to make contact, and he could not rise to the occasion.

Contrast this soporific situation, if you will, with the atmosphere attendant upon A.N. Whitehead entering the classroom at Harvard University, beautifully captured by the late Hilton Page:

By his eager, enthusiastic and emphatic manner, his evident inner excitement, Whitehead was eminently successful in conveying the impression that lecturing on philosophy was the highest state of human enjoyment, the very summit of human felicity....One could not help taking pleasure in his pleasure and so feel pleased oneself....the cheerfulness, the good humour, the zest and vitality were obvious from the moment his voice was heard coming in through the door.[8]

Page surmised that Whitehead was presenting material from what was to become *Process and Reality* (1929) and the ideas were truly formidable, but the students were drawn in and carried along by the irresistible force of Whitehead's own enthusiasm for the subject *and* for teaching it. Not surprisingly, this attitude found a powerful echo in Whitehead's own educational theory,[9] and his "cursed be the dullard who destroys wonder" makes plain the importance he attached to enthusiasm in teaching.

Perhaps, however, these paradigm examples are misleading if they suggest that the presence or absence of enthusiasm is always obvious. Whitehead himself, after a lifetime involved with making university appointments, confessed that nothing is more difficult than distinguishing between a loud voice and vigour.[10] Whitehead had in mind the difference between appearance and reality, pretence and sincerity, quantity and quality, and the difficulty of making these distinctions in a relatively brief session when people are being interviewed for appointments. It is easy to be taken in and to discover too late that one's judgment was faulty. Similarly, enthusiasm can be feigned, largely because it has certain typical forms of expression in any culture. Many textbooks give students advice on voice inflection, physical movement, gesturing, eye contact and the like.[11] In fact, a number of research studies in the literature dealing with enthusiasm in teaching are not studies of genuine enthusiasm at all, but rather of actors simulating an enthusiasm which they do not really have.[12]

It takes skill, of course, to appear enthusiastic when one is not, but enthusiasm is not itself a skill. It is not something in which we can be trained or drilled. We can, certainly, learn to recognize and eliminate mannerisms and habits which interfere with our genuine enthusiasm

being appreciated, but this is quite different from learning to be enthusiastic. The latter can only mean having enthusiasm develop in us for
some activity or work we are engaged with.[13] It is worth emphasizing
this point about skills at a time when the dominant conception of
teacher education is one which views the process as the acquisition of
general teaching skills.[14] It is in connection with qualities such as
enthusiasm that we see the truth in David Solway's observation that
teachers cannot be trained, they must be found.[15]

Even though enthusiasm can be simulated, it is also true that
students can in time see through such false attitudes and sense the
difference between the sham and the genuine.[16] Have we not all known
teachers whose exclamations and gesticulations did not ring true? It
may take time for this awareness to emerge, if only because we tend to
assume that people would not be teaching that which they themselves
do not find worthwhile and stimulating. The ultimate result, however,
is cynicism and disillusionment when students realize that their teachers
simply do not share the excitement they are supposedly trying to
communicate. There is a fundamental dishonesty involved when
teachers purport to have enthusiasm which in reality is absent.

Lack of enthusiasm is considered a fault in certain circumstances,
but hardly a moral fault. We are not led by the absence of enthusiasm
to make an adverse moral judgment about a person's character as we
are by the absence of courage or humility, though we may fault an
individual for continuing to work in a context which calls for enthusiasm when that is absent. If we are told on occasion that we might have
shown rather more enthusiasm, perhaps about an invitation or an offer,
the mild moral rebuke suggests that in the circumstances politeness and
harmony required that we feign an enthusiasm which we did not really
feel.[17] Typically, however, an observation about enthusiasm, or lack
thereof, involves a judgment about an individual's personality which is
revealed in his or her manner.

Enthusiasm can be attributed to an individual in different ways. A
person can respond with enthusiasm to a particular suggestion, invitation, comment or request. On occasion, perhaps, a certain remark may
be so striking or powerful that it continues long after it was uttered to
fill one with enthusiasm when it is recalled.[18] Often, however, it is a

temporary matter, fleeting though nonetheless real. Our enthusiastic response was genuine, but it was tied to a particular context or moment. We can, however, also attribute enthusiasm to someone in a more general way, say in a letter of recommendation, as a comment on his or her overall personality, much as we might say that someone is invariably friendly.[19] Typically, perhaps, a particular context or subject matter is implicit and understood, such as teaching, research, sports, travel and so on, because perfectly general enthusiasm about everything is odd. Enthusiasm has a certain narrowing effect, leading to a concentration on those things one finds *particularly* interesting and rewarding, such as a certain kind of work, hobby, reading material, or whatever. Enthusiasm is a special or heightened interest and typically involves an ordering of interests.

John Dewey sometimes discussed enthusiasm in the context of what he called whole-heartedness or single-mindedness.[20] He saw enthusiasm in teaching as bringing about a state of being absorbed in the material or topic being studied, and it operated as an intellectual force presumably by focussing attention and engaging the student in a willing pursuit of ideas. We should understand these remarks as directed against the kind of divided interest which leads to what Dewey called an external, perfunctory attention being paid to one's studies, and remember also that Dewey is speaking of an attitude in somewhat ideal and exaggerated terms. A genuine enthusiasm for science or history or philosophy does not demand an exclusive or fanatical commitment, and Dewey's use of the term "single-minded" should not be taken in this way.

To have enthusiasm for something is to have a disposition to engage in that activity directly, or to be disposed to talk about it, or plan for it. As a disposition, enthusiasm may not be manifest at a particular moment, but one's enthusiasm will show itself at various times in the manner of one's performance or talk or anticipation, in an intense interest and eagerness which we communicate. It would make no sense to say that someone had enthusiasm for such and such if he or she did not typically show enthusiasm when doing, or contemplating, the activity in question. To have enthusiasm for research is to be someone who shows enthusiasm when engaged in, or thinking about, research activities. It comes in degrees, of course, and we can be quite or very enthusiastic about things. Enthusiasm is something one can be full of, or bursting with, such that it is always likely to spill over into action. There is a paradoxical element in being "slightly enthusiastic" which effectively defeats the assertion.

Imagination and creativity are, of course, also shown, but these are shown in the kinds of products which emerge when we work imaginatively and creatively. Having imagination, for example, is shown in one's ability to produce imaginative work, that which is novel and valuable. One's enthusiasm, however, does not consist in creating a product which is enthusiastic, though one's enthusiasm may come through in that product. A person's enthusiasm for a subject can be felt in a book or painting, because we can hear it in the way in which the author speaks or sense it in the artist's achievement. Enthusiasm is found in the way in which one goes about one's work, in the manner of one's performance.

It might be said that we can tell that a person is enthusiastic in some area from the sheer number of works, or even the complexity of a single work, produced. Could anyone seriously deny, for example, that the late Isaac Asimov was an enthusiastic writer when he had more than 400 books to his credit? If this does not count as being enthusiastic about writing, what would? Here, however, we need a distinction between that disposition which is essentially a matter of regular and consistent application, and that disposition which represents a felt desire of some intensity to engage in a certain activity. To feel enthusiasm for something is to feel inclined to do it, support it, think about it, talk about it, and so on. It is to be keenly interested in whatever is in question, and not to take up suitable opportunities for engagement and involvement gives reason to doubt one's enthusiasm.

Enthusiasm, like skills, can be a power for good or evil depending upon what captures one's enthusiasm, and whether or not one's enthusiasm is judicious. Like so many of the virtues, enthusiasm has a dark side to it. We might recall the etymological connection with divine possession, and the disparaging sense which has often been thereby associated with the attitude, showing up especially in the word "enthusiast" with its implication of being naive and deluded, and caught up in a dubious cause. Excessive enthusiasm can shade into fanaticism, where one's commitment is unchecked by reasonable constraints.[21] If Emerson is right that nothing great was ever achieved without enthusiasm, it is equally true that many horrendous deeds have been similarly inspired.[22]

## Enthusiasm in Teaching

The general sentiment in favour of enthusiasm as a desirable quality in teachers has led some commentators to lose sight of the supportive role that the attitude plays in the educational context and to view it as an unalloyed good. Kevin Ryan and James M. Cooper, in a burst of enthusiasm of their own, state that: "We would rather see an enthusiastic teacher teaching Turkish military history or macramé than an uninspired teacher teaching Shakespeare."[23] Waiving an immediate objection to such facile, either/or thinking,[24] and leaving aside any comment about the actual examples employed here, it does need to be noted that this remark tends to distort the value of enthusiasm in the context of teaching. It is as if enthusiasm can somehow redeem the situation *whatever is being taught*, so that the content is immaterial. On the contrary, however, it matters very much what is being taught and how. Trivial work is not magically transformed into an educational experience simply because the teacher, like so many, is a great champion of pedantry and busywork. Indeed, to the extent that such enthusiasm may rub off on the students, the situation is even worse. If we follow Ryan and Cooper, we are on our way to ignoring questions about the quality of what it is the students are actually learning.

Similarly, indoctrination is not made more palatable because it is done with genuine enthusiasm. We might recall here Tussman's warning that eagerness for teaching may well be a sign of unfitness if it betrays an enthusiasm for imposing one's own beliefs on others.[25] Gage and Berliner quote with approval Ware's description of the enthusiastic teacher as one who "sees himself as a salesman", with no apparent recognition of the negative aspects of this simile nor of how it ought to suggest an important qualification to the value of enthusiasm in the context of teaching.[26] Teaching can degenerate into propaganda, and the propagandist is often zealously seeking converts offering whatever arguments will succeed. Similarly, a teacher may passionately advocate views which are prejudiced and biased. Here again, to the extent that enthusiasm is infectious, the problem is compounded. Mary Warnock has stated that the first rule of teaching is sincerity, and we have seen in considering empathy that this quality is vitally important. But even a genuine enthusiasm is subject to other guiding ideals such as open-mindedness, humility, and impartiality.[27]

This is not to say that teachers must conceal their enthusiasm by cloaking their views in a neutrality designed to shield the student from acquaintance with the teacher's own beliefs, values and ideals. The best teachers, Russell declared, have "strong enthusiasms, to which they wish to give expression in their teaching."[28] Russell was concerned that conventional and established opinions would dominate education, that truth would be equated with what is commonly believed; and he recognized that one effective way to undermine this tendency was to have students exposed to teachers who hold very different views.

To make his point emphatically, Russell went so far as to say that the best teachers were *not* impartial, but this remark needs to be understood in the context of a false notion of impartiality which Russell was anxious to refute, one where impartiality was assumed to be a matter of accepting the orthodox views of the education establishment.[29] Russell's advocacy of strong enthusiasms presupposed teachers "fired by certain ideals of life", especially intellectual honesty, tolerance, broad-mindedness, and love of knowledge, what Russell called the intellectual virtues.[30] We might perhaps say that the teacher's enthusiasm for a particular substantive position or view needs to be tempered by an overriding commitment to the sorts of ideals Russell mentions. This would accommodate the point made by Kilpatrick that the teacher is not there "to gain converts to his partisan cause; he is there to help those under his care learn to think reliably for themselves."[31]

To concede that enthusiasm *may* lead to fanaticism and indoctrination, is not to say that being enthusiastic entails an abandonment of reason. In her interesting discussion of this point, Susan Stebbing notes that a certain vagueness and emotive force which attaches to the word "enthusiasm" in ordinary usage leads some to conclude that it means something like "unreasoning passionate eagerness", at which point the alleged incompatibility with reason follows inevitably. Stebbing, however, takes it to mean "intense eagerness" and observes: "We can be enthusiastically *for* a cause *about* which we have reasoned dispassionately." Nevertheless, Stebbing wisely notes that "our enthusiasms stand in need of being from time to time revised; like our other mental habits, they are all the better for being occasionally overhauled."[32]

In addition to triviality and indoctrination, another way in which enthusiasm can go astray in teaching is exemplified in the behaviour of a teacher like Miss Price whose overeager attempts to help an unpopular and disadvantaged student backfire tragically, with the result that the student becomes "a victim of the teacher's pity".[33] In this case, the teacher's actions spring more from a sense of mission than from a genuine interest in and concern for the student as a person, and overzealousness clouds her judgment. Miss Price is too clearly keen to help and her attempts to be subtle are, we are told, painfully obvious.

These examples would appear to give some support to the view cited earlier that enthusiasm is rather dubiously posited as a criterion of good teaching, but such a conclusion is premature. Hickcox moves too quickly from the claim that there isn't much relationship between enthusiasm and *amount* of learning to a controversial conclusion about the nature of good teaching, as if the latter were simply a function of how much is learned.

First, however, what *do* we know about the relationship between teacher enthusiasm and the amount of learning which takes place? As with almost all empirical research into teaching, the findings are confused, contradictory and inconclusive.[34] In one often cited study in 1963, Victor Mastin found that in nineteen out of twenty sixth- and seventh-grade classes observed, the mean achievement was higher where the lesson had been taught with apparent enthusiasm.[35] These general findings were supported in experimental studies carried out by Coats and Smidgens in 1966 where they found evidence that "students did remember much more from the dynamic lecture than from the static one".[36] Further support came from the widely discussed study by Ware in 1974.[37] In 1982, however, Abrami, Leventhal and Perry, reviewing previous research, reported that the effect of expressiveness, i.e. a display of apparent enthusiasm, on achievement was not significant in five of ten cases. There was, they claimed, a stronger link with student satisfaction as reflected in ratings than with actual achievement. Content coverage, by contrast, *was* found to be significantly related to achievement in almost every case.[38]

The findings in the literature are simply not consistent. We need to remember also that we are dealing with a quality which researchers call "highly inferential", meaning that it has to be judged on the basis of a wide variety of behaviours which may or may not reliably indicate its presence. Inevitably, to attain precision and observable agreement, enthusiasm is operationally defined in terms of specific behaviours; but when enthusiasm is translated into eye contact, voice inflection and gesture, it is not evident that these behaviours really capture the quality in question. Most of the studies, moreover, involve teachers or actors *making an effort to appear* enthusiastic, and it is not clear that we can generalize from these findings to the effect of genuine and natural enthusiasm displayed consistently in the course of regular teaching. These points suggest an intractable problem in finding "hard data" in this area. We can, of course, observe teachers in natural settings but we are brought back to the kind of personal judgment and impressions, such as the recollections of Whitehead's teaching cited earlier, which we can all "test" in our own ordinary experience. In any event, there is no warrant for the brash conclusion of Hickcox that we *know* there is little relationship between enthusiasm and amount of learning.[39] We do *not* know that a genuinely enthusiastic approach to teaching, manifested consistently over an entire course, would not lead to students paying greater attention, taking more interest, and ultimately learning more than they otherwise would from competent but dull instruction.

Some have held that even if the empirical findings did indicate that enthusiastic teaching was significantly related to student achievement, this would not be particularly useful for teacher-education programmes because high-inference studies "do not tell us how a teacher should behave in order to be stimulating".[40] There could hardly be a better illustration of the trap which lies in wait here, for the assumption is that there is nothing useful for teachers to learn unless it is turned into specific behavioural criteria. Student teachers, however, could usefully reflect on the problems inherent in trying to reduce enthusiastic teaching to specific behaviours, could review examples of enthusiastic teaching (on video, for example) to become clearer about the range and nature of such teaching, and could start to identify some general principles which would call for intelligent application in their own particular situation.

The matter, however, does not stand or fall on empirical research. We need to keep in mind the central aims and purposes of education when we judge good teaching. Our interest is not simply in how much the students have learned, even if the material is worthwhile, but also in the attitudes which they have developed with respect to the subject in question. If we believe that one central objective is to have students come to care for what they have learned, to develop an interest which they are keen to pursue, and to see the subject as important and worthwhile,[41] then enthusiasm surely is a vital quality in teachers. It is part of that desirable, albeit hidden, curriculum which influences the students. The teacher with enthusiasm for science, philosophy or any other subject serves as a critically important example to the student. Dewey put the point clearly:

> Collateral learning in the way of formation of enduring attitudes, of likes and dislikes, may be and often is much more important than the spelling lesson or lesson in geography or history that is learned....The most important attitude that can be formed is that of desire to go on learning.[42]

It is, Dewey observed in the same context, the greatest of all pedagogical fallacies to think that the person is only learning the particular thing being studied at the time.

Dewey's point helps us to see why enthusiasm is naturally thought of as important in some roles and not others. Sometimes, our interest is quite understandably in sheer competence. Can the person perform the necessary task successfully or not? It is of no particular concern how he or she feels about the task in question. The example of the enthusiastic dentist strikes one as slightly odd if we think of those aspects of that work involving procedures which are necessary but unpleasant for the patient. In these cases, we want the dentist to perform the operation quickly, competently and painlessly. Aspects of the dentist's manner are important, of course, since the patient needs to be treated with consideration and understanding. Enthusiasm, however, is not required, and it would in any case exist uneasily with the patient's apprehension and discomfort. It is quite different if we think of preventive dental care. Enthusiasm in this area strikes one as quite appropriate, since this attitude may be picked up by the patient where it may serve to ensure that unpleasant procedures will never be necessary.

Teaching is not *simply* a matter of competently and efficiently transmitting information and skills to students. Acquiring information is not the same as developing a love of learning; developing skills is not the same as becoming committed to certain activities and pursuits. When it becomes apparent, however, that the schools are simply failing to teach basic information and skills, as high rates of illiteracy indicate, then competency and efficiency become the watchwords in education, and reference to enthusiasm begins to sound suspiciously like an excuse for incompetence. We expect to be told that what a teacher lacks in ability, he or she makes up for in enthusiasm. What is happening, of course, is that certain necessary aspects of education such as skills and information, because they are not being satisfied, are transformed into sufficient conditions, with the result that attitudes, appreciation and commitment get short shrift as educational outcomes. If these are not thought of as important objectives of teaching, they will not be thought of as important qualities in the teacher. We can surely expect this view to gain ground as the value of education comes increasingly to be thought of in terms of economic benefits and global competitiveness.

If we return to the traditional view that enthusiasm in teachers is important, we discover the surprising point that many who would agree with this also believe that enthusiasm *for the subject itself* is either not important or even undesirable. Arthur Bestor reported in the 1950s that many student teachers had told him that professors of education and principals of schools were of the view that enthusiasm for the subject was outdated and useless. Some, apparently, were heard to proclaim that "we teach children not subjects".[43] It is quite easy to find similar views in print. Michael Hutchinson and Christopher Young, for example, were prepared to say: "To be 'sound' as a teacher of English is almost certainly to be dull and so to bore children."[44] This would seem to mean that excellent preparation in the subject matter will mean that one cannot present it in an interesting way. Subject mastery is an impediment to good teaching.

These views rest on the unexamined and unargued assumption that a love of knowledge would somehow entail a lack of interest in sharing that knowledge with others. On the contrary, however, a keen interest in one's subject would quite naturally involve an interest in talking about it. One common way in which enthusiasm finds an outlet is in discussing it with others. There may be particular reasons why an individual does not enjoy teaching, but other things being equal, why would one *not* want to explore with others a subject one finds fascinating? Moreover, how *could* one be interesting and stimulating about a subject one does not understand very well? One thinks of Solway's comments on the new breed of instructors who have become experts in transmitting what they themselves have failed to master, "forced to scurry quickly, like cortical centipedes, over those regions of their subject which they do not command with the authority and sureness which compel genuine respect."[45]

John Wilson has argued that the very idea of "making a subject interesting" is deeply paradoxical. Either the subject is given an attractive external appearance, in which case we are not presenting the subject itself but some false image; or we change the inner constitution of the subject so as to capture interest, in which case we are not making the original subject interesting.[46] Possibly, however, the common injunction to "make the subject interesting" can be understood in terms of attracting the student's attention to what is at the moment not especially or immediately interesting perhaps but which, it is to be hoped, will prove to be so as the student becomes more familiar with the material. One factor in attracting attention will be the teacher's own enthusiasm for the subject.

Wilson's own solution to the problem is in terms of a *presentation* or *arrangement* which expresses the ideas more fully or accurately so as to make them more interesting than they might otherwise be. In teaching, one can be interesting by thinking up good examples and problems, showing unsuspected implications, elaborating on basic ideas, picking up and developing suggestions offered, connecting the topic with some other so as to illuminate both, and so on. These things will, of course, only be done by teachers who are keen enough to make these efforts. They can only be done by those who know the subject well enough to be able to branch out in these ways and by those who possess imagination and that sense of judgment which allows them to seize the moment in the teaching context.

# CHAPTER NINE

# *Judgment: Utilizing Ideas*

xxxxxxxxxxxxxxxxxxxxxxxxxxxxxxxxxxxxxxxxxxxxxxxxxxxxxxxxxxxxx

> Neither, though we have mastered all the arguments of Plato and Aristotle, if yet we have not the capacity for passing a solid judgment on these matters, shall we become philosophers.
>
> René Descartes, *Rules for the Direction of the Mind*

## *Judgment and Education*

Some philosophers appear to suggest that if an individual lacks judgment, the situation cannot really be remedied. Hume, for example, remarks that "the defects of judgment can be supplied by no art or invention".[1] It is worth noting, however, that the immediate contrast Hume has in mind in this context is with *memory*, and possibly the thought that deficiencies in judgment are not to be remedied in the same way as deficiencies in memory may have translated into the thought that they cannot be remedied at all. It is surely impossible to believe that Hume would have held that if a person were supplied with, and grasped, a useful distinction, say that between is and ought, he or she would be in no better position to judge the merits of an argument in ethics. We should be wary of placing too much weight on a particular remark about judgment and reading into it a general theory.

Consider also the claim of Kant that the faculty of judgment is a special talent which cannot be taught but must be practised.[2] This will not do as it stands, mainly because it implies a rather narrow view of teaching. Again, however, the direct contrast is with *rules* and, one suspects, the correct idea that judgment cannot be taught as rules are taught has become the dubious idea that judgment cannot be taught at all. Kant is surely right that judgment cannot be *reduced* to rules, since judgment is what is required when we need to determine whether or not something falls under a particular rule, what to do when two rules conflict, whether a certain rule is satisfactory, and so on. A distinction such as that between is and ought, or whatever, can be given a rule-like formulation, but it remains necessary to *recognize* that the distinction is ignored in a certain argument, which is not always obvious, to assess the significance of the distinction in a particular context, and the like.

Sometimes, of course, the application of a rule is so clear and straightforward that the notion of judgment in that situation reaches the vanishing point. Incidentally, the same applies to the notion of critical thinking, as we might expect, since judgment and critical thinking are intimately connected.[3] On the view, for example, that critical thinking is thinking which adequately reflects relevant reasons,[4] there is some danger of collapsing thinking and critical thinking unless we build in a reference to the need for an ability to go beyond a memorized rule. Knowing that the dimensions of a room are 15' x 10', we have a relevant reason for concluding that the area is 150 sq. ft. This conclusion, however, hardly calls for critical ability. It is a routine calculation.[5] Similar factors will eliminate the need for judgment. In a case involving the falsification of an expense account, the chairperson of a school board admitted to "an error of judgment";[6] but does one need *judgment* to know that claiming a non-existent item as an expense is wrong? "Do not invent items for the expense account" is a learnable rule with, normally at least, a straightforward application.[7]

In judging, we utilize what we know in order to reach a conclusion which we cannot merely calculate.[8] Armed with various rules, examples, distinctions, ideas and information, and given suitable opportunity to practise under experienced and critical supervision, judgment may develop. Kant recognized this too. In his *Thoughts on Education*, he introduces the notion of judgment in order to emphasize its centrality in education. A person without judgment, says Kant, is merely a walking dictionary, and he suggests how judgment may be cultivated: When someone quotes a general rule, we may ask for examples drawn from history or fable in which this rule is disguised, passages from the poets where it is expressed, and thus encourage the exercise of intelligence and memory.[9] It seems that in the more dramatic assertion that judgment cannot be taught, Kant had slipped into a narrow account of teaching, explicit instruction perhaps, and is not in fact maintaining that teachers cannot develop judgment in their students.[10]

It would be wrong to leave the impression that rules are anathema to the development or the exercise of judgment. Notice that Descartes' comment on becoming philosophers in our own right comes in a book entitled *Rules for the Direction of the Mind*. R.S. Peters notes that one important task of teachers and coaches is to comment on and encourage the performances of others, and they do so very often by reiterating rules.[11] This is a useful reminder. The fundamental point, however, is that it is one's orientation to the rules which matters. It is not the mastering of rule and routine which is the problem, but what Dewey terms their *blind observance*. If we master a rule when we are learning a certain activity, such mastery is not incompatible with being able to modify and vary the rule in practice according to our best judgment. As in music, we can improvise on what we have mastered.

A sense of judgment is vital if we are to be able to reflect intelligently on what we have learned, not simply accept it. There is a difference, as Descartes points out in the comment which heads this chapter, between understanding what other philosophers have had to say and assessing for ourselves the merits and significance of such views. When we read Plato and Aristotle, we encounter certain standards, criteria and principles which enable us to make distinctions, support judgments and revise opinions. We begin to develop a sense of what constitutes a good reason and a sound argument. But we also need to be willing and able to reflect critically on the very standards, criteria and principles we are acquiring.

In this way, the development of judgment includes a necessary *familiarity* with the information and ideas on which we draw in framing our own views, but also a critical *distance* from what we are learning so that we can assess these ideas, discarding, modifying and applying them as appropriate. Dewey put it this way:

> Judging is the act of selecting and weighing the bearing of facts and suggestions as they present themselves, as well as deciding whether the alleged facts are really facts, and whether the idea used is a sound idea or merely a fancy.[12]

We cannot judge at all if we have nothing to go on, just as judgment is not needed if the answer is already in. But the subject matter we learn is not itself exempt from critical scrutiny and judgment.

There is, as Kant and other philosophers have brought out, a close connection between the possession of sound judgment and being an educated person. Dewey, for example, held that someone with sound judgment in any context is *ipso facto* an *educated* person as respects those matters, whatever that person's schooling or academic standing.[13] This is a way of reminding us that we can pay too much attention to credentials and qualifications, to surface aspects of education, and forget what is at the heart of the enterprise. There is a further connection between judgment and education which Aristotle brings out in his famous remark that it is a mark of the educated mind to expect that amount of exactness which the nature of the subject admits.[14] In other words, it is not just being *able* to judge which distinguishes the educated person, but *appreciating* that judgment is called for in a certain context. When precise calculation necessarily eludes us, it is crucial that we understand that we have to rely on judgment.

We have seen in earlier chapters that teachers and school officials can, unfortunately, lose sight of their main task, which is to further the educational development of their students, allowing the acquisition of information, the inculcation of dogmatic views, or even sheer attendance to become the be-all and end-all. This last, desperate position should perhaps be passed over in silence; but amassing information and doctrinal persuasion deserve a further word in connection with judgment.

Indoctrination overrides the individual's own judgment and substitutes that of some authority, with the result that those who have been indoctrinated cannot think for themselves about certain issues. It is a mark of the insidious and offensive nature of indoctrination that the person who has been indoctrinated is generally not aware of his or her true state. One's ability to reflect critically on various ideas has been impaired, and intellectual autonomy has been undermined. The answers produced to objections are, in effect, someone else's answers to which those who have been indoctrinated have blind allegiance, such that they cannot independently judge the merits of the objections raised. It would be a serious mistake to think that this problem arises only when a zealot finds his or her way into the classroom, and to console ourselves with the optimistic thought that this is relatively uncommon. The same effect occurs when the hidden curriculum of schooling teaches that students should defer uncritically to authorities and experts, whether they be textbooks or teachers. It happens also at the teacher's level when fashionable educational theories prevent the teacher from thinking independently.

Dewey was concerned that "in school, amassing information always tends to escape from the ideal of wisdom or good judgment."[15] Not that the acquisition of information was unimportant. Dewey said plainly that "suggestions and inferences can occur only to a mind that possesses information as to matters of fact."[16] Too often, however, the acquisition of information was treated as an end in itself rather than as the basis for intelligent decision-making. It is clear, then, to any fair-minded critic that Dewey is not open to the charge, levelled at contemporary proponents of critical thinking in education by E.D. Hirsch, that the goal of teaching shared information is under attack.[17] Indeed, Dewey would surely condemn Hirsch's sharp dichotomy between cultural literacy and critical thinking as yet another exaggerated and misleading either/or.

The problem is to hold information (and skills) and judgment in proper balance in our conception of education when, as Passmore has warned, it is virtually a law that all subjects in the school context tend towards an instructional state.[18] When this happens, we are back to what Dewey called "covering the ground". The teacher is content to provide information with little attempt made to engage the students' judgment or have them display their own judgment. One is reminded of Russell's complaint that the modern teacher had become a civil servant, suggesting an image of the teacher cheerlessly dispensing "wisdom" to the masses as efficiently as possible.[19] Wisdom, of course, cannot be dispensed at all.

Whitehead's comment that the *merely* well-informed person is the most useless bore on God's earth has not always been taken in the proper spirit.[20] Indeed, the word "mere" has tended to become associated with facts and information creating the impression, which alarms critics like Hirsch, that content as such has come to be considered unimportant. If we read Whitehead correctly, however, it is evident that, like Kant, he means only to say that information alone is *insufficient*. Without a store of information, of course, we will not be able to make critical judgments. For example, I am never asked to review books in physics, with good reason. The possession of information alone, however, will not ensure that we know how to deploy that information intelligently, nor that we know when to revise it should it become suspect. Whitehead's own memorable dictum about education reveals that he did not disparage content. Education, he said, is the acquisition of the art of the utilization of knowledge.[21] The notion of utilization is crucial if the problem of inert ideas is to be avoided, but we cannot intelligently employ what we do not have.

It is a fallacy, therefore, to think that content and critical judgment represent an either/or choice,[22] though this point obviously leaves room for dispute about the appropriate time to emphasize one rather than the other. Indeed, this calls for judgment. There are those who believe that elementary and secondary education should *largely* be made up of relatively non-controversial information and skills, a position buttressed by the undeniable fact that many students fail to master even the basic skills of reading and writing in school.[23] Witness the high rate of illiteracy, and the alarming drop-out statistics, in Canada and some other developed countries.

The problem here, however, is that in trying to postpone the development of independent judgment until the college years, we may not in fact succeed at that later date. Russell and others have pointed out that in the course of giving instruction, habits of mind are inevitably imparted.[24] In avoiding critical reflection and judgment, the message may go out that criticism is unimportant, with the result that unthinking acquiescence sets in. I have shown elsewhere that the argument that there is *no time* to teach critical thinking in school because the curriculum is already overcrowded,[25] fails because it assumes that *additional* lessons are needed rather than teaching in a different way.[26] A different spirit would permeate teaching if it were approached critically, such that information would not be presented as settled beyond all possibility of revision but as tentative and representing our best estimates today. Skills would not be inculcated as if they necessarily had ready and obvious application, but would come with some emerging sense that judgment was required with respect to occasions which might be appropriate.

To say that teachers need to have a sense of judgment is *not* to say that common sense is more important than, or could replace, sophisticated theoretical understanding. Of course, common sense is invaluable, for teachers and everybody else, and can prevent us from foolishly following ideas which we have been persuaded to accept by "experts". R.M. Hare brings this home when he remarks: "You even hear parents saying something [that they should give their children something to rebel against] which I think they must have got from popular psychologists who write in the newspapers—for they would never have thought up anything so silly themselves."[27] In other words, if we could stop for a moment to *notice* what we are saying, and free ourselves from the influence of trendy rhetoric, we could all see that this is puerile.

Judgment and common sense, however, are not the same. Indeed, when something is a plain matter of common sense, such as wearing a seat belt when driving, or not baking one's skin in the midday sun, one does not need judgment to make appropriate decisions, even though these and similar matters became part of common sense as a result of expert inquiries which did demand judgment. Common sense contrasts with specialized knowledge.[28] We don't need to be experts to know those things which are a matter of common sense. Nevertheless, we do need specialized knowledge in particular areas, and an uncritical appeal to "common sense" can lead us to think that we know when we only have a prejudice. Teachers need the specialized knowledge which psychologists, sociologists, historians, philosophers and others have developed, but they need judgment to apply these findings intelligently in particular situations.[29]

## Judgment in Teaching

I meet first-year university students every year in my Introduction to Philosophy class who have not written a single essay on any subject in high school. A sufficient number of students have independently and solemnly assured me that this is true that I have come to believe that it must be so, despite its incredible nature. The class in question is a so-called writing course,[30] one in which written work is considered frequently and in detail. This takes the form of critical essays on philosophical topics where students are expected to examine a problem and defend the position they adopt. For almost all students philosophy is a new subject; but for many students the task of formulating a critical point of view in an extended piece of prose is also a novel, confusing and intimidating experience.

Their teachers at school had favoured "fill-in-the-blank" or multiple-choice tests, what Stephen Toulmin rightly dismisses as "a way of testing the appearance of knowledge in the absence of the ability to express the content of knowledge".[31] Not to mention, we might add, the absence of any opportunity to formulate in a careful way one's own considered views about the content being studied, and to have those views critically assessed. There may be a number of explanations here, including the possibility that teachers are simply so overburdened that they have no time to devote to the demanding task of reading and assessing essays. Horace's compromise comes to mind again. It may be, however, that some teachers fail to recognize the truth in Aristotle's observation referred to above, and have come to believe that everything does or should admit of precise measurement. Combined with the prevalent view that the teacher's task is to provide information, this leads to the idea that there is one correct answer which can then be offered among the multiple choices which comprise the test.

In practice, such testing produces notorious horror stories. One which came to my attention quite recently appeared on a grade-eight test in a subject entitled "Personal development and relationships". The question read: "Alcohol is a ___ , it can kill you." I have tried this out on a number of my B.Ed. students and, like me, they all got it "wrong". Everyone I know favours the answer "drug", but the "correct" answer was deemed to be "killer"—turning the assertion into a miserable tautology in one sense, or a very dubious claim in another.[32] Why, one asks, is this the correct answer? Because, quite simply, the teacher has declared it to be so. Indeed, the student might recall that the correct response had been provided in class some time prior to the test.[33] This teacher does not use judgment to assess the merits of the students' answers, and the students learn that their own judgment is not appreciated. This teacher has lost perspective, and the students have lost an opportunity to develop a reflective point of view in a subject which eminently calls for one's best judgment.

To be able to exercise judgment with respect to the quality of a student's work presupposes a degree of competency in the subject matter which, regrettably, many teachers simply do not possess. When teachers lack the necessary background and depth in the subject they are assigned to teach, inevitably they fall back on the textbook, the answer book, and multiple-choice, fill-in-the-blank, tests. The possession of knowledge does not guarantee that one can teach that material, nor that one will be able to exercise judgment with respect to work in that area. Still, subject-matter competency *is* an absolute prerequisite. No one, to my knowledge, has ever successfully challenged R.F. Dearden's blunt reminder that "to teach something in ignorance of it is not just difficult: it is logically impossible."[34] Many school boards, however, continue to ignore this logical truth when they knowingly assign teachers to subject areas in which they have no demonstrated competence.[35]

Other factors inimical to the exercise of judgment may also be at work. Once teachers abandon the relatively safe territory of the precise and correct answer, they enter the dangerous waters of "subjective assessment" where their opinions on the quality of the students' work are more readily open to challenge. It is not easy, or pleasant, to explain to an irate student that his or her work is simplistic, unimaginative, one-sided or in any number of ways inadequate, when these comments presuppose the very judgment which the essay plainly reveals the student lacks.[36] It takes a certain amount of courage to make a critical judgment and defend it in the face of a hostile reaction.[37] These matters, as Aristotle pointed out, do not admit of proof, and yet the teacher may be challenged to defend his or her judgment *as if* it could be rigorously demonstrated.[38] The predictable consequence is that teachers fall back on their authority to carry the day, and judgment loses out again.

In addition to these problems, a fashionable but foolish relativism has persuaded many teachers that the very idea of defensible judgment is spurious. What Dewey would have called the thoughtful selection and weighing of facts and suggestions is, on this view, nothing more than indulging or slipping into one's biases and prejudices.[39] From such teachers, students learn to echo Protagoras in thinking that what seems true for anyone *is* true for that person.[40] Students anxiously inquire if their own *opinion* is required. If so, how can their work be evaluated? It does, after all, present their opinion. Surely many teachers are familiar with this line of questioning. The idea that opinions can be assessed in terms of how well they are defended is a foreign concept, and this shows that the notion of intelligent judgment is itself not understood. The classic rebuttal to these confused ideas was given by Socrates. If relativism were true, why would any student need to have a teacher at all? Where is the student's comparative ignorance?[41] One cannot even say that one might learn the truth of relativism, since such a notion is clearly self-contradictory.

The very idea of education as a process of gradually improving our understanding through the exercise of judgment and on-going reflection on the judgments we make, gives way to a situation in which any opinion is deemed as good as another since all are inscribed with bias, devices for exercising power over others, ideological constructs, or something equally disreputable. How *these* judgments escape the net of self-condemnation is never explained. Teachers who fall victim to these confusions will either assert their own opinion authoritatively, for it is as good as any other, or cleave to a dogged neutrality, refusing to offer any opinion at all since their own view is no better than anyone else's. Both options are disastrous. The first tends in the direction of indoctrination, where the student's own emerging judgment is compromised. The second encourages a retreat towards a fast-disappearing realm of firm facts, where information displaces wisdom.

What is needed are teachers who recognize when judgment is called for, who are courageous enough to offer a judgment, who do so in the right spirit, i.e. tentatively and with a degree of humility, who support their judgments with facts and reasons, and who convey to the students the idea that judgments are important, evidential, and revisable. The teacher, Dewey remarked, is not to stand off and look on.[42] The tendency to exclude the teacher from full participation in the group was, he thought, absurd, since it denied the contribution of the most mature member. Massialas and Zevin, sketching an "ideal-type" of teacher to foster inquiry in the classroom, speak of teachers who "try to minimize to the extent possible their own talk in class."[43] It is not, however, the amount of talk which is crucial, but the kind. Dewey observed that some teachers were afraid even to make suggestions as to what the students might do with the materials supplied for fear of infringing on the students' freedom. But then why supply any materials at all, since they too are suggestive?[44]

A popular caricature of progressive education suggests that students should simply follow their own interests, and that the authenticity of such choices is undermined by the teacher's overt or covert influence.[45] The founders of progressive education, however, were not taken in by such tempting extremism. It was clearly recognized early on that the teacher's judgment was necessary to see when one interest was petering out and another beginning to emerge. Here Dewey spoke of "striking while the iron was hot" so that the moment would not be lost. Similarly, the teacher needs a sense of where an interest may lead, so that appropriate guidance may be given.[46] Relativists, of course, would not agree with Dewey that experiences differ with respect to their educational value. But if there is a distinction between education and miseducation, then it is part of the teacher's responsibility to try to judge in which direction an interest is heading.

Such exercise of judgment is often immediate. Teachers need to make decisions quickly during the course of a lesson. Something comes up and the teacher with judgment seizes on it at once, with no time to wonder about the wisdom of one's choice. This kind of spontaneous reaction does not, however, mean that judgment should be seen as an intuitive matter, at odds with rationality. What the teacher is able to *notice* in the classroom is a function of the understanding and conceptual framework which the teacher brings to the task. Noticing occurs all at once, but it does not just happen. Similarly, a well-thought-out lesson plan is not inimical to the exercise of judgment. As Dewey noted: "Because the kind of advance planning heretofore engaged in has been so routine as to leave little room for the free play of individual thinking or for contributions due to distinctive individual experience, it does not follow that all planning must be rejected."[47]

Good judgment in the context of teaching requires that the teacher have a sense of the fundamental nature of the educational enterprise, especially a philosophical perspective on the aims of education. Particular decisions about what will be effective or useful with a certain group of students presuppose a grasp of the outcome desired in terms of the educational development of the students. This is why reflections on the philosophy of education are pivotal in teacher-preparation programmes. It would be much more difficult for ideological fervour to spring up around particular approaches and methods, such as neutrality in teaching, if teachers could remind themselves *why* neutrality ever came into the discussion at all. With clarity on this point, teachers could recognize when a departure from neutrality would be a wise move. Lacking a sense of the overall purpose, particular approaches become ends in themselves.

One reason why neutrality cannot be endorsed as a fundamental principle in teaching is simply that education itself has values written into it about which teachers cannot be indifferent. Teachers must insist on certain moral norms in their own classrooms, such as respect for others, fairness and honesty, and must refuse to condone prejudice, bias and discrimination. In reaction to the extreme relativism with respect to values which was endemic in the 1970s, some educational theorists rightly said that there was a time to be angry, and to be seen to be angry, when certain practices occurred.[48] Here too, however, there is an important point about the need for judgment, first clearly made by Aristotle: "But to be angry...with the right person and to the right extent and at the right time and for the right purpose and in the right way—that is not easy and it is not everyone who can do it."[49]

## Judgment and Independence

Teachers can, however, become so captivated by certain approaches or practices that their sense of judgment with respect to the *application* of these ideas vanishes. If individual teachers try to think critically about such matters, the profession can mount considerable pressure to secure conformity. At the present time, for example, to raise a critical question about whole-language methods is to invite ridicule and vilification.[50] One can still hear conservative voices blaming

Dewey for the sorry situation of modern education, but Dewey at least was clear that intelligent educational practice could not be based on watchwords. To say, for example, that we favour a whole-language approach is, as Dewey might say, to set ourselves a *problem*: what exactly do we mean, and how are we to achieve the results which the approach promises?[51] This problem calls for critical reflection, not slavish commitment.

One contribution of philosophy is to help uncover the general principles which lie behind such approaches. Once uncovered, they are available for discussion and consideration. If the teacher can grasp the justification and rationale which lies behind the approach, he or she is in a position to follow the approach more intelligently: "Only knowledge of the principles upon which all methods are based can free the teacher from dependence upon the educational nostrums which are recommended like patent medicines, as panaceas for all educational ills."[52]

The general point here was not a new one when Dewey made it almost one hundred years ago. Writing in the 1st century A.D., Quintilian warns his readers:

> Let no one however demand from me a rigid code of rules such as most authors of textbooks have laid down....Most rules are liable to be altered by the nature of the case, circumstances of time and place, and by hard necessity itself....Rules are rarely of such a kind that their validity cannot be shaken and overthrown in some particular or other.[53]

The difficulty, of course, is to apply this insight to those rules we ourselves are most fond of, or to those which currently constitute the conventional wisdom. It is the problem of recognizing the difference between a rule and a guideline, and of seeing that a guideline needs to be interpreted by appeal to general principles in the light of particular circumstances.

Consider a typical piece of advice found in a better-than-average text for teachers. Following an extended piece of teacher/student classroom dialogue, the authors observe that the teacher seldom called on students who had not volunteered, and they comment: "Often it is useful to call on students who do not raise their hands." They offer various reasons why this might be a desirable practice. Students may be shy; they may be anxious to avoid ridicule if they do not know the answer; or they may learn to "tune out" if the teacher confines his or her attention to those who volunteer.[54] Behind these particular points lies the sound principle that teachers need to try to involve all the students in the learning experience.

This advice comes in an opening chapter which begins by stating that one of the book's two chief purposes is to provide teachers with "concrete suggestions". This latter phrase is, I think, crucially important but potentially problematic, containing within itself a certain tension. A *concrete* suggestion holds the promise of something firm and definite, not vague or tentative. A suggestion, on the other hand, is something to be considered, reflected on, not something to be religiously followed. It *might* be useful. Teachers have to hold both of these ideas together as they review the practical suggestions offered. Certainly, the observations offered on the textbook example itself may stimulate teachers to review their own practice more critically. Which students are being called on and why? Furthermore, there *are* reasons for calling on students who do not volunteer. But there is no simple rule here which eliminates the need for judgment. There will be occasions when a sensitive teacher will not call on a particular student who has not volunteered. It is a sign of the good teacher, Quintilian remarked, to be able to differentiate the abilities of one's various students.[55]

Certainly, there are some absolute prohibitions in teaching, such as those against abuse and discrimination, but these identify what is intolerable. They do not begin to identify excellence in teaching. Textbooks for teachers are full of useful advice of the kind mentioned above. Give students a reasonable opportunity to respond to your questions; introduce challenging statements as a variant on questions; avoid questions which suggest the correct answer; set students problems rather than mere exercises; permit and encourage students to choose their own themes for writing assignments. And so on. *All* of these, however, call for thoughtful and intelligent application. Robin Barrow comments that "what distinguishes the good from the bad teacher is *knowing when* to question, listen to, correct, inform, etc., *which* pupils in *what* manner for *how long*."[56] This is why teachers need to learn to work independently of the guidelines, no matter how useful these may be.

Even critical thinking itself can degenerate into an affair of routine. We read books on critical thinking, but do we read them critically? It is with some trepidation that one encounters attempts to capture critical thinking in a list of handy prescriptions. A recent contribution includes among such guidelines: Don't oversimplify.[57] Valuable advice, certainly, but when is a simplification an oversimplification? One needs critical judgment. The advice is almost a truism and needs to be interpreted critically if it is not to lead to a refusal to simplify when simplification is just what is needed. (The same point applies to guidelines which are drawn up for teachers in addressing matters of bias in textbooks. These can be helpful and suggestive but can also be applied mechanically with deplorable results.) In the end, the advice about oversimplification demands a sense of judgment or it will turn upon itself.

Perhaps it is the fact that their implementation demands judgment which makes the observations of philosophers of education seem inadequate and feeble when compared with the confident prescriptions of pundits. Consider, for example, Whitehead's advice about teaching something thoroughly, and not teaching too many subjects. This is excellent practical advice which grows out of a critical assessment of educational practice in the light of a fundamental point about education itself, namely that education is not the "passive reception of disconnected ideas".[58] Of course, one will look in vain in Whitehead for an answer to the question how many subjects is too many. But then *no one* can answer this question in a general, context-free way, and to think that it can be answered is to be on our way to that mental dry rot which Whitehead deplored.

# CHAPTER TEN

## Imagination: Open Possibilities

***************************************************************************

> New ideas thrive in the imagination, which negates what is
> and ponders what might be.
> Israel Scheffler—In *Praise of the Cognitive Emotions*

## Imagination and Critical Thinking

In the wealth of material which has appeared on critical thinking
in recent years, there is precious little attention paid to imagination.
"Critical thinking" has become the latest educational slogan and everyone, it seems, subscribes to the view that teachers need to have, and to
foster, critical ability. Imagination has had fewer champions.[1] Some
philosophers of education, of course, have long claimed a link between
criticism and imagination, notably John Passmore who took the view
at the very outset of the modern debate on critical thinking that a critical person must possess initiative, independence, courage and imagination.[2] Not surprisingly, Dewey had also resisted the tempting dichotomy between criticism and creativity, pointing out that criticism,
especially self-criticism, was the road to the release of creative activity.[3]
Gilbert Ryle reminded us that "there are hosts of widely divergent sorts
of behaviour" which can be appropriately described as imaginative,
including the business of criticism itself.[4] On the whole, however, these
suggestions have not been pursued, and it is often assumed that imagination and criticism are in conflict.

No one who has followed recent educational theory can have failed
to notice that critical thinking has effectively supplanted creativity as
the pre-eminent aim of education. During the 1980s, there was a
veritable deluge of articles and books on critical thinking, and a parallel
decline in work on creativity which had so captured the headlines a
generation ago.[5] It may be that imagination has suffered by association

with creativity and the sense that critical thinking and creativity are unrelated, even incompatible. This is quite mistaken. Ideas which genuinely deserve to be considered creative, or imaginative, must be critically evaluated and deemed to meet an appropriate standard.[6] Similarly, critical thinking can take us beyond our present beliefs and practices to new possibilities, and thus involve a creative element. It is something which can be done mechanically or imaginatively.

Teachers who value the imagination need to see critical ability and imagination as complementary, as Dewey clearly did when he described one vital phase of reflective thought as involving "anticipation, supposition, conjecture, imagination".[7] Robert Ennis, one of the leading writers on critical thinking, has attempted to catalogue the dispositions which distinguish the critical thinker, calling attention to the importance of *looking for alternatives*, a disposition which translates into a number of relevant abilities.[8] That, indeed, is the heart of imagination, since an essential feature of the imaginative person is being both disposed and able to think up numerous possibilities.[9] In Ennis' list of abilities, we find such items as: formulating alternative solutions; considering alternative interpretations; seeking other possible explanations; thinking up questions to elicit possible meanings; designing possible experiments, and so on. As far as I can see, Ennis makes no *explicit* mention of imagination, though he does say that his current definition incorporates "creative elements".[10] Clearly, however, the sorts of activities mentioned do call for imagination. All that is needed is to bring the connection into the open.

Laura Duhan Kaplan has recently argued, however, that critical thinking texts and courses tend to teach political *conformity*, contrary no doubt to the expressed intention of teachers and authors.[11] Her conclusion is that the whole conception of critical thinking, and the movement inspired by this conception, is deficient if we are concerned, as she puts it, about "the ability to envision alternative events and institutions".[12] I take this to mean, although again it is not made explicit, that the student's imaginative capacity is impaired by courses and texts in critical thinking. To learn conformity is, after all, to have one's eyes closed to other possibilities. It is also clear from Kaplan's glowing endorsement of *critical pedagogy* as "a means of awakening the student's awareness that the world contains unrealized possibilities for thought and action", that the notion of imagination is implicit in her argument and fundamental in her scheme of values.[13]

The nub of her objection is that critical thinking merely teaches the student to practise certain skills with respect to given and fixed alternatives, whereas students ought to be encouraged to "create alternatives, not merely to choose between them".[14] Her case is supported by reference to a few texts in the general area of critical thinking.[15] None of her claims, however, is at all persuasive. Against her objection that David Kelley's approach, for example, teaches that choice exists among clear-cut options, determined by the author or teacher, it is surely obvious that critical thinking *can* show, and *must* allow, that *none* of the options presently before one is defensible, and therefore some other option will have to be found. It does not take long, as writers on critical thinking have shown, to discover that the question "How am I to get in?" nicely ignores the question "Are you to get in at all?", and there is a *general* lesson to be learned here about the fallacy of many questions which is then available for use in other contexts.[16] Awareness of fallacies such as oversimplification, the black-or-white fallacy, and begging the question, can also awaken in students an appreciation that a context or argument can be rigged or unfairly circumscribed, closing off other avenues.[17] One of the basic lessons in critical thinking is that alternatives may have been arbitrarily denied and consequently that we have to *imagine* other possibilities.

Kaplan observes that most major and many minor life choices do not present themselves as opportunities to select among clear-cut options. Surely, however, students can distinguish between the context of teaching and the context of ordinary experience. They can practise their skills on the examples offered, and recognize that, once learned, such skills can be employed in other contexts and even turned against the very examples on which the skills were honed,[18] or against the teacher's views, real or apparent.[19] On the assumption that students have some capacity for independent, critical judgment,[20] we need not be concerned that the examples we choose may be inadvertently slanted *if* the students are not only permitted but encouraged to assess the merits of these same examples.

In her classic and still useful primer on clear thinking, Susan Stebbing offered the following cautionary word to the reader, touching on this point: "I ought to avoid making elementary mistakes in logic, since I have been thinking about the conditions of sound reasoning and have been trying to teach logic for years. But eager haste to establish a conclusion may lead me to make elementary blunders....Naturally I cannot provide an example of my own failure in this respect; to have recognized the error would be to have avoided it."[21]

Every good author and teacher concerned with the development of critical thinking will ensure that a similar self-referential doubt is cultivated. We can readily imagine that we have committed errors even if we cannot imagine what they are; and we can encourage our students and readers to try to imagine alternative positions to the ones we confidently defend. Would any self-respecting teacher of critical thinking disagree with Stebbing when she remarks: "I do not hope to succeed in escaping bias either in my selection or in my exposition of these examples."?[22] Even more pointedly Stebbing observes: "It may even be that you can find in this book some evidences of my having used crooked arguments. Certainly I am not aware of having done so, but in that I may be self-deceived, I cannot hope to have avoided altogether the defects of twisted thinking."[23]

One text rejected by Kaplan as seriously deficient is *An Introduction to Reasoning* by Stephen Toulmin, Richard Rieke and Allan Janik.[24] I readily confess that Kaplan's opinion that this book "teaches reasoning in the sense that we say the Sophists in ancient Athens taught reasoning",[25] immediately struck me as unlikely in the extreme, given that distinguished philosopher Stephen Toulmin is senior author. Still, stranger things have happened and, as Carl Sagan points out, one's scepticism imposes a burden, i.e. a responsibility to find out. Kaplan's interpretation of the book is that it teaches students to adopt those reasons which are socially acceptable, in her words "how to behave in the courtroom, the health spa, the realtor's office, and the office party, in order to be accepted as a member of the petty bourgeoisie."[26] Again, the alleged lesson is conformity and the result is the demise of imaginative speculation about alternatives.

An examination of *An Introduction to Reasoning* reveals that

Kaplan's reading of the book is a complete misrepresentation. As one might have predicted, it is *not* the authors' view (how could it be?) that a good reason is whatever is generally thought to be a good reason in a particular social situation. Why would one need to *study* critical thinking if that were the case when informal socialization would suffice? Their point is the quite different one that the appropriateness and necessity of giving and searching for reasons varies from one context to another: "The trains of reasoning that it is appropriate to use vary from situation to situation."[27] It is made perfectly clear that appeals to "well-founded" authority may be challenged and supposed authority cannot be taken for granted. Moreover, to say that reasons "relevant" to a certain situation must be given is *not* to say that what is traditionally and socially *regarded as* relevant *is* relevant. It is explicitly acknowledged that such reasons may be disputed.[28] The notion of relevance is itself controversial. Similarly, the distinction between what appears to be quite acceptable and proper and what is acceptable and proper is always clear. What is *not* clear is how Kaplan could have so completely misinterpreted this book.[29] I hope it is not unfair to comment that she has herself been rather unimaginative concerning the ways in which the lessons such books teach might be used.

One final point about imagination and critical thinking. One hears much less these days about brainstorming. Perhaps it is yet another example of a practice which is occasionally useful but by no means the panacea which enthusiasts once proclaimed.[30] The general idea at work is that judgment should be deferred as ideas are produced so that those involved will not be inhibited by the concern that their ideas are foolish or irrelevant. It may indeed be that the technique is sometimes effective, as researchers have claimed, but whether or not imaginative suggestions have in fact been produced can only be determined by judging their merits *at some point*, and this requires critical assessment. The great danger is that simply being *prolific* in producing ideas (regardless of their merit) will be equated with being imaginative. Nevertheless, the strategy of getting our ideas on the table before deciding too quickly that they are not worth mentioning seems sensible. This does *not* mean, however, that we have only to play down critical reflection to allow our imaginations to flourish. That is once again to set up a dubious dichotomy.

## Teachers With Imagination

Teachers need to use their imagination in many ways in their work. If they are not to be trapped in narrow and negative views, they will need to entertain the possibility that either/or choices can be challenged and overcome; that there might be ways in which they can do justice to critical thinking *and* cultural literacy, to knowledge for its own sake *and* vocational studies, to competence *and* imagination, to moral rules *and* moral thinking, and so on. Fanaticism on either side of these divisions in educational theory encourages teachers to take refuge in whatever fortified position they can, and the idea of an imaginative resolution is lost. At times, as with the present conflict over whole-language approaches versus "phonics", the atmosphere is so hostile and the respective positions so uncompromising that it takes an effort of the imagination to conceive that there might be "a new order of conceptions".[31]

Again, a vital imaginative capacity involves the teacher grasping and sharing the perspective of the student coming to a new subject which may seem impossibly difficult or uninteresting.[32] It is important for the teacher to try to appreciate the difficulties and frustration students may experience, and all too easy to forget these in practice.[33] The teacher, we may hope, now understands the material well, and perhaps no longer even recalls similar problems he or she may have encountered when the subject was first studied. It may take an imaginative leap to place oneself in a certain situation, even if we ourselves once occupied that situation. Louis Arnaud Reid observes that one great benefit of student teachers studying some *new* subject during their professional programme is being placed thereby in much the same situation as the children they will teach, thus gaining a new sense of their students' perspectives.[34] Imaginative teachers are able to think of various reasons why students might have difficulty grasping or appreciating the material, and this puts them in a position to look for imaginative solutions. There is no point merely informing the student that the solution to a problem is obvious if the student doesn't find it obvious; there is nothing to be gained by merely asserting the value of the work if the student does not appreciate this.

Related to this, teachers need to be able to see what their students are getting at even though their questions and comments are poorly phrased, awkward and hesitant. It is a common complaint by students that their teachers "missed the point" they were trying to make, and dismissed an idea too quickly. The teacher needs to consider the possibility that the student has a valuable point, albeit clumsily expressed, and also to wonder if there may be a further and deeper meaning which the student is reaching towards. Isaiah Berlin has noted, for example, that children frequently raise questions which contain the germs of philosophical ideas, and are often told to stop asking silly questions.[35] They need teachers (and parents) with an imaginative grasp of the possible meanings in their questions, philosophical or otherwise, and with the ability to respond in such a way that their sense of wonder is not destroyed. Teachers also need to avoid being so locked into particular anticipated responses that they cannot entertain some other answer to the problem or issue.[36] Tests, for example, which permit only one correct response deprive children of the opportunity to articulate an idea they have, and also prevent teachers from trying to look imaginatively at the student's response.[37]

Teachers need to be able to see possibilities for the future in the behaviour and interests of their students. Of course, judgment also comes into this, especially when it is a matter of seizing the moment.[38] As Dewey noted, however, "other acts and feelings are prophetic; they represent the dawning of flickering light that will shine steadily only in the far future. As regards them there is little at present to do but give them fair and full chance, waiting for the future for definite direction."[39] It takes some imagination to *see* the potential indicated by such "flickering light", but it needs to be recognized if the opportunity for development is to be provided. We know, unfortunately, how easy it is in practice for children in school to be labelled and streamed in such a way that teachers in the end simply *cannot* imagine *any* promising future for them. One thinks here of Jill Solnicki's impassioned plea to her department head whose cynicism is overwhelming: "How can it be that you've never seen past their 'unclear, incorrect sentences' to the expressiveness in their writing, the humour, the insight, the God damn humanity?!"[40] The educator, said Dewey, more than other professionals is concerned to take a long look ahead.[41] We need to recognize that this forward-looking perspective often takes the form of imaginative speculation.

Everything which has been said in this book about the impossibility of reducing teaching to rule and routine suggests that teachers will need imagination to think of ways of satisfying conflicting needs and claims *in their own teaching situation.* There is no ready-made rule to follow which will satisfy the demands of authority and freedom in education, for example, and Russell is surely right to insist that teachers will simply have to *find* a way of exercising authority in the spirit of liberty.[42] Tact, sensitivity and judgment will be required here, but also imagination. Like Russell, Dewey set himself against recommending methods and strategies to be "slavishly copied", as he put it, in other contexts.[43] Moreover, fundamental educational principles, such as the freedom of the learner, did not carry self-evident implications for practice either; they needed *interpretation* in one's own situation.[44] They did not constitute answers so much as problems; and solutions would only be found by those with the imagination to break out of traditional ways of thinking, and to adapt "tried and true" ideas to the unique situations they find themselves in: "No teacher can know too much or have too ingenious an imagination in selecting and adapting...to meet the requirements that make for growth in this and that individual."[45]

Imaginative teachers are capable of seeing unexpected possibilities in teaching moments. Eisner brings this out with great clarity when he observes that teachers need to be inventive and innovative as they deal with unpredictable contingencies, and in creating ends *as they proceed.*[46] Max van Manen also stresses the importance of teachers knowing how to *improvise*, knowing at once what is the right thing to say.[47] Some writers, however, have misconstrued the need for improvisation and interactive decision-making as meaning that imaginative teachers must avoid intending at the outset to achieve a specific result in teaching. Ruth Mock speaks of the teacher who "intends, unimaginatively, to obtain a predetermined result".[48] The teacher who has a goal in mind, however, is not thereby prevented from seizing an *opportunity* which comes along. Once again, an unnecessary dichotomy looms before us, this time planning versus improvisation. Eisner gets the point exactly right when he comments that "the exclusive use of such a model of teaching (i.e. predetermined ends) reduces it to a set of algorithmic functions."[49] The crucial term here is "exclusive".

There is still a tendency to think of imaginative teaching as necessarily involving the kind of unusual, innovative *strategy* which succeeds sometimes precisely because it is so unusual that it captures the student's imagination. John Keating, the charismatic teacher in the film *Dead Poets Society*, comes to mind. As with courage, the *dramatic* examples may dominate our conception of imaginative teaching and blind us to other forms. Imagination, however, can be displayed in teaching which follows commonly employed methods such as instruction, discussion, and question-and-answer sessions. If these approaches as such are not imaginative, imaginative *variations* may well be introduced.[50] In the course of teaching in these ways, the teacher can show his or her imagination in the examples, cases, references, analogies, connections, metaphors, allusions, and diagrams introduced. The hoary examples give way to fresh ones which open up the issue for teacher and student alike. These possibilities for imaginative teaching, however, are ignored by those who take the simplistic view that classroom teachers who value and emphasize creative learning will "minimize to the extent possible their own talk in class".[51] There may be good reasons why on occasion teachers should minimize their own talk, but this is not a general guideline for imaginative teaching. It is the quality, not the amount, of talk which matters. Some teachers show their imagination by being able to think of another way of explaining a point or demonstrating a principle when other teachers would be defeated.

On a related matter, there is currently a popular view which holds that if children are to write imaginatively and honestly, they *must* choose their own topics. If the teacher assigns a topic, the students' own imagination is compromised. Moreover, imaginative writing must not be constrained by conventional norms such as correct spellings.[52] These are recognizable themes in the contemporary whole-language approach. Clearly, there is much to be said for the student trying to identify a worthwhile topic; this is itself an imaginative exercise. We need to stop short, however, of the absurd situation where a teacher is afraid to make suggestions as to possible topics. Moreover, as a general policy, this view underestimates the value of the teacher showing great imagination in the kinds of topics assigned. If the teacher can think up problems, situations, tasks, questions, dilemmas, puzzles and projects which are interesting, provocative and novel, where the students have to *use* what they know, he or she may challenge the students and excite their imagination. Too often teachers set assignments which are little more than busy work, such as the dull and deadly worksheets which are so common. Naturally, too, it would be foolish to be so obsessed with incorrect spelling that one missed the imaginative ideas, as Jill Solnicki points out. On the other hand, the possession of basic writing skills means that one is able to concentrate one's attention on the ideas.[53]

Elliot Eisner reminds us that we can become so concerned about "engaged time" and counting the minutes spent on what is thought of as serious business, that wonder and imagination are undermined.[54] Many schooling practices, Eisner points out, especially assessment practices, militate against the development of the imagination. It is helpful, I think, to recall here Aristotle's point that philosophy itself began with wonder and that the person who is puzzled and wonders considers himself or herself ignorant.[55] This suggests a link between imagination and some of the other virtues we have examined, especially humility and open-mindedness. The teacher with imagination can entertain the possibility that he or she is mistaken, that there are alternative positions which may well turn out to be right, that his or her own knowledge is really quite limited, and that students need time simply to wonder about what they have been learning. All of this can help to offset the tendency towards interpreting teaching as no more than the authoritative transmission of certain knowledge.[56]

Many of these aspects of imagination in teaching will be missed if we think only of the imagination as entering into the formation of utopian visions. Burbules, for example, anxious to point out the dangers of utopianism, reminds us that the capacity to imagine and describe better possibilities is not itself a way of attaining these objectives.[57] He remarks that "utopian thinking avoids the tragic sense by substituting our imagination for our sense of reality."[58] The imagination, however, does not only come into play in conceiving of ideals and visions, but also into thinking of the means by which these goals might be achieved or approached. Burbules also indicates that there will be inevitable trade-offs between competing ideals in the real world, and the implication may be that our imaginative horizons will have to be limited. Again, however, we should remember that the imagination will play a vital role in coming up with creative compromises when such conflicts occur.

## *Believing in Imagination*

In addition to resisting the false dichotomy between imagination and critical thinking examined earlier, teachers who value imagination need to reject the suggestion that our imaginations cannot overcome allegedly insuperable barriers resulting from our gender, race, ethnic background, or life experiences. An increasingly popular view is that those who have not directly and personally experienced certain events cannot really understand what it is like to have those experiences, and thus one's right to contribute to policy decisions with respect to such matters is called into question. Without the personal experience, we simply do not know what we are talking about. This has already translated into proposals for restricting the teaching of certain classes and topics to those who belong to certain groups,[59] and we have met the view earlier in chapter four that members of certain groups should not address certain topics at all.[60]

The effect of this, perhaps the intent also, is to silence opinion, and to dismiss certain suggestions without benefit of serious examination. If someone does not, and cannot, understand an issue, it is scarcely sensible to pay attention to what he or she has to say about it. The thesis is that people only understand if they have themselves experienced the matter in question; for example, the oppression suffered by minority groups in societies which discriminate against them.[61] It is asserted more than argued that we simply cannot imagine what such experiences are like if we have not had them ourselves; and if it is grudgingly conceded that one might have an abstract, intellectual grasp of the experience, it is strongly denied that any genuine imaginative and sympathetic awareness at the emotional level could occur.[62]

This view, which is now part of conventional wisdom, flies in the face of all ordinary experience which tells us that by means of appealing to similarities in our own experience with those experiences we have not directly had, we *can* enter imaginatively into those other situations.

Some people, moreover, have the ability to assist us by virtue of their capacity to create and present a vivid and striking imaginative world which we can enter vicariously. Imaginative teachers can help students do this too.[63] It is not difficult at all to show that direct, personal experience is *not* a prerequisite for understanding. In many cases, we know that the person in question did not in fact undergo the experience he or she describes. Consider, for example, Hortense Calisher's achievement in portraying life in a space shuttle on an extended mission.[64] Her own lack of direct experience here seems to have been no bar whatever to her imagination. By her own account, she went to the library for a very short time and read some NASA publications: "When the book was published, John Noble Wilford, who is head of the science news for the *New York Times*, came to interview me. He asked me how long I had researched, I told him what I had done, and he said he couldn't fault me on what was there. I think you just put yourself in any environment that you write in."[65] In other cases, we know that the individual has not had the experience in question since it has never occurred. We are convinced, nevertheless, that he or she has given us some idea of what that situation might be like and feel like. In some cases, what we could not previously imagine becomes imaginable through someone else's gifts. A devastating virus capable of destroying rice, wheat, barley, oats and other basic food crops has so far not infected the world, but can anyone doubt that John Christopher in *The Death of Grass* has given us a sense of that world, its social and moral characteristics, if such a calamity were to occur?[66] Nor is it plausible to suggest that the author must have had some familiarity with famine conditions and their effects on human beings as the principles which comprise civilized society gradually give way to anarchy. Quite simply, he was able to imagine various possibilities and present them with great plausibility. Endless examples of similar imaginative works could be given, but it is enough just to mention books such as Golding's *Lord of the Flies* and Huxley's *Brave New World*, and to note that science fiction would effectively disappear as a genre on this view, for the position to collapse into absurdity.

Teachers should reject this alleged limitation on imagination not just because it is false but because such a belief may be self-fulfilling.

Barriers to the imagination arise easily enough. We hear of customs and lifestyles very different from our own and declare that we simply cannot imagine anyone living that way. We hear of a new scientific notion, and find it unimaginable. It may indeed be psychologically impossible for us to imagine these things because everything we have ever learned has built up the conviction that only what we already believe is possible. If we do not use our imagination, if we are not encouraged to try to imagine certain things, if our imagination is not given full rein as children, then it may be that we cannot imagine what we might otherwise have been able to imagine.[67] If we are led to believe that we cannot imagine certain things, we may not *try* to imagine them with the result in time that indeed we cannot do what we might otherwise have done.[68] Those who encourage us to believe that we cannot enter imaginatively into the lives of those whose cultural experiences we have not shared, endanger values such as respect for persons and other cultures. For how can we respect that which we do not understand?

It is important for teachers to believe in the value of imagination in their own work, whatever subject they are teaching. Imagination can characterize our efforts in teaching any subject, and we need to put behind us the idea that a concern for developing the imagination is the prerogative of teachers in certain areas. The view persists, however, that some subjects are especially connected with imagination, and the favourite candidate is literature.[69] The difficulty involved in ridding ourselves of this view can perhaps be illustrated by noting that while Robin Barrow, for example, recognizes that one can exercise imagination in *any* context, he insists nevertheless that history and literature have *special* value in the development of imagination.[70] *Why*, however, would literature and/or history be more likely to develop philosophical imagination than imaginative philosophy? Russell argued persuasively that basic scientific information can stimulate the imagination if people will take the time to reflect on it. He wanted people to ponder the fact, for example, that the largest star measures six hundred million miles across.[71] Is there any reason to think that history would do more than science to develop our imaginations in this direction? It surely will not do to say, as Barrow does, that imaginative mathematics only feeds the imagination in respect of mathematics. All imagination takes some form, and literature and history will satisfy some and not others.[72]

Finally, I would say that teachers who believe in the value of the imagination in education should resist the suggestion that the term "imaginative" cannot in any reasonably strict sense be applied to the activities and ideas of young children.[73] Barrow is surely right to insist that the word is bandied about loosely in much educational theory, and that the necessary connection with relevant standards of quality is often absent. Nevertheless, just as he properly admits that what we allow as imaginative at an earlier period of history would not necessarily count as imaginative today, so too the application of standards in connection with the work of students needs to take into account the child's level and knowledge. An unusual and valuable suggestion from a five-year-old counts as imaginative even if it would not count as such if uttered by an adult.[74] This is simply because what counts as unusual is a reflection in part of what the child knows. We need to keep this in mind as teachers so that we are encouraged to go on looking for and promoting such ideas in our students.

# Concluding Comment

~~~~~~~~~~~~~~~~~~~~~~~~~~~~~~~~~~~~~~~~~~~~~~~~~~~~

The virtues of the teacher are those which enable him or her to achieve excellence in that role, especially in educating his or her students. They are both desirable in themselves, as revealing aspects of the teacher as an educated individual and admirable person, and also effective in creating the conditions and context which help promote the goals of teaching and education.

The qualities examined here are surely among the ones we should look for in our teachers. Dewey was right that education will always be in the hands of ordinary men and women, but these excellences are not unattainable if we take them seriously. My own children have known a few teachers who have exemplified these qualities in considerable measure. Unfortunately, they have also had to endure far too many teachers who were arrogant, dogmatic, unfair, cowardly, uninspiring, insensitive, and excruciatingly boring.

In teacher-education programmes, we need to be less concerned with counting the number of weeks students spend in schools on field experience, and more concerned with the moral, intellectual and personal qualities they exemplify in their teaching practice. It is, as Dewey said, a certain quality of practice, not mere practice, which produces the expert and the artist. We need to be less concerned about their allegiance to particular methods and more concerned about their grasp of the principles which lie behind whatever educational approaches seem appropriate in their situation. Our primary interest should not be in particular strategies, methods, techniques and approaches. These are fashionable for a time only to be replaced by other practices, so we need to look for individuals who can intelligently review new ideas which come along. When applicants for teaching positions are being considered, we need to be less concerned with hearing allegiance paid to whatever happens to be the fashionable trend at the time. Any candidate who claims to believe in critical thinking, cultural literacy, whole language, mainstreaming, student empowerment, anti-racism, consciousness-raising, a community of inquiry, standards, or whatever, should be invited to say exactly what he or she takes these to involve, and to explain how they relate to the fundamental idea of educational development. Our notion of the "good teacher" needs to shift from superficial, behavioural criteria to more fundamental human excellences.

We need teachers who have a Socratic awareness of their own ignorance but who are at the same time not afraid to defend central educational values; teachers who are committed to fair decisions based on relevant evidence, but who are also prepared to go on thinking about decisions they have made; teachers who are genuinely interested in and concerned about the well-being of their students, but who are at the same time passionately committed to the subjects they teach; teachers who are able to weigh the complex factors which enter into the particular decisions which face them, but who are capable of stepping outside the boundaries set by present realities. These qualities would go a long way towards restoring meaning and dignity to the idea of teaching.

# Notes

xxxxxxxxxxxxxxxxxxxx

## NOTES FOR PREFACE

1. See Plato, *Apology* 20B. Reprinted in Hugh Tredennick (trans.), *The Last Days of Socrates* Harmondsworth: Penguin Books, 1969.
2. Which is not to say that important ethical questions do not arise in the case of these and other animals.
3. See Immanuel Kant, "Thoughts on education", in Steven M. Cahn (ed.), *The Philosophical Foundations of Education* New York: Harper and Row, 1970: 183.
4. Kant, op. cit.: 182.
5. John Dewey, "What psychology can do for the teacher", in Reginald D. Archambault (ed.), *John Dewey on Education* New York: Random House, 1964: 201. (From John Dewey and James A. McLellan, *The Psychology of Number* 1895.)
6. Dewey, op. cit.: 201.
7. Dewey, op. cit.: 198.
8. Suitable adjustments to be made for other jurisdictions with different systems.
9. See Robert Bérard and William Hare, "Investment in excellence: paid study leave for teachers", *The Teacher* (Nova Scotia) Feb. 29, 1984.
10. Bertrand Russell, "Why fanaticism brings defeat", *The Listener* September 23, 1948: 452-3.

## NOTES FOR CHAPTER ONE

1. Theodore R. Sizer, *Horace's Compromise: The Dilemma of the American High School* Boston: Houghton Mifflin Company, 1984.
2. David Braybrooke, "The possibilities of compromise", *Ethics* 93, 1982: 139-50.
3. Nicholas Rescher, *Ethical Idealism* Berkeley: University of California Press, 1987, especially ch. 6.
4. Reported in *Canadian School Executive* 9, 3, 1990: 36. Similar cases will come up when the notion of judgment is discussed in chapter two.

5.  Maxine Greene, *Teacher As Stranger* Belmont: Wadsworth Publishing Company, 1973. For a memorable example of lost perspective in the workplace, consider the example of the telephone operator who stayed on duty though she could see the house, in which her mother lay bed-ridden, on fire. See Chester Barnard, *The Functions of the Executive* Cambridge: Harvard University Press, 1938: 269.

6.  Peter Singer, *Animal Liberation* New York: New York Review Company, 1975.

7.  See Edward H. Humphreys, "Policy and privacy of student information in Canada", in *Canadian Journal of Education* 7, 3, 1982: 25-38.

8.  See Stanley I. Benn, "Privacy, freedom and respect for persons", in J. Roland Pennock and John W. Chapman (eds.), *Privacy* Nomos, Vol. 13, New York: Atherton Press, 1971: 1-26.

9.  A.N. Whitehead, *The Aims of Education* New York: Mentor Books, 1949: 13. (Essay originally published in 1916.)

10. John Stuart Mill, *On Liberty* 1859.

11. See Ivor Shapiro, "Devil's advocate", *Saturday Night* December 1989: 25-8. Apparently these remarks, and the comments attributed to Professor Gillers, were made in a documentary shown on PBS television in 1989 entitled "Ethics in America". In recent years, some lawyers in the United States have been jailed for refusing to defend clients planning to lie on the witness stand. See the case of Ellis Rubin reported in *Time* July 21, 1986: 52. In a special section on ethics in *Time* May 25, 1987, Lisa Milord, ethics counsel for the American Bar Association, is reported as admitting that all too many lawyers are "looking out for their own interests rather than the integrity of the legal system". Depressing as this is, the comment at least suggests a growing awareness of and concern about the problem.

12. Plato, *Apology* 35C, in Hugh Tredennick (trans.), *The Last Days of Socrates* op. cit. I was glad to find my own unease about contemporary attitudes echoed by John Passmore in "Academic ethics?", *Journal of Applied Philosophy* 1, 1, 1984: 63-77.

13. See Brenda Jo Bredemeier and David L. Shields, "Values and violence in sports today", *Psychology Today* October 1985: 23-32.

14. See an article in *Life* February 1991. Librarians have also been tempted on occasion to hold that general ethical principles have no relevance in their professional work. See a discussion in Melissa Watson, "The unresolved conflict", in *The Reference Librarian* 4, 1982: 117-21.

15. See *The Mail Star* (Halifax), March 20, 1990.

16. See *The Globe and Mail* January 27, 1987.

17. John Dewey, "What psychology can do for the teacher", in Reginald. D. Archambault (ed.), *John Dewey On Education* op. cit.: 201.

18. See my discussion in "Limiting the freedom of expression: The Keegstra case", *Canadian Journal of Education* 15, 4, 1990: 375-89.

19. Bertrand Russell, *Bertrand Russell Speaks His Mind* Westport, CN: Greenwood Press, 1974: 141.

20. See John Dewey, "What psychology can do for the teacher", in Archambault (ed.), op cit.: 201. Also Bertrand Russell, *Unpopular Essays* London: George Allen and Unwin, 1940: 147. And Israel Scheffler, *Reason and Teaching* Indianapolis: Bobbs-Merrill, 1973.

21. Israel Scheffler, *In Praise of the Cognitive Emotions* New York: Routledge, 1991: 128.

22. Clive Beck, "Some arguments and a procedure for democratizing the central decision-making structure of educational institutions", in Michael J. Parsons (ed.), *Philosophy of Education 1974* Edwardsville: Southern Illinois University, 1974: 318.

23. Consider, for example, the curriculum offered by the Halifax District School Board in its four high schools. There are 77 courses in the area of business education and not a single course anywhere in classical literature. Surely, something is out of perspective here. See Halifax District School Board, Senior High School Course Selection Guide, 1992-1993.

24. John Passmore, "On teaching to be critical", in R.S. Peters (ed.), *The Concept of Education* London: Routledge and Kegan Paul, 1967: 198. One of the finest essays in the literature on philosophy of education.

## NOTES FOR CHAPTER TWO

1. The document is reprinted in James A. Johnson et al. (eds.), *Foundations of American Education: Readings* Boston: Allyn and Bacon, 1972: 557-9.

2. See "The code of ethics of the education profession", a document produced by the National Education Association, reprinted in Johnson et al. (eds.), *Foundations of American Education* op. cit.: 554-7. It would be interesting to see how other professions fare in this respect.

3. Jacques Maritain, *Education at the Crossroads* New Haven: Yale University Press, 1943: 4.

4. B.F. Skinner, "Freedom and the control of men", *American Scholar* 25, 1, 1955-6: 47-65.

5. See "The ethics of higher studies", in Anton C. Pegis (ed.), *A Gilson Reader* New York: Image Books, 1957: 25.

6. John Dewey, *How We Think*, reprinted in Jo Ann Boydston (ed.), *John Dewey: The Later Works, 1925-56* Vol. 8: 1933 Carbondale: Southern Illinois University Press, 1986: 163. (This is the 2nd edition, published in 1933.)

7. Bertrand Russell, "Education for democracy", *Addresses and Proceedings of the National Education Association* 77 (1939): 533.

8. Paul Weiss, "Adventurous humility", *Ethics* 51, 3, 1941: 337-48.

9. I would not agree with Patricia White that cases like the courageous villain can be ignored in the context of education for democracy. Such cases do occasionally occur, the protagonists see themselves as fighting

for truth and justice, and we have to be able to admit that they are courageous but find the courage ourselves to oppose them. See her interesting paper, "Educating courageous citizens", in Clive Harber and Ronald Meighan (eds.), *The Democratic School* Derbyshire: Education Now Books, 1989: 7-16.

10. Plato, *Apology* 32B, in Tredennick, op. cit.

11. See Constance Holden, "Textbook controversy intensifies nationwide", *Science* January 2, 1987: 19-21.

12. Edward Wynne, "Moral courage and moral learning", *Ethics in Education* 7, 5, 1988: 13-14.

13. See a W5 programme, "Tales out of school", broadcast on CTV, April 21, 1991.

14. John Passmore, "On teaching to be critical", in R.S. Peters (ed.), *The Concept of Education* op. cit.: 199.

15. John Searle, *The Campus War* Harmondsworth: Penguin Books, 1972: 193. Searle employs the notion of Sacred Topics and views the student movement of the time as quasi-religious in character.

16. For a flavour of the times in the early 1990s, see "Taking offense", *Newsweek* December 24, 1990: 48-55. Also, "Upside down in the groves of academe", *Time* April 1, 1991: 62-4. And, "The silencers", and "A war of words", *Maclean's* May 27, 1991: 40-50.

17. Bertrand Russell, "The place of science in a liberal education", in his *Mysticism and Logic* Harmondsworth: Penguin Books, 1953: 46. (Essay originally published in 1913.)

18. David Pratt, "The social role of school textbooks in Canada", in Elia Zureik and Robert M. Pike (eds.), *Socialization and Values in Canadian Society* Vol. 1 Toronto: McClelland and Stewart, 1975: 120.

19. Donald Marshall is a Mikmaq who spent eleven years in prison for a murder he did not commit. He was released in 1982, exonerated, and compensated by the Nova Scotia government. This example would not have suited my purposes here were it not for the fact that the textbook in question *has* succeeded in addressing many of the faults identified in traditional books in this area.

20. See my paper, "What can philosophy say to teachers?", in William Hare (ed.), *Reason In Teaching And Education* Halifax: Dalhousie University School of Education, 1989: 51. To his credit, Joe Clark, then Minister for External Affairs, quickly denounced the interference. The historical incident in question, i.e. the Armenian massacres, is often relegated to the status of an *allegation* rather than a fact in much commentary. For example, John Gray, writing about the dispute between Armenia and Azerbaijan, speaks of the Armenians "who blame the Turks for the slaughter of hundreds of thousands of Armenians during and after the First World War". See *The Globe and Mail* May 11, 1992. This wording would surely not be used with reference to the Nazi holocaust.

21. Harvey Siegel, *Educating Reason: Rationality, Critical Thinking, and Education* New York: Routledge, 1988: 107.

22. John H. Trueman, "Lest we offend: The search for a perfect past", in *The History and Social Science Teacher* 23, 4, 1988: 194-9.

23. Cited in Trueman, op. cit.: 195. From an article in the *New York Times Magazine*, November 17, 1985: 56.

24. Cited in Trueman, op. cit.: 196. From Allan Nevins, *The Gateway to History* Chicago: Quadrangle Books, 1962: 57. Nevins goes on to point out (p. 59) that the writer of history has "the duty of striving to attain the greatest possible degree of objectivity and impartiality".

25. The prevalence of the false assumption led Russell to declare that the best teachers are not impartial! Bertrand Russell and Dora Russell, *Prospects of Industrial Civilization* New York: Century, 1923. For a discussion of this point, see further chapter seven. Richard Paul and Joel Rudinow, in a mistake which echoes Nevins, are prepared to say that their own discussion is biased, i.e. biased in favour of the truth. This is paradox-mongering and a kind of false humility. To be in favour of the truth is precisely to be opposed to bias. See their paper, "Bias, relativism and critical thinking", in *Journal of Thought* 23, 1988: 125-38.

26. *Standards for Evaluation of Instructional Materials with Respect to Social Content* Sacramento: California State Department of Education, 1986: ?

27. *Standards* op. cit.: 3.

28. Curiously, William Honig, the superintendent under whose direction the California standards were issued, has published an article in which he condemns relativism in values. See Bill Honig, "Teaching values belongs in our public schools", *NASSP Bulletin* 74, 528, 1990: 6-9.

29. John Dewey, *How We Think* op. cit.: 136.

30. John Stuart Mill, *On Liberty*, ch. 2.

31. Karen J. Warren, "Critical thinking and feminism", *Informal Logic* 10, 1, 1988: 31-44.

32. I have made these points myself elsewhere, for example, in rejecting the claims of creation science to equal time. See my *In Defence of Open-mindedness* Montreal: McGill-Queen's, 1985: 96. The point is made with characteristic directness by Carl Sagan when he faces up to the objection that he has closed his mind to the truth by ignoring the evidence that the earth is six thousand years old: "Well, I haven't ignored it; I considered the purported evidence and *then* rejected it." See his paper, "The burden of skepticism", *The Skeptical Inquirer* 12, 1, 1987: 38-46. This is all that Warren needs to say about certain views.

33. Stephen Toulmin, "The new philosophy of science and the 'paranormal'", *The Skeptical Inquirer* 9, 1, 1984: 48-55.

34. Warren is no doubt right to say that a patriarchal framework is biased because it involves false and faulty generalizations; but she cannot thereby claim that feminist theory is necessarily free of such biases. See

Warren, "Critical thinking and feminism", op. cit.: 39. Nor is she correct to assert that open-mindedness (properly understood) *is* a commitment to feminism, unless this claim is made trivially true by so defining feminism. Warren refers us to the work of Alison Jaggar on this point, but I have shown elsewhere that *aspects* of Jaggar's own feminist theories are actually incompatible with open-mindedness. See my *In Defence of Open-mindedness* op. cit.: 61-2.

35. My impression is that schools are not terribly sensitive to the matter of student humiliation. It is not uncommon, for example, in elementary schools for teachers to write the names of those given detentions on the board. This is done not to remind those students of the detention but to humiliate them. Consider also the elementary-school teacher who identified in the class yearbook by name and photograph those students alleged *not* to have contributed to the yearbook. What could her educational objectives be? Humility and humiliation are quite different.

36. Bertrand Russell, *Power: A New Social Analysis* London: George Allen and Unwin, 1938: 304.

37. Thomas Nagel, *What Does It All Mean?* New York: Oxford University Press, 1987: 69.

38. See R.M. Hare, *Moral Thinking: Its Levels, Methods and Point* Oxford: Clarendon Press, 1981: 137.

39. Israel Scheffler, *In Praise of the Cognitive Emotions* op. cit.: 98.

40. David Hume, *An Enquiry Concerning the Principles of Morals*, Section 2, Part 1. (Originally published, 1751.) Reprinted in Alasdair MacIntyre (ed.), *Hume's Ethical Writings* London: Collier Books, 1965: 29.

41. Nicholas Rescher, *Unselfishness* Pittsburgh: University of Pittsburgh Press, 1975: 8.

42. See Robin Barrow, *Understanding Skills: Thinking, Feeling, and Caring* London, ON: The Althouse Press, 1990: 125-30.

43. See P.H. Hirst and R.S. Peters, *The Logic of Education* London: Routledge and Kegan Paul, 1970: 102. Hirst and Peters speak of the teacher allowing glimpses of himself as a human being to slip out (p. 100). Why *glimpses?*

44. John Dewey, "What psychology can do for the teacher", in Archambault, op. cit.: 199.

45. The text of the discussion is reproduced in Bryan Magee, *Men of Ideas* Oxford: Oxford University Press, 1982. An appreciation of the point I am making about Berlin's obvious enthusiasm really requires that the programme be seen.

46. Carl Sagan, "Why we need to understand science", *Skeptical Inquirer* 14, 3, 1990: 263-9.

47. On a related point, Berlin observes that children's questions are often philosophical in character, and parents find these a nuisance, with the result that children are conditioned to repress them. See Magee, *Men of Ideas* op. cit.: 14-5.

48. See "Askov decision intended as guideline, top court says", *The Globe and Mail* March 27, 1992.
49. Quoted in "NWT battle brewing over alcohol policy", *The Globe and Mail* July 27, 1991.
50. My position is that school detentions are not justified at all, though this is independent of my view that the school's interference in this student's behaviour off the school premises was totally unwarranted and an infringement of his civil liberties, and the number of detentions imposed utterly ridiculous. In serious cases of breach of rules, students should be suspended from school. In this particular incident, it is the school and school board officials who should have been suspended.
51. See *The Globe and Mail* June 17, 1992. These officials have no doubt forgotten Dewey's comment on traditional schooling practices and assumptions: "If he (the student) engaged in physical truancy...he was held to be at fault. No question was raised as to whether the trouble might not lie in the subject-matter or in the way in which it was offered." *Plus ça change.* See Dewey, *Experience and Education* New York: Collier Books, 1963: 46. (Originally published, 1938.) (Our attitudes to punishment are hard to fathom. According to a recent report, a nine-year-old involved in an armed robbery of a pizzeria in Toronto will not face *any charges at all.* The police noted: "The most we can do is pick him up and take him home to his parents". See *The Chronicle Herald* July 14, 1992. One wonders if the Supreme Court will again have to remind the lower courts and other officials to use their judgment.)
52. See, for example, "University professors get lessons in teaching", *The Globe and Mail* June 25, 1988.
53. See chapter four.
54. Cf. A. Phillips Griffiths, "A deduction of universities", in R.D. Archambault (ed.), *Philosophical Analysis and Education* London: Routledge and Kegan Paul, 1965: "'Imaginative', 'wise', 'logical', and 'intelligent' are adjectives which derive their sense from the adverbial form", p. 203.
55. R.F. Dearden, "What is general about general education?", *Oxford Review of Education* 6, 3, 1980: 284.
56. John Dewey, "What psychology can do for the teacher", in Archambault (ed.), op. cit.: 205.

## NOTES FOR CHAPTER THREE

1. Joseph Tussman, *Government and the Mind* New York: Oxford University Press, 1977: 165.
2. Op. cit.: 166.
3. David Bercuson and Douglas Wertheimer, *A Trust Betrayed: The Keegstra Affair* Toronto: Doubleday, 1985.

4.   See Gilbert Highet, *The Immortal Profession* New York: Weybright and Talley, 1976: 69.

5.   Bertrand Russell, *Principles of Social Reconstruction* London: Allen and Unwin, 1916: 147.

6.   John Dewey, *Democracy and Education* New York: The Free Press, 1966: 184. (Originally published, 1916.)

7.   Bertrand Russell, "Education for democracy", *Addresses and Proceedings of the National Education Association* 77 (2-6 July) 1939: 152.

8.   Alfred North Whitehead, "Harvard: The future", in A.H. Johnson (ed.), *Whitehead's American Essays in Social Philosophy* Connecticut: Greenwood Press, 1959: 160.

9.   Jean Ruddock, "A strategy for handling controversial issues in the classroom", in J.J. Wellington (ed.), *Controversial Issues in the Curriculum* Oxford: Basil Blackwell, 1986: 6. There is an echo here of Russell's reaction to William James' "will to believe". See Bertrand Russell, "Free thought and official propaganda", in *Sceptical Essays* London: George Allen and Unwin, 1960: 151. Russell proposed the "will to doubt".

10.  John Dewey, *Experience and Education* op. cit. See the famous opening lines.

11.  Ruddock, op. cit.: 7.

12.  David Hume, *An Inquiry Concerning Human Understanding* Indianapolis: Bobbs-Merrill, 1955, Section 10, Part one. (Originally published, 1748.)

13.  Donald C. Orlich et al., *Teaching Strategies: A Guide to Better Instruction* 2nd ed. Lexington, MA: D.C. Heath, 1985: 171. Emphasis in original.

14.  David Sadker and Myra Sadker, "Is the o.k. classroom o.k.?", *Phi Delta Kappan* Jan. 1985: 358-61.

15   Robert Hoffman, "The irrelevance of relevance", in Sidney Hook, Paul Kurtz and Miro Todorovich (eds.), *The Idea of a Modern University* Buffalo: Prometheus Books, 1974: 107-18.

16.  Jay F. Rosenberg, *The Practice of Philosophy: A Handbook for Beginners* 2nd ed. Englewood Cliffs, NJ: Prentice-Hall, 1984.

17.  Dennis Gunning, *The Teaching of History* London: Croom Helm, 1978: 51.

18.  Jerome A. Popp, "Teaching the ways of inquiry", *Illinois Schools Journal* 57, 3, 1977: 54-9.

19.  Russell, *Principles of Social Reconstruction* op. cit.: 154.

20.  Harvey Siegel, "Epistemology, critical thinking, and critical thinking pedagogy", *Argumentation* 3, 1989: 127-40.

21.  Henry Sidgwick, *The Methods of Ethics* London: Macmillan, 1962: 334. (Originally published, 1874.) For a recent discussion which links humility with ideals, see Jay Newman, "Humility and self-realization", *Journal of Value Inquiry* 16, 4, 1982: 275-85.

22.  Patricia White, "Self-respect, self-esteem and the 'management' of schools and colleges", *Journal of Philosophy of Education* 21, 1, 1987: 85-92.

23. Helen Oppenheimer, "Humility", in James F. Childress and John MacQuarrie (eds.), *The Westminster Dictionary of Christian Ethics* Philadelphia: Westminster Press, 1986: 284. Hume cautioned, however, that if people were to openly *proclaim* the merits they properly *believe* themselves to possess, "a flood of impertinence would break in upon us". See David Hume, *An Enquiry Concerning the Principles of Morals* Section 8, in Alasdair MacIntyre, *Hume's Ethical Writings* op. cit.: 106. (Originally published, 1751.)

24. Cf. Immanuel Kant, *Critique of Practical Reason* (trans. T.K. Abbot) London: Longmans, Green and Co., 1954: 178. (Originally published, 1788.)

25. Plato, *Protagoras* 318A, in W.K.C. Guthrie (trans.), *Protagoras and Meno* Harmondsworth: Penguin Books, 1975. Hugo McCann and Bevis Yaxley have commented that Plato created a character, Socrates, who humiliates his opponents to some degree, and that humiliation is of doubtful educational value. It might be said, however, that overweening arrogance invites humiliation. It is the inevitable consequence of the attitude the arrogant person has adopted. See their paper, "Retaining the philosophy of education in teacher education", *Educational Philosophy and Theory* 24, 1, 1992: 51-67.

26. Plato, *Apology* 21E, in Hugh Tredennick (trans.), *The Last Days of Socrates* op. cit. See also my discussion in "Reading the *Apology* in school", *The Classical World* 80, 1, 1986: 25-9.

27. Plato, *Crito* 46B, in Tredennick, *The Last Days of Socrates*, op. cit.

28. Notice how naturally the word "trust" came into the title of the book on the Keegstra affair cited in fn. 3 above.

29. Russell, *Principles of Social Reconstruction* op. cit.: 147

30. Joel Feinberg, "The child's right to an open future", in William Aiken and Hugh Lafollette (eds.), *Whose Child? Children's Rights, Parental Authority, and State Power* Totowa: Littlefield, Adams and Co., 1980: 140-51.

31. R.M. Hare, "Adolescents into adults", in T.H.B. Hollins (ed.), *Aims in Education: The Philosophic Approach* Manchester: Manchester University Press, 1964: 47-70.

32. Neil Postman, "The teacher with wisdom", in Allan C. Ornstein, *Strategies for Effective Teaching* New York: Harper and Row, 1990: 546.

33. Plato, *Apology* 23A, in Tredennick, *The Last Days of Socrates*, op. cit.

34. Diogenes Laertius, *Lives of Eminent Philosophers* (Loeb edition, trans. R.D. Hicks) London: Heinemann, 1972. Vol. 1, 160-1. Gregory Vlastos suggests that when Socrates disclaims knowledge, he is in effect saying that "any conviction he has stands ready to be re-examined in the company of any sincere person who will raise the question and join him in the investigation." See his "The paradox of Socrates", in Vlastos (ed.), *The Philosophy of Socrates* New York: Doubleday, 1971: 10.

35. Plato, *Meno* 86C, in Guthrie (trans.), *Protagoras and Meno*, op. cit.

36. Robert Gilpin, *American Scientists and Nuclear Weapons Policy* Princeton: Princeton University Press, 1962: 4.

37. Israel Scheffler, "Moral education and the democratic ideal", in *Reason and Teaching* op. cit.: 142.

38. See James Randi, *Flim-Flam!* New York: Lippincott and Crowell, 1980. Cf. John Dewey, *How We Think* in Boydston, op. cit.: 135: "It is a matter of common notice that men who are expert thinkers in their own special fields adopt views on other matters without doing the inquiring that they know to be necessary for substantiating simpler facts that fall within their own specialities."

39. See Theodore R. Sizer, *Horace's Compromise: The Dilemma of the American High School* op. cit.: 187.

40. D.C. Phillips, "Philosophy of education: *In extremis?*" *Educational Studies* 14, 1, 1983: 1-30.

41. Carl Sagan, "The burden of skepticism", *The Skeptical Inquirer* 12, 1, 1987: 45.

42. Michael Oakeshott, "Learning and teaching", in R.S. Peters (ed.), *The Concept of Education* op. cit.: 176.

43. Kant, op. cit.: 169.

44. Epicurus, *Fragments* 74. Cf. Socrates' attitude in Plato, *Gorgias* 458, Walter Hamilton (trans.), Harmondsworth: Penguin Books, 1973.

45. The attitude required is suggested very effectively by Samuel Walters Dyde (1862-1947) in one of the earliest articles in philosophy of education in Canada in the twentieth century: "Humility of mind...is not an abject and slavish abdication of one's reason, not a burial of one's judgment in a napkin, but rather a sense of the treasure to be known and possessed." See his paper, "Should there be a faculty of education in the university?", *Queen's Quarterly* 12, 2, 1904: 165-77.

## NOTES FOR CHAPTER FOUR

1. There are numerous such examples in Douglas N. Walton, *Courage: A Philosophical Investigation* Berkeley: University of California Press, 1986. Few teachers are mentioned in Walton's study. I noted references only to Socrates and Stephen Hawking, and the latter case is not really an example of courage in teaching though it is an example of a teacher with courage.

2. One sign of the times is the fact that the Los Angeles School Board in 1991 reversed an earlier decision to expel students found bringing guns to school. Apparently, there were so many offenders that a revised policy was deemed necessary. See *Maclean's* September 30, 1991.

3. Thomas Jefferson High School in East New York has a burial fund to help cover the funeral expenses of students killed at school. According to a recent report, "in the past four years, 70 students have been killed,

shot, stabbed or permanently injured on the school grounds." See "Childhood's end", *Time* March 9, 1992: 24-5. See also "A blackboard jungle", *Maclean's* March 16, 1992: 30.

4. Cf. the point made by John Passmore cited in fn. 14 in chapter two. See also Dennis M. Adams, "Literature for children: Avoiding controversy and intellectual challenge", *Top of the News* 42, 3, 1986: 304-8.

5. Walton makes the point that "courage is a concomitant of the nasty, the awful, and the annoying....The wish to be courageous is somehow absurd." See his *Courage* op. cit.: 194.

6. See Brand Blanshard, *The Uses of a Liberal Education* London: Alcove Press, 1974: 365-78. Especially what he calls "the fears of oneself".

7. Philippa Foot, *Virtues and Vices* Oxford: Basil Blackwell, 1978: 16.

8. David Solway, *Education Lost: Reflections on Contemporary Pedagogical Practice* Toronto: OISE Press, 1989: 35.

9. Aristotle, *Ethics* Book 3, ch. 7.

10. See reports in *The Gazette* and *The Globe and Mail* for February 8, 1991.

11. Epictetus, *Moral Discourses* (ed. Thomas Gould), New York: Washington Square Press, 1964: 76.

12. See my paper, "Limiting the freedom of expression: The Keegstra case", *Canadian Journal of Education* 15, 4, 1990: 375-89.

13. I allude to a column entitled "Principles" by William Christian, *The Globe and Mail* April 16, 1991, and I take the opportunity to pay tribute to my late colleague at Dalhousie University, George Grant. Grant resigned from the Department of Philosophy at York University in 1960, though he had no alternative employment at hand, on a matter of academic principle, namely his unwilllingness to use a text he judged to be unacceptable on scholarly grounds.

14. Harper Lee, *To Kill a Mockingbird*. I cannot discuss this excellent book here, but the errors in thinking which lead to it being condemned as racist are essentially the same as those which I have examined in detail with respect to *The Slave Dancer*, by Paula Fox. See my paper, "Bias in stories for children: Black marks for authors", *Journal of Applied Philosophy* 2, 1, 1985: 99-108. When sensitive and courageous books such as these are labelled racist, one can understand why teachers would hesitate before dealing with such issues at all. It is reassuring to be able to report that "Neither the Department of Education nor the District 20 School Board banned the novel; it continues to be included as an option on a list of approved resources for Senior High English Language Arts in the province of New Brunswick." (Personal communication from the Minister of Education, September 15, 1992.) For an excellent discussion of *To Kill a Mockingbird*, see Don Gutteridge, "The search for presence: A reader-response to postmodern literacy", *Our Schools/Our Selves*, 4, 1, 1992: 90-110.

15. Deanne Bogdan, "Toward a rationale for literary literacy", *Journal of Philosophy of Education* 24, 2, 1990: 209.

16. Peter Singer reports that since 1989 he has been unable to lecture openly in Germany, Austria and Switzerland because protestors, incensed by his support for euthanasia in the case of severely disabled newborn infants, cause disruptions. Singer speaks of an atmosphere of repression and intimidation such that it takes real courage to work in applied ethics in Germany and Austria. "Academics should be the first to rally in defence of those whose freedom of expression is restricted, whatever we may think of the content of what is said, or of its 'political correctness'." See "A German attack on applied ethics: A statement by Peter Singer", *Journal of Applied Philosophy* 9, 1, 1992: 85-91.

17. Moreover, the excuse can be made that a certain book "has merely taken a well deserved rest from centre stage for a time". See Bogdan op. cit.: 210. But did anyone judge that a rest was in order before the brouhaha erupted?

18. Cf. an observation made in David Bercuson and Douglas Wertheimer, *A Trust Betrayed: The Keegstra Affair* op. cit.: 132.

19. R.M. Hare, *Moral Thinking: Its Levels, Method and Point* op. cit.: 200. Hare makes the point that there are principles proper to our vocation, and for some these will be fairly stringent though "others would be foolish to aspire to these". This latter remark, I take it, must refer to principles understood as *stringent*, because some commitment to these same principles is surely necessary, if one is to pursue the vocation at all. See Hare, op. cit.: 201.

20. Stephan Thernstrom, Winthrop professor of history at Harvard, accused of being "racially insensitive" by students in 1988, is quoted as saying: "I expected the university to come to my defense....Instead I was left out there by myself, guilty without being proven guilty. I could not even defend myself because the charge of racism or racial insensitivity is ultimately unanswerable." Quoted in Dinesh D'Souza, *Illiberal Education: The Politics of Race and Sex on Campus* New York: Vintage Books, 1992. Thernstrom had read from Southern plantation owners' journals, and quite reasonably pointed out that students need to know what kind of justifications the owners offered. In a particularly unfeeling commentary on the Thernstrom case, Rosa Ehrenreich picks up on John Taylor's words that Thernstrom "found it hard not to imagine the pointing fingers, the whispers", and she adds: "The operative word here is 'imagine'." Does one have to be paranoid, however, to fear for one's reputation and good name when one is charged with being racially insensitive in the campus newspaper? See Rosa Ehrenreich, "What campus radicals?", *Harper's Magazine* December 1991: 57-61.

21. D'Souza, *Illiberal Education*, op. cit.

22. Even an unsympathetic commentator like Susan Crean acknowledges curator Jeanne Cannizzo's good intentions, and makes it clear that she herself does *not* claim that the curator and the organizers condone the white supremacist rhetoric depicted. See Crean's vulgarly entitled "Tak-

ing the missionary position", *This Magazine* 24, 6, 1991: 23-28. Incidentally, Crean asks at the beginning of her article, Why *did* the Royal Ontario Museum impose a white perspective on an exhibition about Africa? The simple answer to this question-begging question, which suggests a sinister motive, is surely that the point of the exhibition was to reveal the white perspective at the time. Crean accuses various defenders of the exhibition of arrogance and insufferable superiority in insisting on the vital distinction between what is displayed and what is endorsed, but manages not to notice her own patronizing dismissal of "the vast majority [who] tend to drift in and out of such presentations; relatively few pay strict attention all the way through" (p. 25). Crean makes much of the fact that clues and warnings can be missed, but she doesn't hesitate to *make up* an incriminating statement which she attributes to Cannizzo, presumably counting on people to be sophisticated enough to distinguish between this "quote" and a real quote (p. 25). Crean castigates the ROM for refusing "to take any criticism whatsoever" (p. 28), which seems to mean refusing to agree that those who falsely accuse you of racism are correct. She finds this especially distressing when objections come "in such number and with such unanimity from the very community whose past you are displaying" (p. 28). Other commentators report that the demonstrations usually drew fewer than forty persons, and that unanimity was *not* to be found. On this, see Robert Fulford, "Into the heart of the matter", *Rotunda* 24, 1, 1991: 19-28. In any case, a *judgment* about racism is not made by counting heads but through reflection and deliberation.

23. It is worth noting that the charge of racism cannot be explained away as the kind of exaggeration which appears during the heat of controversy. Months later, in May 1991, spokespersons for the International Women's Day Coalition in Toronto repeated, as if it were self-evident, the assertion that the exhibition was racist. See "Gender isn't everything—*all* issues are women's issues", *The Globe and Mail* May 14, 1991.

24. The case raises issues which have been very well discussed in John H. Trueman, "Lest we offend: The search for a perfect past", op. cit.: 194-99. As Trueman observes, "real history is often offensive and messy: that's the way it happpened." Robert Fulford, however, seems to believe that when a museum displays an artifact, it is assumed that the object is presented for *admiration*. He should visit the Museum of National Relics in Nicosia, Cyprus, and ask himself if the British gallows on display there is intended to excite admiration. See Fulford, "Into the heart of the matter", op. cit.: 28.

25. Crean, "Taking the missionary position", op. cit.: 25.

26. I can also report that my own then twelve-year-old had no difficulty at all drawing the distinction between what is reported and what is approved.

27. The case was presented on the CTV programme W5 on Sunday, March

10, 1991 in a segment appropriately entitled "Hounded Out", produced by Michael Lavoie. Host Eric Malling introduced the item with the apposite remark that it concerns courage or the lack of it on university campuses. One young black woman interviewed on the programme said that the *title* "Into the heart of Africa" was Cannizzo's "big mistake". Titles, however, can be read in different ways, and we are not obliged to accept the particular interpretation placed on the title by this critic. And if Cannizzo, curator, made a mistake, why was retribution meted out to Cannizzo, teacher? Socrates, of course, has some useful things to say about the way we should deal with people who have made mistakes. See Plato, *Apology* 25D. There is an excellent editorial entitled "The pillorying of a curator" in *The Globe and Mail*, October 20, 1990 which points out the undeniable fact, which many seem anxious to overlook, that "a respected and competent scholar has been driven from the classroom in a crude display of intolerance".

28.  It is worth recalling here that the word "racist" had been spray painted on her house. The threat of bodily harm must have seemed real.

29.  Aristotle, *The Politics* Book 3, ch. 9.

30.  Fulford, "Into the heart of the matter", op. cit.: 26. Jerry Zeidenberg, in an article on the case of Professor Leopold Infeld in the 1950s, reminds us that the Cannizzo affair was not the first time that the University of Toronto failed to defend one of its professors. See "Persecuted professor", *The Globe and Mail* March 16, 1990.

31.  Michael Keefer, "Tensions exist but Maclean's article not acceptable account of developments", *University Affairs* August/September, 1991.

32.  Thelma McCormack, "Politically correct", *CAUT Bulletin* April 1992. She does comment that "administrators are not courageous about cases of academic freedom, and would like them settled quickly and quietly, disguised as something else." But the telling examples are not provided.

33.  Peter Gzowski was speaking with Paddy Stamp, Sexual Harassment Officer, and Rhonda Love, Faculty of Medicine, University of Toronto. Unfortunately, Gzowski did not raise the Cannizzo case, but his very next guest, Robert Fulford, did. He immediately pointed out the tremendous irony involved in the earlier denial of repression in the Canadian academic context.

34.  There were honourable exceptions, of course, such as Ron Blair referred to earlier.

35.  "The right to intellectual freedom: A statement by the Philosophy of Education Society", *Educational Theory* 3, 2, 1953: 185-6.

36.  Thomas Henry Huxley, "Agnosticism", in Alburey Castell, *Selections from the Essays of T.H. Huxley* New York: Appleton-Century-Crofts, 1948: 89

37.  Huxley, "Agnosticism and Christianity", in Castell (ed.), *Selections from the Essays of T.H. Huxley* op. cit.: 92.

38.  See *Time* Oct. 21, 1991. It has been pointed out to me that it is not

unheard of for the police to manufacture the necessary evidence when they "know" the accused is guilty. One would think that anyone with a concern for liberty and justice would be cautious before suggesting that some people just know.

39.   Notwithstanding the absence of corroborating evidence, David Olive was ready to observe that "in the days ahead, we will learn if Mr. Thomas is capable of...coping with the more prosaic task of managing with honour the women who work under his supervision." See *The Globe and Mail* Oct. 13, 1991. I should perhaps make it explicit here that I am NOT claiming, nor am I implying, that the complaints brought against Clarence Thomas were false. Disagreements between people as to whether Hill or Thomas is being truthful are not disagreements about *values* at all.

40.   Huxley, "Agnosticism", op. cit.: 91.

41.   D'Souza, *Illiberal Education* op. cit.: 143.

42.   See also an article entitled "When a child cries wolf", by Timothy Appleby, in *The Globe and Mail* April 18, 1992 for evidence that this is by no means an isolated case. And Marjaleena Repo, "Fairytales of abuse make for nightmares", *The Globe and Mail* July 28, 1992, where Repo draws attention to "the relatively new belief, approaching an unchallengable orthodoxy, that accusations made by a child must be true." Recall here the chilling statement from the University of Michigan with respect to false accusations of racism. In a response to Repo, Bruce Rivers, Executive Director of the Children's Aid Society, and Colin Maloney, Executive Director of the Catholic Children's Aid Society, of Metropolitan Toronto, assert that "the well-being and safety of the child is the children's aid societies' primary concern". Agreed, but not at the expense of justice for all. See *The Globe and Mail* Aug. 1, 1992.

43.   See Bryan Magee, "Conversation with Karl Popper", in Magee's *Modern British Philosophy* Oxford: Oxford University Press, 1971: 90.

44.   See Ray Conlogue, "Quebec diary", *The Globe and Mail* Mar. 4, 1992.

45.   It will come as no surprise that the woman in the painting is *not* smiling. What Shira Spector can or cannot imagine is an uninteresting comment about herself and has nothing to do with art appreciation. Some people have a limited imagination. Incidentally, if Lyn Robichaud is deemed incapable of interpreting the experiences of non-whites, and ought not to paint these subjects at all, how is it that these white critics are capable of knowing that her work is racist, and why do *they* speak for women of colour? For a related matter, see chapter five, fn. 22.

46.   On the matter of absurdity, bear in mind that a government agency in Britain will no longer describe any plants or trees as native or alien, a decision which some have apparently welcomed as a victory against "biological racism".

47.   Sharon Bailin, *Achieving Extraordinary Ends: An Essay on Creativity* Dordrecht: Kluwer Academic Publishers, 1988: 5.

48. E.H. Gombrich, *The Story of Art* 15th ed., Englewood Cliffs, NJ: Prentice-Hall, 1990: 3.
49. I have demonstrated this elsewhere with respect to the phrase "scrambling rats" as it occurs in Paula Fox's *The Slave Dancer*. See my "Bias in stories for children", op. cit.: 100-1.
50. Allan Hutchinson, "Giving smaller voices a chance to be heard", *The Globe and Mail* Apr. 14, 1992.
51. Zemans made this statement in an interview on CBC's Morningside, April 1, 1992.
52. Thomas Hurka, "Should whites write about minorities?", *The Globe and Mail* Dec. 19, 1989. Hurka teaches philosophy at the University of Calgary.
53. Lenore Keeshig-Tobias appeared on CBC's Morningside Apr. 1, 1992, together with Neil Bissoondath, Michael Bliss, Heather Robertson, Patricia Smart and Rudy Wiebe, in conversation with Peter Gzowski. Keeshig-Tobias has discussed related issues in an essay with the self-explanatory title "White lies?", *Saturday Night* Oct. 1990: 67-8. During the Morningside debate, the absurdity in the debate came out clearly in the course of an example designed to illustrate how a white artist was given prominence in a certain art gallery while the work of a local, native artist was confined to a small, backroom. Gzowski inquired as to whether the "white" artist was not in fact a Métis, which led to general confusion and near farce.
54. See his very moving piece "I'm just a 'writer'—that's the voice that matters", *The Globe and Mail* Apr. 4, 1992.
55. "Don't trust the writer, trust the tale." Iris Murdoch, in conversation with Bryan Magee in the series of BBC television programmes which led to Magee's *Men of Ideas* op. cit. Her specific point has to do with not accepting the author's judgment or interpretation of his or her book as final or definitive, but the advice has more general application.
56. *The Globe and Mail* Mar. 28, 1992.

## NOTES FOR CHAPTER FIVE

1. P.T. Geach, "Plato's *Euthyphro*", *The Monist* 50, 3, 1966: 369-82.
2. See *Sexism in Children's Books: Facts, Figures and Guidelines* London: Writers and Readers Publishing Cooperative, 1976.
3. See Greg Sheridan, "Arrogant science threatens to realize a Brave New World", *The Weekend Australian* Feb. 4-5, 1989: 26.
4. Cf. Act 590, Arkansas 1981, "Balanced treatment for creation-science and evolution-science act". Prohibited by District Court injunction, 1982. See also Stephen J. Gould, "Darwinism defined: The difference between fact and theory", *Discover* 8, 1, 1987.
5. Robert Irvine Smith, "Values in history and social studies", in Peter

Tomlinson and Margret Quinton (eds.), *Values Across the Curriculum* London: Falmer Press, 1986: 83.

6. See "The Webber case at Memorial University", *CAUT Bulletin* 26, 4, 1979: 17.

7. Plato, *Phaedo* 74E, in Tredennick, *The Last Days of Socrates*, op. cit. See Alan R. White, *The Philosophy of Mind* New York: Random House, 1967: 25-7.

8. David Layton, "Revaluing science education", in Tomlinson and Quinton (eds.), *Values Across the Curriculum* op. cit.: 170.

9. Cf. Bryan Wilson, "Values in mathematics education", in Tomlinson and Quinton (eds.), *Values Across the Curriculum* op. cit.: 104. And Patrick Wiegand, "Values in Geographical Education", ibid.: 62.

10. Wiegand, op. cit.: 63.

11. *Interim Guidelines for Evaluation of Instructional Material with Respect to Social Content* Sacramento: California State Department of Education, 1981: 7. In the *Standards for Evaluation of Instructional Materials with Respect to Social Content* which superseded the *Interim Guidelines* in 1986, the explanatory note has been deleted but the guideline remains the same (except that "such portrayal" has become "portrayals").

12. *Interim Guidelines* op. cit.: 1. In the 1986 *Standards*, op. cit.: 1, reference to the United States and to other contemporary cultures has been deleted, and the admonition, now restricted to the *teacher's* edition, reads:"...although a particular attitude toward women or a minority group was prevalent during a certain period of history, that attitude has changed or is in the process of change." This obviously does not circumvent the difficulties. Is this attitude changing everywhere? Will the literature in the curriculum not include material dealing with other cultures which, at the present time, do *not* show evidence of moving in the direction of equality for women and other groups? Will not such omissions constitute, by implication, an adverse reflection on them? Are schools to pretend that all cultures are moving ahead progressively on these fronts? Why *not* criticize those cultures which do not share these basic values?

13. David Bridges, "So truth be in the field", in David Hicks and Charles Townley (eds.), *Teaching World Studies* London: Longman, 1982: 47.

14. *Interim Guidelines* op. cit.: 1. Cf. Bertrand Russell, "On keeping a wide horizon", in *Russell* 33-34, 1979: 5-11.

15. *Interim Guidelines* op. cit.: 8. This particular line does not appear in the 1986 *Standards*, but it remains a requirement that minority persons be depicted in the same range of socioeconomic settings as persons of the majority group. The qualification "when accurate" is not appended. See *Standards* op. cit.: 3.

16. An infamous case is the wholly unwarranted criticism of *The Slave Dancer* by Paula Fox. See my discussion in "Bias in stories for children: Black marks for authors", op. cit.: 99-108.

17.　One somewhat surprising example is that of Russell in his "Can men be rational?", in Bertrand Russell, *Sceptical Essays* op. cit.: 51. Here Russell suggests that our objective reports invariably betray our biases. In many other places, however, Russell maintains that critical reflection can free us from what he sometimes calls the prison of prejudice. Cf. Russell, *The Problems of Philosophy* London: Oxford University Press, 1973: 91. (Originally published, 1912.)

18.　Layton, "Revaluing science education", op. cit.: 162-3. Layton draws on the discussion of this case in Robert Gilpin, *American Scientists and Nuclear Weapons Policy* Princeton: Princeton University Press, 1962.

19.　In addressing bias effectively, we do need to know what biases people have or may have. In being so informed or persuaded, however, we may ourselves become biased against such persons and fail to give their ideas serious consideration. Joseph Tussman discusses this dilemma and recognizes that "interpretive aid" may take our attention away from *what* is said and turn it towards *who* said it. Tussman, however, shrugs this off with the thought that life is short and the comforting suggestion that attention to the person is a "legitimate short-cut". Surely, however, the dilemma points up the need for students and teachers to learn the difference between being intelligently alert and prejudiced. Such information can help us to make an intelligent judgment *if* we do not conclude that it makes judgment redundant. We have seen earlier in chapter four how tempting it can be to slide over the crucial matter of evidence in our anxiety to convict or dismiss. See Tussman, op. cit.: 112-3.

20.　See *Guidelines For Selecting Bias-Free Textbooks and Storybooks* New York: Council on Interracial Books for Children, 1980. I have found that my own students are incredulous when I tell them that one criterion, seriously advanced, for detecting bias is the copyright date. (In principle, however, this is no different than "judging" a book on the basis of the author's skin colour or racial/ethnic background. Both moves ignore the book itself.) See p. 26 of these guidelines. They also contain the outrageous assessment of Paula Fox's *The Slave Dancer* mentioned in fn. 16 above.

21.　I have discussed aspects of this claim as it concerns men teaching courses in women's studies in my *In Defence of Open-mindedness* Montreal: McGill-Queen's, 1985, op. cit.: ch. 5. See also related matters in chapter four.

22.　See John Howard Griffin, *Black Like Me* New York: Signet Books, 1960. What should we say of whites who have themselves been slaves? R.M. Hare begins a paper on slavery with the words: "Nearly everybody would agree that slavery is wrong; and I can say this with greater feeling than most, having in a manner of speaking *been* a slave." Hare was in Japanese prison camps during the Second World War, and worked on the Burma railway "in conditions not *at the time* distinguishable from slavery". See R.M. Hare, "What is wrong with slavery?", *Philosophy and Public Affairs*

8, 2, 1979: 103-21. Women who are forced into prostitution would be another group who could claim first-hand acquaintance with conditions not distinguishable from slavery.

23. Gilpin, op. cit.: 327. Gilpin follows the view of James Conant, *Modern Science and Modern Man* New York: Doubleday, 1952.

24. See Kai Neilsen, "The very idea of a religious education", *Journal of Education* (Nova Scotia) 2, 2, 1974-5: 36-8. Similar remarks appear in Bertrand and Dora Russell, *Prospects of Industrial Civilization* New York: Century Co., 1923: 255.

25. Godfrey L. Brandt, *The Realization of Anti-racist Teaching* London: Falmer Press, 1986: 38.

26. For an excellent discussion of this point, see John H. Trueman, "Lest we offend: The search for a perfect past", op. cit.: 194-9. I discuss some related matters in "What can philosophy say to teachers?", in William Hare (ed.), *Reason in Teaching and Education* op. cit. The case at Harvard involving Professor Stephan Thernstrom, mentioned in chapter four, fn. 20, illustrates how the criterion of truth and accuracy in the historical record is nowadays on shaky ground.

27. Bertrand Russell, "The place of science in a liberal education", in *Mysticism and Logic* Harmondsworth: Penguin Books, 1953: 38-49. (Essay originally published, 1913.)

28. Richard Pring, "Aims, problems and curriculum contexts", in Tomlinson and Quinton (eds.), *Values Across the Curriculum* op. cit.: 107.

29. Bernard Crick, "On bias", *Teaching Politics* 1, 1, 1972: 3-12.

30. See Everett Dean Martin, *The Meaning of a Liberal Education* New York: W.W. Norton, 1926, ch. 3.

31. See Edgar H. Henderson, "Toward a definition of propaganda", *Journal of Social Psychology* 18, 1943: 71-87.

## NOTES FOR CHAPTER SIX

1. See my *Open-mindedness and Education* op. cit.: 9.

2. Plato, *Crito* 46B. Cf. Plato, *Gorgias* 506.

3. Nicholas Rescher, *Ethical Idealism* Berkeley: University of California Press, 1987: 133.

4. Cf. John Passmore, "On teaching to be critical", in R.S. Peters (ed.), *The Concept of Education* op. cit. Passmore comments on attempts to confine critical thinking to certain "approved" topics and areas. See especially p. 205.

5. Cf. John Dewey, *Democracy and Education* op. cit.: 175.

6. Thomas Nagel, *What Does It All Mean?* New York: Oxford University Press, 1987: 69.

7. Homer, *The Odyssey* Harmondsworth: Penguin Books, 1983. Trans. E. V. Rieu. See Book 12.

8.   Richard W. Paul (with A.J.A. Binker), "Glossary: An educator's guide to critical thinking terms and concepts", in Richard Paul, *Critical Thinking: What Every Person Needs to Survive In a Rapidly Changing World* Sonoma State University: Centre for Critical Thinking and Moral Critique, 1990: 540-71.

9.   See John Dewey, *How We Think* op. cit.: 30-1. And Bertrand Russell, *Principles of Social Reconstruction* op. cit.: 152.

10.  Robert H. Ennis, "A taxonomy of critical thinking dispositions", in Joan Boykoff Baron and Robert J. Sternberg (eds.), *Teaching Thinking Skills: Theory and Practice* New York: W.H. Freeman, 1987: 12.

11.  Strike, Haller and Soltis present a challenging case where a teacher is drawn further and further into a discussion in class about the morality of sexual relations with children and the limits of tolerance with respect to free speech in the classroom are pressed. See Kenneth A. Strike et al., *The Ethics of School Administration* New York: Teachers College Press, 1988: 23-7.

12.  Bertrand Russell, "An Outline of Intellectual Rubbish", in *Unpopular Essays* op. cit.: 126.

13.  Nathaniel Ward, "Against toleration", in Norman Cousins (ed.), *Great American Essays* New York: Dell Publishing, 1967: 185-9. Ward was writing in pre-revolutionary America.

14.  Jay Newman, *Foundations of Religious Tolerance* Toronto: University of Toronto Press, 1982: 8.

15.  T.H. Huxley, *Science and Christian Tradition* New York: D. Appleton and Company, 1898, ch. 11.

16.  Peter Gardner, "Religious upbringing and the liberal ideal of religious autonomy", *Journal of Philosophy of Education* 22, 1, 1988: 89-105. Gardner's mistake has been exposed in T.H. McLaughlin, "Peter Gardner on religious upbringing and the liberal ideal of religious autonomy", in *Journal of Philosophy of Education* 24, 1, 1990: 107-25. The point was noted by Robert Louis Stevenson in his remark: "To state one argument is not necessarily to be deaf to all others." See, "An apology for idlers", reprinted in Bernard Johnston (ed.), *Issues in Education: An Anthology of Controversy* Boston: Houghton Mifflin, 1964: 356-62.

17.  David Suzuki, "Science and Society", *The Canadian Encyclopaedia* Vol. 3, 1985: 1655-8. See also Avrum Stroll, "Scepticism and religious toleration", *History of Philosophy Quarterly* 5, 3, 1988: 221-32. Stroll speaks of "the sceptical stance of open-mindedness".

18.  Bertrand Russell, *Philosophy* New York: W.W. Norton and Company, 1927.

19.  Nelson Goodman, *The Languages of Art* Indianapolis: Bobbs-Merrill, 1968.

20.  See Norman Malcolm, "Knowledge and belief", *Mind* 51, 1952: 178-89.

21.  Alan R. White, "On Claiming to Know", *Philosophical Review* 66, 1957: 180-92.

22. John Chadwick, *The Decipherment of Linear B* Harmondsworth: Penguin Books, 1961.

23. Gilbert Harmon presents one version of this idea in his *Thought* Princeton: Princeton University Press, 1973: 148.

24. G.K. Chesterton, *Orthodoxy* New York: John Lane Company, 1909: 58.

25. Descartes, *Discourse on Method Book 1*. See René Descartes, *Discourse on Method and Meditations on First Philosophy* (trans. Donald A. Cress) Indianapolis: Hackett Publishing Company, 1981. (Originally published, 1637.)

26. Irving Thalberg, "Visceral racism", *The Monist* 56, 4, 1972: 43-63.

27. See Frederick Schauer, *Free Speech: A Philosophical Enquiry* Cambridge: Cambridge University Press, 1982.

28. The legal situation in Canada was changing rapidly in the early 1990s. In a decision handed down in December 1990, the Supreme Court of Canada, by a vote of 4-3, determined that Section 319 of the Criminal Code which deals with the promotion of hatred and discrimination *is* constitutional. The Court upheld the conviction of Jim Keegstra, the former Alberta teacher. On the other hand, a further 4-3 Supreme Court ruling in August 1992 held that Section 181 of the Criminal Code, which prohibits the wilful publication of "false news" that the publisher knows to be false and that harms the public interest, placed *unjustifiable* limits on the guarantee of free speech in the Charter of Rights and Freedoms. The Court overturned the conviction of Ernst Zundel who had published a pamphlet entitled *Did Six Million Die?*

29. Gabriel Weiman and Conrad Winn, *Hate On Trial* Oakville: Mosaic Press, 1986. It is worth noting that the authors assume that answers to the question "Would you say that Jews have too much power in Canada?" allow one to measure the respondent's anti-semitism. For my part, I believe that these short cuts are problematic and controversial. But if they are right, their own comment that Anglo-Scottish Canadians have a special place in the corporate boardrooms of the nation represents the kind of thinking they should seek to *discourage*. See p. 112.

30. Joel Feinberg, *Social Philosophy* Englewood Cliffs, NJ: Prentice-Hall, 1973.

31. See *Maclean's* Dec. 25, 1978: 44.

32. Plato, *Apology* 28B.

33. H.J. McCloskey, "Limits to freedom of expression", *Journal of Value Inquiry* 16, 1982: 47-58.

34. See John Dixon, "The politics of opinion", *The Canadian Forum* 66, April 1986: 7-10.

## NOTES FOR CHAPTER SEVEN

1. David Hume, *An Enquiry Concerning the Principles of Morals* in Alasdair MacIntyre (ed.), *Hume's Ethical Writings* op. cit.: 66. I shall not be concerned here with subtle differences among the concepts caring, empathy, sympathy, fellow-feeling and so on, since the general points I wish to make do not depend upon any such distinctions.

2. See Alan R. White, *The Philosophy of Mind* op. cit.: 79-82.

3. On pity, see Eamonn Callan, "The moral status of pity", *Canadian Journal of Philosophy* 18, 1, 1988: 1-12.

4. Contrast Marcus Aurelius. See A.S.L. Farquharson (ed. and trans.), *The Meditations of the Emperor Marcus Antoninus* Oxford: Clarendon Press, 1944: 223. For an echo of this, see Nel Noddings, *Caring: A Feminine Approach to Ethics and Moral Education* Berkeley: University of California Press, 1984: 19-20.

5. Noddings, op. cit.: 51-8.

6. Noddings, op. cit.: 89, 91, 195 et passim. Also Nel Noddings, "Believing and disbelieving persons: Response to Krolikowski", in Robert E. Roemer (ed.), *Philosophy of Education: 1983* Normal, Ill. : Illinois State University, 1984: 275-8.

7. Noddings, *Caring*, op. cit.: 176 et passim.

8. Cf. Robin Barrow, *Understanding Skills: Thinking, Feeling, and Caring* op. cit.: 128.

9. T.W. Rolleston (trans.), *The Teaching of Epictetus* London: Walter Scott, 1893: 89.

10. Op. cit.: 97.

11. Adam Smith, *The Theory of Moral Sentiments*, reprinted in L.A.Selby-Bigge (ed.), *British Moralists* Indianapolis: Bobbs-Merrill, 1964: 278. (Originally published, 1759.)

12. Noddings, *Caring* op. cit.: 8.

13. Op. cit.: 28.

14. Carol Gilligan, *In A Different Voice: Psychological Theory and Women's Development* Cambridge: Harvard University Press, 1982, ch. 2.

15. Noddings, *Caring* op. cit.: 20.

16 Gilligan, op. cit.: 32.

17. Noddings speaks frequently of "an ethic of caring".

18. Cf. Israel Scheffler, *In Praise of the Cognitive Emotions* New York: Routledge, 1991: 98.

19. Noddings, *Caring* op. cit.: 1-2.

20. Op. cit.: 5, 25, 37.

21. Op. cit.: 56.

22. Op. cit.: 5. Universalizability is the principle which holds that if we form a moral view of a certain action done by a particular person, then we must take the same view of a similar action performed by another person, including ourselves, in similar circumstances.

23. R.M.Hare, "Language and moral education", in Glenn Langford and D.J.O'Connor (eds.), *New Essays in the Philosophy of Education* London: Routledge and Kegan Paul, 1973: 160.

24. Noddings, *Caring* op. cit.: 30.

25. Nicholas Rescher, *Unselfishness* op. cit.: 8.

26. I refer, in particular, to the Birmingham Six, the Guildford Four, and the Maguire family.

27. Val Mulkerns, "The World Outside", in Malcolm Ross and John Stevens (eds.), *Man and His World* Toronto: J.M. Dent and Sons, 1961: 272-80.

28. This story also illustrates R.S. Peters' wise remark about the value of humour in allowing teacher and student to "step out of the shadows of self-reference cast by age, sex and position". The students are willing to laugh with the teacher when they detect the kind of caring in question. See Peters, *Authority, Responsibility and Education* London: George Allen and Unwin, 1973: 101.

29. Hortense Calisher, "A Wreath for Miss Totten", in Hortense Calisher, *In the Absence of Angels* Boston: Little, Brown and Company, 1951: 78-92.

30. John Dewey, *Democracy and Education* op. cit.: 170. One is reminded, too, of John Wisdom's anecdote about Mr. Flood, the Dublin zookeeper, who attributed his success in breeding cubs to understanding lions, which understanding consisted in knowing that every lion is different. See John Wisdom, *Paradox and Discovery* Berkeley: University of California Press, 1970: 138.

31. Richard Yates, "Doctor Jack O'Lantern", in Richard Yates, *Eleven Kinds of Loneliness* Westport, Conn.: Greenwood Press, 1962: 3-20. (Story originally published in 1952.)

32. Op. cit: 9.

33. On displaying anger, see Andrew Oldenquist, "'Indoctrination' and societal suicide", *The Public Interest* 63, 1981: 87.

34. For related remarks, see Harvey Siegel, "Teaching, reasoning, and Dostoyevsky's *The Brothers Karamazov*", in Philip Jackson and Sophie Haroutounian-Gordon (eds.), *From Socrates to Software: The Teacher as Text and the Text as Teacher* 89th Yearbook, NSSE Chicago: University of Chicago Press, 1989: 115-34.

35. Bertrand Russell, *Power: A New Social Analysis* op. cit.: 304.

36. Cf. my "The roles of teacher and critic", *Journal of General Education* 22, 1, 1970: 43.

37. Noddings, *Caring* op. cit.: 193-6.

38. Op. cit.: 195

39. R.M. Hare, "A school for philosophers", *Ratio* 2, 1959-60: 107-20.

40. Noddings, "Believing and disbelieving persons: Response to Krolikowski", op. cit.: 277. Also, Noddings, *Caring* op. cit.: 178.

41. For a recognition of this point, see the paper cited in fn. 33: "Because morality is as much a matter of emotion and feeling as a matter of

rationality and reasoning, it is an error to think that one should 'play it cool' and never get excited about moral issues in front of children....teachers, parents and juvenile authorities are likely to mislead themselves about morality, as much as they do young people, when they attempt to be unemotional, neutral, and 'objective' when confronted with real issues involving social morality." Oldenquist, "'Indoctrination' and societal suicide", op. cit.: 87-8.

42. Mike Rose discusses the case of a student at UCLA who "had incorporated stretches of old encyclopaedia prose into her paper and had quoted only some of it." Rose offers a number of excuses and explanations for this behaviour. The student's father had discouraged her from expressing her own opinion; she thought she was supposed "to use other people" and was unsure "how to weave quotations in with her own prose"; she was "adrift in a set of conventions she didn't fully understand"; her previous teachers were probably pleased that she had gone to expert sources. And so on. (Notice that in connection with the latter suggestion, Rose clearly does not *know* this, and it is bound to seem that he is inventing a defence.) Rose asserts somewhat testily that he is not asking for soft-heartedness, and comes down rather hard on the professor who accused this student of plagiarism for levelling a moral judgment. Certainly, the factors mentioned by Rose need to be taken into account *where they can be ascertained*. But it is vital to note that we are not dealing here with mere *conventions*. Intellectual honesty is a fundamental principle in academic work, and the professor is fully entitled to discuss this issue in moral terms. It is difficult, too, to believe that any university student is *completely* unaware that copying word for word from a book without appropriate quotation marks is unacceptable. What value can she think there is in this? Whatever may explain the conduct, the paper is worthless as an indicator of the student's independent ability. If her previous teachers have not brought these matters to the student's attention, it is all the more important that someone do this now. See Mike Rose, *Lives on the Boundary* New York: The Free Press, 1989.

43. Noddings, *Caring* op. cit.: 178.

44. Noddings, *Caring* op. cit.: 176.

45. References can be found in my paper, "Teaching: Nature, norm and numbers", in Evelina Miranda and Romulo Magsino (eds.), *Teaching, Schools and Society* London: Falmer, 1990: 195-213.

46. Gilbert Ryle, "Teaching and training", in R.S.Peters (ed.), *The Concept of Education* op. cit.: 119.

## NOTES FOR CHAPTER EIGHT

1. See "30 leading Canadians were asked, 'What are the qualities of a good teacher in the 1990s?'", *Education Today* 3, 4, 1991: 9-26.

2. John Dewey, *How We Think* op. cit.: 32.

3. Bertrand Russell, "The functions of a teacher", in *Unpopular Essays* op. cit.: 154.

4. Gilbert Highet, *The Immortal Profession* op. cit.: 47. For further comments, see Gilbert Highet, *The Art of Teaching* London: Methuen, 1951.

5. Edward S. Hickcox, "Ideas for performance appraisal: Breaking the mold", *Canadian School Executive* 10, 3, 1990: 11-3.

6. An example might be Hilda Neatby, *A Temperate Dispute* Toronto: Clarke, Irwin, 1954. See especially the first essay.

7. For obvious reasons, this "interview" did not make it to air on the regular programme, but was broadcast in an "All-time favourites" segment of a tenth anniversary special. One is reminded of that wonderful line, recalled by Barzun, about the teacher who yawned during his own lecture: "The professor confirms our judgment but usurps our prerogative." See Jacques Barzun, *Teacher In America* Boston: Little, Brown, 1946: 31. Incidentally, "Quirks and Quarks" also illustrates how quickly we recognize genuine enthusiasm when we encounter it. It comes through quite unmistakably as the scientists talk about the projects they have worked on.

8. F.H. Page, "A.N. Whitehead: A pupil's tribute", *Dalhousie Review* 28, 1, 1948: 71-80. Francis Hilton Page (1905-1989) taught philosophy at Dalhousie University for 56 years. In the late 1920s he was a graduate student at Harvard University and attended Whitehead's class.

9. See A.N. Whitehead, *The Aims of Education*, op. cit., especially perhaps ch. 3 on "The rhythmic claims of freedom and discipline". (Originally published, 1923.)

10. A.N. Whitehead, "Harvard: The future", in A.H. Johnson (ed.), *Whitehead's American Essays in Social Philosophy* Connecticut: Greenwood Press, 1959: 168-9.

11. See, for example, Thomas L. Good and Jere Brophy, *Looking in Classrooms* 3rd ed. New York: Harper and Row, 1984: 340-2. And N.L. Gage and David C. Berliner, *Educational Psychology* Chicago: Rand McNally, 1975: 518-21.

12. The most famous example surely is J.E. Ware, Jr., "The Doctor Fox effect: A study of lecture effectiveness and ratings of instruction". Unpublished doctoral dissertation, Southern Illinois University at Carbondale, Ill.

13. I think here of a certain television programme dealing with history and culture, where the host clearly is enthusiastic about the subject but, having been coached presumably in gesture, voice inflection and the like, makes every comment with an intensity and fervour which is ultimately overwhelming, tiring, and self-defeating. The genuineness is compromised by the evident deliberateness. On the matter of how the ritualistic employment of certain skills can be irritating and disturbing, see Robin Barrow, *Understanding Skills: Thinking, Feeling, and Caring* op. cit.: 127.

14. See Robin Barrow, "Skill talk", *Journal of Philosophy of Education* 21, 2, 1987: 187-95.

15. David Solway, *Education Lost: Reflections on Contemporary Pedagogical Practice* op. cit.: 8. See also Robin Barrow, "Teacher education: theory and practice", *British Journal of Educational Studies* 38, 4, 1990: 308-18, especially the section on 'personal characteristics', p. 312.

16. Some readers may have seen the 1990 PBS programme "Schools That Work" in the Learning in America series with Roger Mudd, and will recall the segment on the Northview Elementary School in Manhattan, Kansas. No one I have discussed this with failed to notice the infectious enthusiasm of the teachers.

17. We are criticized for failing to show enthusiasm where "show" has the sense of pretence. The common-sense justification for this kind of deception, which may or may not actually deceive, is to avoid unnecessarily hurting someone else's feelings. See Sissela Bok, *Lying: Moral Choice in Public and Private Life* New York: Vintage Books, 1979, ch. 5.

18. For example, Kennedy's remark in his Inaugural address: "Ask not what your country can do for you; ask what you can do for your country."

19. If we learn that someone is friendly, we are not inclined to ask, to whom? But if someone is said to be enthusiastic, it is natural to inquire, about what?

20. See John Dewey, *How We Think* op. cit.: 31. And John Dewey, *Democracy and Education* op. cit.: 176.

21. Jay Newman, *Fanatics and Hypocrites* Buffalo: Prometheus Books, 1986.

22. Ralph Waldo Emerson, "Circles", in Reginald L. Cook, *Ralph Waldo Emerson: Selected Prose and Poetry* New York: Holt, Rinehart and Winston, 1969: 120. (Originally published, 1841.)

23. Kevin Ryan and James M. Cooper, *Those Who Can, Teach* 4th ed. Boston: Houghton Mifflin, 1984: 316.

24. Ineliminable, it would seem, from educational discourse. In 1992, the Nova Scotia Teachers' Union adopted a resolution that cooperation, not competition, be fostered in visual arts programmes in elementary schools. Why not a judicious balance of the two?

25. Joseph Tussman, *Government and the Mind* op. cit.: 165.

26. N.L. Gage and David C. Berliner, *Educational Psychology* Chicago: Rand McNally, 1975: 518-21. The reference is to Ware's much discussed work on the so-called "Doctor Fox effect", (see fn. 12 above). Perhaps in keeping with the "salesman" image, Ware spoke of enthusiasm as SE (seduction-expressiveness). See also Frederick A. Aldrich, "Commitment is catching", in Edward F. Sheffield (ed.), *Teaching in the Universities* Montreal: McGill-Queen's, 1974: 39-42. The metaphor of teaching as selling turns up with surprising frequency and may seem innocuous, but it contributes subtly to an undermining of the ideals of teaching.

27. Mary Warnock, "The neutral teacher", in William Hare and John P. Portelli (eds.), *Philosophy of Education: Introductory Readings* op. cit.: 185.

28. Bertrand and Dora Russell, *The Prospects of Industrial Civilization* op. cit.: 255.

29. I have addressed this point in my talk on Russell on the tape *Twentieth Century Philosophers of Education* ed. William Hare, Halifax: Dalhousie University, 1990.

30. Russell, *The Prospects of Industrial Civilization* op. cit.: 255.

31. W.H. Kilpatrick, *Philosophy of Education* New York: Macmillan, 1951: 311.

32. L. Susan Stebbing, *Thinking to Some Purpose* Harmondsworth: Penguin Books, 1939: 243-4. Stebbing makes a comment about enthusiasm which has a bearing on the point made by Huxley (see earlier chapter four) on the distinction between faith and knowledge. She writes: "The danger [with enthusiasm] arises from the feeling that the passionateness of a belief provides any guarantee of its truth." Stebbing, op. cit.: 40.

33. Richard Yates, "Doctor Jack-O'-Lantern", in Bernard Johnston (ed.), *The Literature of Learning* op. cit.: 235. See also the discussion of this story in chapter seven.

34. For more on these issues, see Robin Barrow, "Teacher judgement and teacher effectiveness", *Journal of Educational Thought* 18, 2, 1984: 76-83.

35. Victor E. Mastin, "Teacher enthusiasm", *Journal of Educational Research* 56, 7, 1963: 385-6. Mastin reported that 77% of the more than 500 students did better on a multiple-choice test of material presented enthusiastically compared with a similar test on the indifferently taught lesson.

36. William D. Coats and Uldis Smidgens, "Audience recall as a function of speaker dynamism", *Journal of Educational Psychology* 57: 189-91.

37. J.E. Ware, "The Doctor Fox effect", op. cit. Ware's results also seemed to cast doubt on the validity of student assessments of teaching, and this implication was a spur to further research which tried to manipulate the variables more carefully.

38. P.C. Abrami, L. Leventhal, and R.P. Perry, "Educational seduction", *Review of Educational Research* 52: 446-64.

39. His comment "There's a bunch of stuff like that" is aggravatingly smug.

40. Barak Rosenshine, "Enthusiastic teaching: A research review", *School Review* 78, 4, 1970: 506.

41. No one has written more effectively about these matters than R.S. Peters. See his *Ethics and Education* op. cit.: 31. Peters acknowledges here his indebtedness to Whitehead.

42. John Dewey, *Experience and Education* op. cit.: 48.

43. Arthur Bestor, *The Restoration of Learning* New York: Alfred A. Knopf, 1955: 206. When these reports became public, there was a good deal of discussion in the media and apparent confirmation that such views enjoyed wide circulation, though there were equally emphatic denials from professionals.

44. Michael Hutchinson and Christopher Young, *Educating the Intelligent* Harmondsworth: Penguin Books, 1969: 105.

45. David Solway, *Education Lost* op. cit.: 29.
46. John Wilson, "Making subjects interesting", *Journal of Philosophy of Education* 21, 2, 1987: 215-22. Surprisingly, Wilson does not point out that a very similar observation was made by Dewey: "When things have to be made interesting it is because interest itself is wanting. Moreover the phrase is a misnomer. The thing, the object is no more interesting than it was before." See "Interest in relation to training of the will", in Archambault (ed.), op. cit.: 267. (Originally published in National Herbart Society, *Second Supplement to the Herbart Year Book for 1895*, 1896.)

# NOTES FOR CHAPTER NINE

1. David Hume, *An Enquiry Concerning the Principles of Morals*. Reprinted in Alasdair MacIntyre (ed.), *Hume's Ethical Writings* op. cit.: 85.
2. Immanuel Kant, *Critique of Pure Reason*. Reprinted in Arnulf Zweig (ed.), *The Essential Kant* New York: Mentor, 1970: 150. (Originally published, 1781.) I discuss this remark and other aspects of judgment in my paper "The teaching of judgment", *British Journal of Educational Studies* 19, 3, 1971: 243-9.
3. To use one's judgment *is* to critically evaluate the available data, reasons, etc. It is not just to guess. Conversely, to think critically *is* to judge the force of certain considerations. It is not just to offer one's opinion.
4. See Harvey Siegel, "The role of reasons in (science) education", in William Hare (ed.), *Reason in Teaching and Education* op. cit.: 6.
5. Robin Barrow's remark that critical thinking implies "thinking of quality" deserves amplification. See his *Understanding Skills* op. cit.: 80. As John Passmore points out, what once had to be worked out by the exercise of critical thought is now reduced to routine. See his "On teaching to be critical", in Peters (ed.), *The Concept of Education* op. cit.: 202. R.S. Peters observes that if someone fails in the elementary applications of rules, we might think him or her a fool, but we would not praise such a person particularly nor ascribe judgment if he or she were successful. See his "Michael Oakeshott's philosophy of education", in Preston King and B.C. Parekh (eds.), *Politics and Experience: Essays presented to Michael Oakeshott* London: Cambridge University Press, 1968: 55.
6. See "Distasteful dispute may be board's downfall", *The Globe and Mail* May 24, 1991. People are not fond of admitting that they lack judgment, but they will do so to avoid a more serious charge.
7. I do not wish to deny that there are any imaginable circumstances when an exception might be justified. But it is also normally obvious when this possibility does not arise.
8. The best discussion on the general nature of judgment I am familiar with is in Thomas F. Green, *The Activities of Teaching* New York: McGraw-

Hill, 1971: 173-92. Dewey also has much that is interesting and useful to say about judgment in various places, especially *How We Think* 2nd. ed. ch. 8, "The place of judgment in reflective activity", in Jo Ann Boydston (ed.), *John Dewey: The Later Works, 1925-1953*, Vol. 8: 1933, op. cit.: 210-20. There is also his short article on judgment in *The Cyclopaedia of Education*, reprinted in Jo Ann Boydston (ed.), *John Dewey: The Middle Works, 1899-1924*, Vol. 7: 1912-14 Carbondale: Southern Illinois University Press, 1979: 262-4. In the latter work, Dewey defines judgment as "the act (or the power) of weighing facts or evidence, in order to reach a conclusion or decision".

9. Immanuel Kant, *Thoughts on Education*, extracts reprinted in Steven M. Cahn, *The Philosophical Foundations of Education* op. cit.: 189.

10. I do not, however, mean to suggest that the point about the concept of teaching is superficial. The idea we have of teaching influences what we do as teachers, and it is potentially damaging to believe that judgment cannot be taught. See my "Teaching: Nature, norm and numbers", in Evelina Miranda and Romulo Magsino (eds.), *Teaching, Schools and Society* op. cit.: 195-213.

11. R.S. Peters, "Michael Oakeshott's philosophy of education", op. cit.: 56. Theodore Sizer has some excellent remarks about the importance of coaching in the development of judgment in *Horace's Compromise* op. cit.: 191-4

12. Dewey, *How We Think*, in Boydston (ed.), *John Dewey: The Later Works* Vol. 8, op. cit.: 210.

13. Dewey, *How we Think*, in Boydston (ed.), op. cit.: 211.

14. Aristotle, *The Nichomachean Ethics* London: William Heinemann Ltd., 1968, Book 1, ch. 3. (Trans. H. Rackham.)

15. John Dewey, *How We Think*, in Boydston (ed.), op. cit.: 163.

16. Dewey, op. cit.: 163.

17. E.D. Hirsch, Jr., *Cultural Literacy: What Every American Needs to Know* New York: Vintage Books, 1988: 132. It is true that Hirsch points out that Dewey is often unfairly blamed for what his followers have done with his ideas. Nevertheless Hirsch himself leaves the impression in various places that Dewey disdained information. See, for example, Hirsch, op. cit.: xvii.

18. John Passmore, "On teaching to be critical", in R.S. Peters (ed.), *The Concept of Education* op. cit.: 202.

19. Bertrand Russell, "The functions of a teacher", in *Unpopular Essays* op. cit.: 147.

20. A.N. Whitehead, *The Aims of Education* op. cit.: 13. R.S. Peters does not do the remark justice in his brief comment on it in "Education as initiation". See R.D. Archambault (ed.), *Philosophical Analysis and Education* London: Routledge and Kegan Paul, 1965: 104.

21. Whitehead, *The Aims of Education* op. cit.: 16.

22. Cf. Confucius: "Learning without thought is labour lost; thought without learning is perilous."
23. Cf. Richard Rorty, "The opening of American minds", *Harper's Magazine* July 1989: 18-22.
24. Russell, "The functions of a teacher", op. cit.: 150. Cf. Dewey, *How We Think* in Boydston (ed.), op. cit.: 159.
25. Cf. John McPeck, *Critical Thinking And Education* Oxford: Martin Robertson, 1981: 160.
26. See my *In Defence Of Open-mindedness* op. cit. Also my review of McPeck's *Critical Thinking and Education* in *Canadian Journal of Education* 7, 4, 1982: 107-10.
27. R.M. Hare, "Language and moral education", in Glenn Langford and D.J. O'Connor (eds.), *New Essays in the Philosophy of Education* London: Routledge and Kegan Paul, 1973: 157.
28. See L.R. Perry, "Commonsense thought, knowledge and judgement and their importance for education", *British Journal of Educational Studies* 13, 2, 1965: 125-38.
29. Hugh Petrie is overly concerned, I believe, about the notion of "applying" knowledge which he thinks is fundamentally flawed. But application need not imply, as he supposes, a mechanical or routine performance. Applied philosophy or mathematics cannot just be cranked out. See his "Knowledge, practice, and judgment", *Educational Foundations* 6, 1, 1992: 35-48.
30. The fact that such classes need to be designated and required at all is itself revealing.
31. Maria Tapp, "An interview with Stephen Toulmin", in *Liberal Education* 73, 1, 1987: 4-9.
32. I strongly suspect that propaganda is usurping the place of inquiry here.
33. Cf. Dewey: "'Is this right?' comes to mean 'Will this answer or this process satisfy the teacher?'. " See *How We Think* in Boydston (ed.), op. cit.: 161.
34. R.F. Dearden, "Instruction and learning by discovery", in R.S. Peters (ed.), *The Concept of Education* op. cit.: 144.
35. Parents and students are handicapped here by the schools' reluctance to publish the qualifications of teachers.
36. Which is not to say that teachers are not to be expected to make the effort to explain and justify their assessment; only that students must also make the effort to grasp what their teachers' comments mean.
37. I know of high schools which offer courses at different levels but which simply total the students' *raw scores*, whatever level of difficulty the student's course load may have involved, when determining which students should be recommended for university entrance scholarships. This allows the school officials to dodge the difficult matter of judgment, and not surprisingly some students opt for less challenging courses than they are capable of tackling where their mark will be higher. Where external examinations have been replaced by school assessment, this practice is sheer dereliction of duty.

38. "It is equally unreasonable to accept merely probable conclusions from a mathematician and to demand strict demonstrations from an orator." *Nichomachean Ethics* Book 1, ch. 3.

39. See earlier chapter five on impartiality.

40. Plato, *Theaetetus* 170A, reprinted in F.M. Cornford, *Plato's Theory of Knowledge* London: Routledge and Kegan Paul, 1960. See p. 77.

41. Plato, *Theaetetus* 161E.

42. John Dewey, *Democracy and Education* op. cit.: 160.

43. Byron G. Massialas and Jack Zevin, *Teaching Creatively: Learning Through Discovery*, Malabar: Robert E. Krieger Publishing Co., 1983: 235.

44. John Dewey, *Experience and Education* op. cit.: 71. See also his comments in "Progressive education and the science of education", in Archambault (ed.), op. cit.: 179: "The teacher, as the member of the group having riper and fuller experience...has not only the right but the duty to suggest lines of activity."

45. A caricature, of course, but such views are not uncommon in educational theory. They appear quite blatantly in the writings of the late John Holt.

46. On these points, see John Dewey, *The Child and the Curriculum* Chicago: University of Chicago Press ,1956. (Originally published, 1902.)

47. John Dewey, *Experience and Education* op. cit.: 58.

48. For example, Andrew Oldenquist, "Indoctrination and societal suicide", op. cit.: 87.

49. Aristotle, *Nichomachean Ethics* Book 2, ch. 9.

50. Andrew Nikiforuk has done so in a weekly column in *The Globe and Mail* (1991-2) and has been advised to "stay out of the classroom" and that his ideas constitute "an attack on childhood" by critics who seem not to value criticism.

51. Cf. Dewey, *Experience and Education* op. cit.: 22.

52. John Dewey, "What psychology can do for the teacher", in Archambault (ed.), op. cit.: 202.

53. H.E. Butler (trans.), Quintilian, *Institutio Oratoria* Book 2, ch. 13, Cambridge: Harvard University Press, 1963.

54. Thomas Good and Jere Brophy, *Looking in Classrooms* 3rd. ed. New York: Harper and Row, 1984: 9

55. Quintilian, *Institutio Oratorio* op. cit.: Book 2, ch. 8.

56. Robin Barrow, "Teacher judgement and teacher effectiveness", op. cit.: 76-83.

57. Carole Wade and Carol Tavris, "Thinking critically and creatively", *The Skeptical Inquirer* 14, 4, 1990: 372-7.

58. A.N. Whitehead, *The Aims of Education* op. cit.: 14.

## NOTES FOR CHAPTER TEN

1.   There are, of course, some notable exceptions. See, for example, Mary Warnock, *Imagination* Berkeley: University of California Press, 1976. And the various contributors to Kieran Egan and Dan Nadaner (eds.), *Imagination and Education* New York: Teachers College Press, 1988.

2.   John Passmore, "On teaching to be critical", in R.S. Peters (ed.), *The Concept of Education* op. cit.: 198.

3.   See John Dewey, *Construction and Criticism* New York: Columbia University Press, 1930. Reprinted in Jo Ann Boydston (ed.), *John Dewey: The Later Works, 1925-1953* Vol. 5, 1929-30 Carbondale: Southern Illinois University Press, 1984.

4.   Gilbert Ryle, *The Concept of Mind* Harmondsworth: Penguin Books, 1963: 242-3. (Originally published, 1949.) It would not be fair to say, as Egan and Nadaner do in the Introduction to their collection *Imagination and Education* op. cit., that philosophers in general have viewed imagination as "a damaging intrusion upon logic". The point is rather that philosophers have been clear that imagination and logic have different roles to play. Even Ryle is said to have "helped assign low status to nondiscursive forms of thought in education". It was Ryle, however, who showed us that there are many different sorts of behaviour which we can perform imaginatively, one of his favourite examples being the imaginative and intelligent behaviour of the circus clown. It is hard to reconcile such an example with a "bias for strict order" or a reduction of productive thinking to testable propositions, as Egan and Nadaner allege. If Ryle also saw a darker side to imagination, he saw no more than is true of any virtue or excellence.

5.   For a sense of the interest in creativity at that time, see James Freeman, H.J. Butcher and T. Christie, *Creativity: A Selective Review of Research* London: Society for Research into Higher Education, 1968.

6.   I agree with Robin Barrow that the term "imaginative" cannot merely refer to unusual ideas or practices. The praise implicit in the term excludes the bizarre, the absurd, or the incoherent (unless, of course, the context makes *these* appropriate.) In excluding these, however, I do not believe we have to build in the criterion of effectiveness, by which Barrow means "conducive to a good solution to or resolution of the task or problem at hand". Often, proposed solutions may have great intuitive plausibility and generate much interest and excitement before they are eventually shown not to work. Why would we not regard those who advance them as imaginative? See Robin Barrow, "Some observations on the concept of imagination", in Egan and Nadaner, *Imagination and Education* op. cit.: 79-90.

7.   John Dewey, *How We Think* in Boydston (ed.), *John Dewey: The Later Works* Vol. 8: 198. Perhaps this is the place to dissociate myself from the view of Kieran Egan that John Dewey, in stressing the importance of

building on the child's everyday experience, somehow generated pedagogical principles which neglect imaginative activity. See Kieran Egan,
"Relevance and the romantic imagination", *Canadian Journal of Education* 16, 1, 1991: 58-71. It is clear enough, surely, that Dewey included
imaginative activity *within* the everyday experience of the child: "Even
when a person builds a castle in the air he is interacting with the objects
which he constructs in fancy." The environment, Dewey insisted, is
whatever conditions interact with an individual to create the experience.
See John Dewey, *Experience and Education* op. cit.: 44.

8.  Robert H. Ennis, "A taxonomy of critical thinking dispositions and abilities", in Joan Boykoff Baron and Robert J. Sternberg (eds.), *Teaching
Thinking Skills: Theory and Practice* New York: W.H. Freeman, 1987:
9-26.

9.  See Alan R. White, *The Language of Imagination* Oxford: Basil Blackwell, 1990: 185.

10. Ennis, op. cit.: 11.

11. Laura Duhan Kaplan, "Teaching intellectual autonomy: The failure of
the critical thinking movement", *Educational Theory* 41, 4, 1991: 361-
70. Her claim is partly empirical, of course, though it would seem that
the burden of her argument is that the very conception of critical
thinking is at fault. An empirical case, in any event, could not plausibly
be made in terms of two or three examples.

12. Kaplan, op. cit.: 369.

13. Kaplan, op. cit.: 362, echoing Maxine Greene. "Critical pedagogy" is
here used in its technical sense to refer to a movement inspired by the
work of Paolo Freire.

14. Kaplan, op. cit.: 364.

15. David Kelley, *The Art of Reasoning* New York: Norton, 1988; Howard
Kahane, *Logic and Contemporary Rhetoric* Belmont: Wadsworth, 1988;
Stephen Toulmin, Richard Ricke and Allan Janik, *An Introduction to
Reasoning* New York: Macmillan, 1979.

16. See Antony Flew, *Thinking about Thinking* Glasgow: Fontana/Collins,
1975: 99. Other examples of the "many questions" fallacy from the
literature would include: (1) "Is God one person or three?"—from J.P.
White, "Indoctrination", in R.S. Peters (ed.), *The Concept of Education*
op. cit.: 186; (2) "Why must countries having a dictatorship of the
proletariat practise democracy towards the people and impose dictatorship on the enemy?"—from R.F. Dearden, "Controversial issues and the
curriculum", in William Hare and John P. Portelli (eds.), *Philosophy of
Education: Introductory Readings* op. cit.: 174. Of course, White and
Dearden are giving these as *examples* of the fallacy. Kaplan actually
commits the fallacy herself when she invites the student to ask: "If 'guilt
by association' is a fallacy, why do we usually use it successfully to make
decisions?" Do we? Furthermore, any logic course surely will make it
clear that there is a difference between validity and truth.

17. Having mentioned the usefulness of studying fallacies, I should add that I have not been convinced by the current onslaught on this important aspect of the development of critical thinking skills. I provide some reasons in my review of McPeck's *Critical Thinking and Education* in *Canadian Journal of Education* 7, 4, 1982: 107-10.

18. Kaplan seems unaware that she does just this herself! In charging Howard Kahane with indoctrination in his book *Logic and Contemporary Rhetoric* op. cit., she speaks of evaluating his own work by "using the questions he teaches students to ask of conservative politicians". But if these really are critical questions which Kaplan raises, it seems that Kahane has been successful after all. See Kaplan, op. cit.: 366.

19. Philosophers are not reluctant to say that this is one of their fondest hopes. See, for example, R.M. Hare's remark, cited earlier in chapter three, about an educator being pleased when the students disagree. From R.M. Hare, "Adolescents into adults", in Hollins (ed.), *Aims in Education* op. cit. I have not myself detected this kind of humility in the literature on critical pedagogy, with the exception of Freire himself.

20. It is not clear that Kaplan shares my optimism, since she quotes with approval Friedrich Pollock's pessimistic appraisal of "the average citizen" who succumbs to the pressure to accept the issues as defined.

21. L. Susan Stebbing, *Thinking to Some Purpose* Harmondsworth: Penguin Books, 1939: 47-8.

22. Stebbing, op. cit.: 75. (She means "hope" in the sense of "expect". Clearly she *wishes* to avoid bias.)

23. Stebbing, op. cit.: 189-90. Again, I cannot lay my hands on a similar statement in the literature on critical pedagogy.

24. Kaplan, op. cit.: 366. *An Introduction to Reasoning* was published by Macmillan in 1978.

25. Kaplan, op. cit.: 366.

26. Kaplan, op. cit.: 367.

27. Stephen Toulmin et al., *An Introduction to Reasoning* op. cit.: 7.

28. Toulmin et al., op. cit.: 8.

29. Kaplan criticizes critical thinking for not encouraging students to go on to ask about the forces which have shaped the views of those we convict of being illogical. This is false. Consider the following from a primer on critical thinking: "It is perfectly legitimate, at least from the standpoint of sound thinking, to raise and to pursue questions about interests and motivations. In particular it is innocuous, and it can be illuminating, to do this when the original issues of truth and validity have been set-tled....Yet it will not do—notwithstanding that it is all too often done—to offer more or less speculative answers to such consequential questions as a substitute for, rather than as a supplement to, the direct examination of whatever were the prior issues." See Antony Flew, *Thinking About Thinking* op. cit.: 63. To apply this point to the present case, having shown that Kaplan's argument is faulty, we could now go on to ask about

the forces and motives which lie behind her work. That, however, is not germane to our concerns here.

30. It was in its heyday at the end of the 1970s when I reviewed its significance in the context of open-mindedness in my *Open-mindedness and Education* op. cit.: 118-9.

31. John Dewey, *Experience and Education* op. cit.: 5.

32. Similar comments could be made about the possibly intimidating character of the school itself. Clearly Miss Price had no conception of this aspect of Vincent's problems, for example, and a failure of the imagination led to inappropriate actions. See earlier, chapter seven.

33. Dewey thought that the teacher "must...have that sympathetic understanding of individuals as individuals which gives him an idea of what is actually going on in the minds of those who are learning." See *Experience and Education* op. cit.: 39.

34. Louis Arnaud Reid, *Philosophy and Education* London: Heinemann, 1962: 194.

35. Isaiah Berlin in conversation with Bryan Magee, in Magee, *Men of Ideas* op. cit.: 15. Perhaps this negative reaction will prove less common as the philosophy for children movement convinces more and more teachers that even young children really can raise and consider serious philosophical questions. See Matthew Lipman, *Philosophy Goes to School* Philadelphia: Temple University Press, 1988.

36. A point made in an amusing way by Alexander Calandra in "Angels on a pin", in Glenn Smith and Charles R. Knicker (eds.), *Myth and Reality* Boston: Allyn and Bacon, 1972: 4-6.

37. See Elliot W. Eisner, "What really counts in schools", *Educational Leadership* 48, 5, 1991: 10-17. T.P. Nunn also reminded us that "it is fatally easy to condemn as contrary to beauty, truth or goodness what merely runs counter to our conservative prejudices." See Sir Percy Nunn, *Education: Its Data and First Principles* London: Edward Arnold, 1947: 14. (First published, 1920.)

38. See earlier, chapter nine, the section on 'Judgment in teaching'.

39. John Dewey, *The Child and the Curriculum* op. cit.: 14-5.

40. Jill Solnicki, *The Real Me is Gonna be a Shock* Toronto: Lester Publishing Ltd., 1992: 209.

41. John Dewey, *Experience and Education* op. cit.: 75.

42. Bertrand Russell, *Principles of Social Reconstruction* op. cit.: 146.

43. John Dewey, "The university elementary school", in Jo Ann Boydston (ed.), *John Dewey: The Middle Works* Vol. 1 Carbondale: Southern Illinois University Press, 1976: 319.

44. John Dewey, *Experience and Education* op. cit.: 20.

45. John Dewey, "The need for a philosophy of education", in Jo Ann Boydston (ed.), *John Dewey: The Later Works* Vol. 9 Carbondale: Southern Illinois University Press, 1986: 199.

46. Elliot W. Eisner, *The Educational Imagination* 2nd ed. New York: Macmillan, 1985: 176.

47. Max van Manen, *The Tact of Teaching* London, ON: The Althouse Press, 1991: 160.
48. Ruth Mock, *Education and the Imagination* London: Chatto and Windus, 1970: 86. It certainly reads as if it is this very intention which condemns one as unimaginative.
49. Elliot W. Eisner, *The Educational Imagination* op. cit.: 177.
50. Eisner makes the point too that the possession of familiar repertoires allows the teacher to notice emerging ideas in the classroom, thus permitting imaginative work. See *The Educational Imagination* op. cit.: 176.
51. Byron G. Massialas and Jack Zevin, *Teaching Creatively: Learning Through Discovery* op. cit.: 235.
52. See, for example, Donald H. Graves, *Writing: Teachers and Children at Work* Portsmouth, NH: Heinemann, 1983.
53. Cf. Eisner's point in fn. 50 above.
54. Elliot W. Eisner, "What really counts in schools", *Educational Leadership* op. cit.
55. Aristotle, *Metaphysics* Book 1, ch. 2.
56. One is put in mind of Whitehead's famous definition of the teacher as "an ignorant man thinking", and also of his account of the function of the university as the imaginative acquisition of knowledge. See Whitehead, *The Aims of Education* op. cit.: 37, 96. A footnote to Aristotle perhaps?
57. Nicholas C. Burbules, "The tragic sense of education", *Teachers College Record* 91, 4, 1990: 469-79.
58. Burbules, "The tragic sense of education", op. cit.: 472.
59. I have myself been told by more than one student that as a middle-class university professor, I cannot possibly understand the situation of those who live in poverty. In this case, however, I do not have to draw on imagination at all, only memory.
60. See also a reference to this issue in chapter five, section on 'Fashionable confusions'.
61. Even here, of course, it is easy to forget that people may have had at some point in their lives experiences remarkably similar to those normally associated with other groups. See the anecdote about R.M. Hare cited in chapter five, fn. 22, and cf. fn. 34 above.
62. Philip Walkling rightly condemns "a cultural solipsism which, as an explanation of the world, cannot even account for how persons are mutually intelligible across cultures." See his "Multicultural education", in Noel Entwistle (ed.), *Handbook of Educational Ideas and Practices* London: Routledge, 1990: 87.
63. Recall Peter McGlynn, the schoolteacher in Val Mulkerns short story discussed earlier in chapter seven. He was able to bring Spain alive to the students even though he had never travelled there himself.
64. Hortense Calisher, *Mysteries of Motion* New York: Doubleday, 1983.

65. From an interview with Hortense Calisher in Deborah A. Straub (ed.), *Contemporary Authors* New Revision Series, Vol. 22 Detroit: Gale Research, 1988: 66.
66. John Christopher, *The Death of Grass* Harmondsworth: Penguin, 1970. (First published, 1956.)
67. This is not to say that there is no sense in which we *cannot* imagine certain things. Richard Feynman makes the point that "whatever we are *allowed* to imagine in science must be *consistent with everything else we know....We* can't allow ourselves to seriously imagine things which are obviously in contradiction to the known laws of nature." In *The Feynman Lectures on Physics* Reading, Mass.: Addison-Wesley, 1964: 10-20. Feynman is speaking here of what is intellectually impossible *given certain assumptions.*
68. A point made memorably by Spinoza when he commented: "For no one under-estimates oneself by reason of self-hate, that is, no one under-estimates himself in so far as he imagines that he cannot do this or that. For whatever a man imagines that he cannot do, he imagines it necessarily, and by that very imagination he is so disposed that in truth he cannot do what he imagines he cannot do." See Spinoza, *Ethics* Part 3, def. 28 (trans. Andrew Boyle).
69. One well known instance of this view in the literature is in P.H. Nowell-Smith, *Education in a University* Leicester: Leicester University Press, 1958: 8. A similar view had appeared in *General Education in a Free Society* Cambridge: Harvard University Press, 1945, where it was held that "in literature (the student's) imagination is stirred with vivid evocations of ideals of action, passion, and thought." See p. 60.
70. Robin Barrow, *Understanding Skills* op. cit., ch. 5.
71. Bertrand Russell, "On keeping a wide horizon", *Russell* 33-4, 1979: 5-11.
72. Whitehead gets the point right when, speaking of imagination being disciplined by science, he comments: "Of course, it involves only one specific type of imaginative functioning which is thus strengthened, just as poetic literature strengthens another specific type....we must not conceive the imagination as a definite faculty which is strengthened as a whole by any particular imaginative act of a specific type." See "Science in general education", in Whitehead's *A Philosopher Looks at Science* New York: Philosophical Library, 1965: 47.
73. Cf. Robin Barrow, "Some observations on the concept of the imagination", op. cit.: 87-8.
74. Sometimes, indeed, their suggestions are imaginative by any standard. See, for example, some of the remarks of children reported by Ann Margaret Sharp in "What is a 'community of inquiry'?", in William Hare and John P. Portelli (eds.), *Philosophy of Education: Introductory Readings* op. cit: 207-17.

# Index